Dummies 101: WordPerfect For Windows 95

C. SHEET

Fixing Mistakes

If you don't like what's going on, press Esc a few times.

If you have just deleted something and want it back, press Ctrl+Shift+Z or Alt+Backspace.

If you have just given a command and want to undo it, press Ctrl+Z.

Opening, Printing, and Saving

To Do This Task	Do This
Open a document	Choose File⇨Open from the menu bar, press Ctrl+O, or click on the Open button on the Toolbar.
Save a document	Choose File⇨Save from the menu bar, press Ctrl+S, or click on the Save button on the Toolbar.
Print a document	Choose File⇨Print from the menu bar, press Ctrl+P, or click on the Print button on the Toolbar.
Close a document	Choose File⇨Close from the menu bar, press Ctrl+F4, or click on the document close button in the upper-right corner of the document window.
Exit from WordPerfect	Choose File⇨Exit from the menu bar, click on the close button in the upper-right corner, or double-click on the Control-menu box in the upper-left corner of the WordPerfect window.

Mouse Droppings

To Do This	Do This with Your Mouse
Select (highlight) text	Click at the beginning of the text, hold down the mouse button, and drag to the end (in a straight line).
Select a word	Double-click on the word.
Select a sentence	Click in the left margin.
Select a paragraph	Double-click in the left margin.
Move text or graphics	Select it and then click on it and drag.
See a QuickMenu	Click on the right mouse button.
Close a file	Double-click on the Control-menu box in the upper-left corner of the document window.
Close WordPerfect	Double-click on the Control-menu box in the upper-left corner of the WordPerfect window.

Dummies 101: WordPerfect® 7 For Windows®95

CHEAT SHEET

Formatting Tricks

To Get This Effect	Do This
Boldface	Select text and then press Ctrl+B or click on the Bold icon on the Toolbar.
Italics	Select text and then press Ctrl+I or click on the Italics icon on the Toolbar.
Underlining	Select text and then press Ctrl+U or click on the Underline icon on the Toolbar.
Center current line	Press Shift+F7.
Right-align current line	Press Alt+F7.
Indent current line	Press F7.
Hanging indent current line	Press Ctrl+F7.
Look at hidden codes	Press Alt+F3 or choose View⇨Reveal Codes from the menu bar.
Begin a new page	Press Ctrl+Enter.
Set the margins	Press Ctrl+F8 or click and drag dotted blue guidelines.

Accessing the CD-ROM Files

Note: The CD-ROM does not contain the WordPerfect 7 program. You must already have WordPerfect 7 installed on your computer.

Follow the installation instructions at the back of the book or in the Introduction. To access the files that you've installed, follow these steps (see Unit 2 for more detailed information):

1. **With WordPerfect 7 running, choose File⇨Open from the menu bar.**

   WordPerfect displays the Open dialog box.

2. **Click on the List button at the top of the dialog box to see a list of files on your hard drive.**

   If you chose the default directory structure when you installed the files from the CD, make sure that you are looking in C:\MyFiles. (You may want to look at Unit 8 for information on how to look in different folders on your hard disk.)

3. **Click once on the document that you want to open.**

4. **Click on Open.**

IDG BOOKS WORLDWIDE

DUMMIES 101:™
WORDPERFECT® 7
FOR
WINDOWS® 95

**by Alison Barrows
and Margaret Levine Young**

**IDG
BOOKS**
WORLDWIDE

IDG Books Worldwide, Inc.
An International Data Group Company

Foster City, CA ✦ Chicago, IL ✦ Indianapolis, IN ✦ Southlake, TX

Dummies 101™: WordPerfect® 7 For Windows® 95

Published by
IDG Books Worldwide, Inc.
An International Data Group Company
919 E. Hillsdale Blvd.
Suite 400
Foster City, CA 94404

Library of Congress Catalog Card No.:96-75114

ISBN:1-56884-633-9

Printed in the United States of America

10 9 8 7 6 5 4 3 2 1

1B/SY/QW/ZW/IN

Distributed in the United States by IDG Books Worldwide, Inc.

Distributed by Macmillan Canada for Canada; by Contemporanea de Ediciones for Venezuela; by Distribuidora Cuspide for Argentina; by CITEC for Brazil; by Ediciones ZETA S.C.R. Ltda. for Peru; by Editorial Limusa SA for Mexico; by Transworld Publishers Limited in the United Kingdom and Europe; by Academic Bookshop for Egypt; by Levant Distributors S.A.R.L. for Lebanon; by Al Jassim for Saudi Arabia; by Simron Pty. Ltd. for South Africa; by Pustak Mahal for India; by The Computer Bookshop for India; by Toppan Company Ltd. for Japan; by Addison Wesley Publishing Company for Korea; by Longman Singapore Publishers Ltd. for Singapore, Malaysia, Thailand, and Indonesia; by Unalis Corporation for Taiwan; by WS Computer Publishing Company, Inc. for the Philippines; by WoodsLane Pty. Ltd. for Australia; by WoodsLane Enterprises Ltd. for New Zealand. Authorized Sales Agent: Anthony Rudkin Associates for the Middle East and North Africa.

For general information on IDG Books Worldwide's books in the U.S., please call our Consumer Customer Service department at 800-762-2974. For reseller information, including discounts and premium sales, please call our Reseller Customer Service department at 800-434-3422.

For information on where to purchase IDG Books Worldwide's books outside the U.S., contact IDG Books Worldwide's International Sales department at 415-655-3078 or fax 415-655-3281.

For information on foreign language translations, contact IDG Books Worldwide's Foreign & Subsidiary Rights department at 415-655-3018 or fax 415-655-3281.

For sales inquiries and special prices for bulk quantities, contact IDG Books Worldwide's Sales department at 415-655-3200 or write to the address above.

For information on using IDG Books Worldwide's books in the classroom or for ordering examination copies, contact IDG Books Worldwide's Educational Sales department at 800-434-2086 or fax 817-251-8174.

For authorization to photocopy items for corporate, personal, or educational use, please contact Copyright Clearance Center, 222 Rosewood Drive, Danvers, MA 01923, or fax 508-750-4470.

 is a trademark under exclusive license to IDG Books Worldwide, Inc., from International Data Group, Inc.

About the Authors

Alison Barrows

Alison has taken the long route to . . .*For Dummies* writing, most recently thinking she would have a career in economics. But over the years, an irresistible magnetic force has been at work, personified by her friends, Margy Levine Young, Margy's brother John and husband Jordan, friend David Kay (most of whom are also . . .*For Dummies* authors), and many others, pulling her into the world of computers and technical writing.

She has been a serious computer user since high school (although she was too young to play with vacuum tubes, when they were the thing) and continued to use them at Wellesley College. In college, thanks to some of the aforementioned friends, she worked at a software company and, after graduation, went to the World Bank as a software guru (although in only one piece of software, Javelin PLUS). She first wrote training material for software while working at the World Bank (she wrote using an older version of WordPerfect). She has often been the person that people come to with computer problems.

Alison and Margy met many years ago on Star Island and were able to become friends despite the fact that only two showers were allowed during the week-long conference. They have managed to stay friends through Alison's many relocations and have worked together a few times. This is their second book together.

Alison has a Master's degree in Public Policy from the Kennedy School at Harvard University and a B.A. in International Relations from Wellesley College. In real life, she loves to sing, watches *Star Trek* (the newer versions), likes to cook, and dabbles in yoga, rock climbing, and ultimate Frisbee. She currently lives in Gardner, Massachusetts, with her sweetie.

Margaret Levine Young

Margy Levine Young has used small computers since the 1970s. She graduated from UNIX on a PDP-11 to Apple DOS on an Apple II to MS-DOS and UNIX on a variety of machines. She has done all kinds of jobs that involve explaining to people that computers aren't as mysterious as they might think, including managing the use of PCs at Columbia Pictures, teaching scientists and engineers what computers are good for, and writing and cowriting computer manuals and books. She has coauthored *Understanding Javelin PLUS* (Sybex, 1986); *The Complete Guide to PC-File* (Center Books, 1991); *Access Insider* (Wiley, 1992); *UNIX For Dummies; MORE UNIX For Dummies; UNIX For Dummies Quick Reference; The Internet For Dummies*, 3rd Edition; *MORE Internet For Dummies; Internet For Dummies Quick Reference; The Internet For Windows For Dummies Starter Kit;* and *Internet FAQs: Answers to the Most Frequently Asked Questions* (all from IDG Books Worldwide, Inc.).

Margy has a degree in Computer Science from Yale University and lives with her husband, two children, and 13 chickens in Lexington, Massachusetts. In addition to writing books, she lectures and consults on using the Internet.

Dedication

Alison and Margy dedicate this book to Star Island, which is where they first met many years ago and is still their spirits' home.

Alison also dedicates this book to Matt and to her mother, both of whom give her support above and beyond any possible call of duty.

Margy also dedicates this book to her family — Jordan, Meg, and Zac.

Acknowledgments

We'd like to thank Melba Hopper for doing a great job making this book come true, as well as Diane Steele, Mary Bednarek, Judi Taylor, Mary Corder, Allen Clark, Christa Carroll, William Barton, Suzanne Packer, and Stephanie Koutek. Thanks also to Sherry Gomoll and the IDG Books production team for their outstanding efforts on this book.

We would also like to thank TIAC and IECC, our Internet and e-mail providers. Without them, the 50-mile drive to exchange units would have meant we never actually got any work done.

Margy thanks Jordan Young, Barbara Begonis, and Lexington Playcare Center for making it possible for her to get her work done.

Alison thanks Matt, for keeping the computers in such a state that she could actually work on them. She also thanks Margy, Jordan, John, and Eric for getting her into this business. And simple thanks are not enough (but will have to do) for Sheila, who has midwifed Alison's writing over many years and who gave Alison and Margy some good editing suggestions when they began this book.

Publisher's Acknowledgments

We're proud of this book; please send us your comments about it by using the Reader Response Card at the back of the book or by e-mailing us at feedback/dummies@idgbooks.com. Some of the people who helped bring this book to market include the following:

Acquisitions, Development, & Editorial

Project Editor: Melba Hopper

Acquisitions Editor: Tammy Goldfeld

Product Development Manager: Mary Bednarek

Permissions Editor: Joyce Pepple

Copy Editors: Suzanne Packer, Christa J. Carroll, William A. Barton, Stephanie Koutek

Technical Reviewer: Allen Clark

Editorial Manager: Mary C. Corder

Editorial Assistant: Chris H. Collins

Production

Project Coordinator: Sherry Gomoll

Layout and Graphics: E. Shawn Aylsworth, Cameron Booker, J. Tyler Connor, Maridee Ennis, Todd Klemme, Drew Moore, Anna Rohrer, Brent Savage, Michael Sullivan

Proofreaders: Jenny Overmyer, Robert Springer, Carrie Voorhis

Indexer: Steve Rath

General & Administrative

IDG Books Worldwide, Inc.: John Kilcullen, President & CEO; Steven Berkowitz, COO & Publisher

Dummies, Inc.: Milissa Koloski, Executive Vice President & Publisher

Dummies Technology Press & Dummies Editorial: Diane Graves Steele, Associate Publisher; Judith A. Taylor, Brand Manager; Myra Immell, Editorial Director

Dummies Trade Press: Kathleen A. Welton, Vice President & Publisher; Stacy S. Collins, Brand Manager

IDG Books Production for Dummies Press: Beth Jenkins, Production Director; Cindy L. Phipps, Supervisor of Project Coordination; Kathie S. Schutte, Supervisor of Page Layout; Shelley Lea, Supervisor of Graphics and Design

Dummies Packaging & Book Design: Erin McDermit, Packaging Coordinator; Patti Sandez, Packaging Assistant; Kavish+Kavish, Cover Design

♦

The publisher would like to give special thanks to Patrick J. McGovern, without whom this book would not have been possible.

♦

Files at a Glance

Unit 11

11-1: Line spacing   Policy.101.wpd and
Policy2.101.wpd

11-2: Setting margins   Policy3.101.wpd

11-3: Aligning text   Proposal4.101.wpd

11-4: Setting tabs   Tour Group.101.wpd

Unit 11 Exercise   History of
Circuses2.101.wpd

Unit 12

12-1: Centering text   Fire Set
Proposal.101.wpd

12-2: Numbering pages   Fire Set
Proposal.101.wpd

12-3: Adding headers and footers   Fire Set
Proposal2.101.wpd

12-4: Avoiding bad page breaks   Fire Set
Proposal.101.wpd

Contents at a Glance

Table
of Contents

Introduction

Welcome to *Dummies 101: WordPerfect 7 For Windows 95,* part of the new tutorial series from IDG Books Worldwide.

If you're new to computers and word processing, the best way to learn WordPerfect for Windows is to take a course — and that's just what this book is. This book isn't a standard reference: if you want a book that you can use for looking up how to do specific tasks, rush back to your bookstore and get *WordPerfect 7 For Windows 95 For Dummies* by Margaret Levine Young and David Kay (published by IDG Books Worldwide, Inc.). Instead, this book is a series of lessons that take you through each of the most important things you need to know, including running WordPerfect, making documents, printing things, saving files, and doing fancy formatting, from boldface and italics to tables and fonts. This tutorial takes the place of an actual class, with lessons, exercises, and even pop quizzes.

This is the book for you if

- ♦ You've ever thought that computers might be useful if only you could figure them out.

- ♦ What you need to know now is how to use WordPerfect 7 for Windows 95 to create fabulous-looking documents.

- ♦ You want to take a class so that you can learn all the important features of WordPerfect, but you don't have the time to attend a structured, sit-down, teacher-walking-around-in-front class.

- ♦ You want to be proficient at all the basic tasks in WordPerfect — like editing, printing, and formatting — so that you don't have to beg your local expert to help you.

This book includes a CD-ROM that enables us to walk you through real-life (except they're more fun) examples of how to use WordPerfect. We refuse to take WordPerfect, or for that matter, any software, too seriously — life is just too short — and that's what makes this a . . .*For Dummies* book.

Who Are You?

This book is designed for the beginning or intermediate computer user who wants more than just technical talk about WordPerfect 7 for Windows 95. We have to make some assumptions about you in order to put word one into this book. This books assumes that

- ♦ You have a PC with DOS, Windows 95, and WordPerfect 7 for Windows 95 installed.

- ♦ You have some basic information about Windows 95 (the tutorial that comes with Windows 95 should teach you all you absolutely need to know to work through this book — although knowing more certainly won't hurt you).

- ♦ WordPerfect is installed in the normal way and that you aren't trying to make it act like anything other than WordPerfect 7 for Windows 95.

Listen Up, Class!

Notes:

One reason this book is fun to read is that it has character, like all . . .*For Dummies* books. Here's how the *Dummies 101: WordPerfect 7 For Windows 95* course works:

- The course contains 12 *units,* each starting with a general introduction of the topic or topics to be covered. After the introduction to the topic, the unit contains *lessons* that delve into particular topics — where the real learning takes place.

- Topics that are a little more complicated or less widely used are highlighted with an *Extra Credit* icon. These tidbits are less detailed than the regular text, but may give you the edge you need to make the next document look even better.

- When we tell you something especially important, you'll see a little note in the margin, summarizing the point we're making.

- Occasionally in the text, you'll see a paragraph labeled ***Tip.*** These paragraphs highlight shortcuts or caveats about the feature being discussed.

- We try to remind you to pace yourself by using a *Recess* section to indicate a good place to stop and take a breather (you won't learn well when you're tired). When you reach a Recess section, we'll tell you how to wrap up what you're doing and how to get back into the swing of things when you're ready for more.

- At the end of each unit, there's a *quiz* to test your comprehension of the material — and to add some comic relief. You'll also find an *exercise* that lets you practice the skills you've learned in the unit. At the end of each part of the book, we've thrown in a *test* so that you can find out how many WordPerfect features you can still remember and which ones you'd like to review. (Psst — the answers are in the appendix.)

In the text, stuff that you are supposed to type appears in **boldface.** Filenames appear like this: Wpdoc.wpd.

When you have to press more than one key at the same time, we show the names of the keys connected with a plus sign, like this: Ctrl+C. Press down and hold the first key (Ctrl, in this example), press the second key (C), and release them both.

When we show commands that you choose from the menu bar, they appear with little arrows between the parts of the commands, like this: File⇨Save. This means to choose File and then to choose Save. Don't worry — we explain this all again more slowly in Unit 2, but we wanted to mention it here, in case you flip through the book and wonder what all the little arrows mean.

How This Book Is Organized

This book is split into three parts:

Part I: Getting Comfortable with WordPerfect 7

Part I covers the basics that you need to know to create a simple document. You learn how to edit a document after you create it, how to store it on a diskette, and how to print it.

Part II: Editing and Organizing Your Documents

In Part II, you learn more about how to be a savvy WordPerfect user — how to find phrases or documents, how to manage documents, how to spell check a document and use other intelligent tools, and how to move and copy text.

Part III: Adding Pizzazz

Part III covers all the fancy formatting tricks that you'll need to know to make your documents look professional. Fonts, spacing, margins, tabs, page numbers, headers, and footers — they're all here.

Icons Used in This Book

This icon tells you when you need to use a file that comes on the *Dummies 101* CD. The CD-ROM installs all the files on your hard drive for easy access.

Here's an item that you might need to know when you get to the quiz at the end of the unit or to the test at the end of each part! But even if this information isn't "on the test," we think it's important enough to help you become a WordPerfect pro.

When we talk about a more advanced topic, it appears in a sidebar highlighted with this icon.

Heads up! Here's an important piece of information that you don't want to miss. The piece of information may be a warning, or it may be a tip. Whatever it is, keep your head up and eyes forward so that you don't miss it.

Using the CD-ROM

The *Dummies 101* CD-ROM that comes with this book contains all the practice files that you'll need to do the lessons and exercises in the book. By using the files on the CD, you won't have to do too much tedious typing when following the lessons in this book — we've done most of the boring typing for you. The files include letters with typos, reports that look boring, and flyers that need to be jazzed up.

Note: The *Dummies 101* CD-ROM does *not* contain the WordPerfect for Windows program itself. You'll have to buy that from a regular old software store or get it from the computer department at your office and already have it installed on your computer. Our CD-ROM contains document files, not programs.

To install the files from the *Dummies 101* CD-ROM onto your hard disk, you'll need a CD-ROM drive and about 500K of free space on your hard disk. You'll also need to be running Windows 95.

1 Insert the *Dummies 101* CD-ROM (label side up) into your CD-ROM drive.

The CD-ROM drive is the one that pops out with a circular drawer. Your CD-ROM drive is usually called D:, although it might be called some other letter.

Be careful to handle only the edges of the CD-ROM.

Wait about a minute before you do anything else; the installation program should begin automatically if your computer has the AutoPlay feature. If the program does not start after a minute, go to Step 2. If it does start, go to Step 5.

2 Click on the Start button on the Windows 95 Taskbar (which is usually at the bottom of the screen).

A menu pops up.

3 Click on Run in the menu.

The Run dialog box appears, asking you what program you want to run.

4 Type d:install in the text box of the Run dialog box and press the Enter key.

If your CD-ROM drive is called E: type **e:\install** instead. In any case, please substitute the appropriate letter before the colon.

5 Follow the directions on-screen.

The installation program guides you through the process, asking some questions along the way. Unless you know what you're doing (and you folks know who you are), go ahead and accept the defaults shown on-screen by clicking on the Next button when those windows appear. If at any time during the process you need more information, click on the Help button.

If you have problems with the installation process, you can call the IDG Books Worldwide, Inc. Customer Support number: 800-762-2974 (outside the U.S.: 317-596-5261).

Start button

After installing the files

After you complete the installation process, all the files you'll need for this book will be ready and waiting for you in the C:\MyFiles folder. You don't have to do anything with the files yet — we let you know when you need to open the first file (in Unit 2).

Note: The files are meant to accompany the book's lessons. If you open a file to play with it, you may accidentally make changes to the file. Steps in an exercise that use that file may not make any sense if the file has been changed. So if you can't resist opening a file, just make sure that you don't save your changes. (But if you do, you can always re-install the files from the CD.)

Store the CD-ROM where it will be free from harm so that you can reinstall a file in case the one that's installed on your computer gets messed up.

Accessing the CD-ROM files

You'll find detailed instructions on how to access the *Dummies 101* files in Unit 2, where you first need to open a file. The files are installed in WordPerfect's default directory, unless

- ♦ You chose another folder during the installation process.

- ♦ On your computer, WordPerfect has a different default folder (the usual one is C:\MyFiles, although if WordPerfect is installed on a different drive — not C — but the rest of the folder names are the same, you shouldn't have any problem). If you need to change your default directory, skip right to Unit 8 to find directions on how to do it. You can also leave the files in a folder other than the default, but you'll have to learn how to find them when you need them.

Removing the CD-ROM files

After you install the *Dummies 101* files onto your hard drive, you can uninstall them by clicking on the Start button on the Taskbar, clicking on Programs, clicking on Dummies 101, and clicking on Uninstall *Dummies 101 Windows 95* Files. To remove all files, click on the Automatic button in the Uninstall window. If you feel comfortable doing a custom uninstall, click on the Custom button. If you create new files with new names, they will not be deleted.

Caution: As soon as you click on the Automatic button, your files are as good as gone, and the only way to get them back is to go through the original installation process again. If you want to keep any of the files that were installed, move them to a different folder before beginning the uninstall process. You should be absolutely certain that you want to delete all the files before you click on Automatic.

Notes:

Send Us E-mail

Please give us feedback about this book! If you can send e-mail, address messages to us at 101wp7win@dummies.com. We can't answer all your questions about WordPerfect, but we'd love to hear how the course worked for you. If you can access the World Wide Web, you can get updates to this book at http://net.dummies.com.

If you want to know about other . . .*For Dummies* books, contact IDG Books at info@idgbooks.com or if you have access to the World Wide Web, visit us at http://www.idgbooks.com.

If you can't send e-mail, you can always send plain old paper mail to us using the reader response form in the back of the book. For your trouble, you'll get an attractive full-color catalog of other . . .*For Dummies* books (collect them all!).

Getting Comfortable with WordPerfect 7

Part I

In this part...

Learning a new word processor can be traumatic. "What? Give up my old Selectric? Replace my old word processor? No way!" After all, you spend many happy (or not so happy) hours typing away, creating lyrical prose, or crunching out boring reports. Whatever you use it for, your word processor has become your friend. You know its in's and out's; and even if your word processor is difficult to use, it's familiar.

And WordPerfect 7 may still be a stranger, and not such a friendly-looking stranger at that. What are all those little buttons on the screen for, anyway? And how can I use this thing just to type a simple letter?

Don't worry — this part of the book is just for you. In the first four units, you make friends with WordPerfect 7. You learn what to say to WordPerfect to get it to do your bidding. You learn which keys to press and mouse buttons to click. And you learn some basics about word processing that will stand you in good stead no matter what word processor you use. In fact, by the end of the very first unit, you have written, saved, and printed a letter! And by the end of Unit 4, you know all the basic skills you need to learn about the more advanced WordPerfect features.

So get comfortable, limber up your typing fingers, and here you go with Unit 1.

Once Around the Block

Objectives for This Unit

✓ Opening WordPerfect

✓ Creating a short document (a letter)

✓ Saving your document on disk

✓ Printing your document

✓ Exiting WordPerfect

Prerequisites

▶ WordPerfect 7 is installed on your PC

▶ You can turn on your computer and Windows 95 comes up

▶ You have installed the diskette that comes with the book (see the Introduction for instructions)

▶ Your printer is hooked up and ready to print (optional)

This unit is a preview of what WordPerfect will do for you. When you finish it, you'll know how to use WordPerfect to create and print a short document — the rest of the book is just icing on the cake! But remember that we can't cover every detail in just a few lessons, so read the rest of the book to find out more. In particular, Unit 2 describes the items on the WordPerfect screen and how to use WordPerfect commands, menus, buttons, and dialog boxes to tell the program what to do.

So what is a document, anyway? Any time you type something in WordPerfect, you're working on a document. A *document* is the unit in which WordPerfect saves information — each file that's created in WordPerfect and saved to disk is a document. A document can contain a letter, a report, a poem, a novel, or any other bunch of text you type.

What do you do with documents? Well, you make them by typing some text, that is, words or characters, in WordPerfect. You save them on disk so that you can work on them again later. You print them so you have copies to pass out to friends and coworkers.

Each document has a name called a document name, or *filename*, which you give it the first time you save it in a file on the disk. In the past (in the bad old days of DOS and Windows versions, before Windows 95), filenames could only be eight characters with an extra three tacked on for variety. No longer. Windows 95 lets you name your files with up to 255 characters, and that number can include spaces and punctuation. Even in Windows 95, though, for the sake of convenience, you may give your filename an *extension* — a dot (.) followed by three additional characters that tell you (and the computer) what kind of file it is. Most programs add the extension for you. WordPerfect

Notes:

documents usually have the extension *.wpd* (we'll let you guess what that stands for), and WordPerfect adds that extension for you every time you save a file (as long as you don't turn that option off). The sample files that come with the book all have a kind of double extension *.101.wpd* to indicate that they came with this book (which is part of the *Dummies 101* series) and that they are WordPerfect documents.

heads up

We need to take a step back and do a tad bit of explaining here. In the world as we've known it, a document has been something that consists mostly of words — so creating one with a word processor makes perfect sense. But Microsoft is playing with our minds — in Windows 95, a document is any file that is created with software (more or less) — so that definition can include word processing files, spreadsheet files, graphics files, and so on. In this book, when we refer to documents we mean something that you (or we) make with WordPerfect — but we thought a definition was in order.

You're ready to fire up WordPerfect and start the first lesson. Although we do give you a chance to take a break in the middle, we encourage you to finish this whole unit in one sitting. Other units have obvious points for a recess, and we'll always tell you how to get back to where you are in case you need to stop and continue later, but this unit is kind of special. It gives you a preview of what is to come as well as the confidence to continue through the book — and may even encourage you to use this great new tool to write that novel you have in mind!

Lesson 1-1 — Running WordPerfect for Windows

The very first step to creating a document is to open the WordPerfect program. You must first turn on your computer, and you (or someone else) must have installed WordPerfect 7 on your hard disk.

After WordPerfect is installed and your computer is on, we can help you with every step. Although this book is mainly about WordPerfect, this lesson also gives you some very rudimentary skills that you need to know to use Windows 95, which is the system that WordPerfect uses to run.

Notes:

The next few paragraphs are background information that will help you with the numbered steps that follow. You don't need to do anything quite yet.

In this unit, you learn how to run WordPerfect, create a letter, save it, print it, and exit WordPerfect. You don't need to learn how to use all the parts of the WordPerfect window to follow these steps. In fact, we use only two parts of the window:

 ♦ The typing area (the large, white space in the middle of the window)
 ♦ The Toolbar (the row of little pictures near the top of the window)

The Toolbar is the row of boxes with little pictures on them, toward the top of the WordPerfect window. If no one has customized your version of WordPerfect, the Toolbar should be immediately below the menu bar — that is, the line of words, each with an underlined letter. (If WordPerfect has been customized, you may want to ask the person who installed it to return it to its virgin state — without customization — so that it matches the figures in this book.) Those boxes are called *buttons*, and each one gives you an easy way to do something (if you want to be technical, each button is a shortcut to a menu command).

Let's talk briefly about your mouse. When you are in Windows (and your mouse is working), you will notice that as you slide the mouse around your desk, a mark on the screen moves too — it's called the mouse pointer. In the Windows 95 Desktop (which is what you see when you start Windows 95) the mouse pointer always looks like a diagonally pointing arrow. The mouse pointer sometimes changes shape in an application to indicate what kind of job it's ready to do.

To use a button on the Toolbar, point to it with the mouse. After your mouse pointer has rested on a button for an instant, a little box appears, telling you the name of the button and a brief description of what clicking on it will do — a convenient reminder. When you're ready to take the plunge and use the button, click on it once with the mouse. Incidentally, when we say *click on something,* we always mean with the left button — if we mean the right button, we'll be sure to tell you that!

Now you know enough about what you see on-screen — and in the WordPerfect window in particular — to create, print, and save a letter. Unit 2 describes the other parts of the WordPerfect window and explains how to use them.

To start these steps, you should see the Windows 95 Desktop on-screen (that's what you usually see when you first run Windows 95, after you get past the opening screens). You have more than one way to start WordPerfect — we mention a couple here, but you may find another that you prefer. In the meantime, after you see the Desktop, follow these steps to get WordPerfect running:

1 **Get psyched.**

Think of how much easier WordPerfect is going to make your life! Pet your mouse, make it your friend, and give it a name (we have a friend who named his mouse Squeak). This is the beginning of an entertaining partnership between you, us, and WordPerfect.

2 **Find the Start button.**

It is probably in the bottom left corner of your desktop (although the Taskbar, which contains the Start button, may be on any edge of the screen).

3 **Click on the Start button with the left button of your mouse. Move your mouse pointer to the item called Corel WordPerfect Suite 7.**

Corel WordPerfect Suite 7 should have a rightward-facing triangle on it. That arrow means that when the cursor is on it, another menu appears. When your cursor is on Corel WordPerfect Suite 7, you see another menu with Corel WordPerfect Suite programs. At this point your screen should look something like Figure 1-1. If your list of Corel WordPerfect Suite programs isn't exactly the same as ours, don't fret — as long as you have WordPerfect 7, you're all set.

Toolbar: row of buttons you can click on

click on the Start button, move to Corel WordPerfect Suite 7, and click on Corel WordPerfect 7

Figure 1-1: Find Corel
WordPerfect Suite 7
when you click on the
Start button.

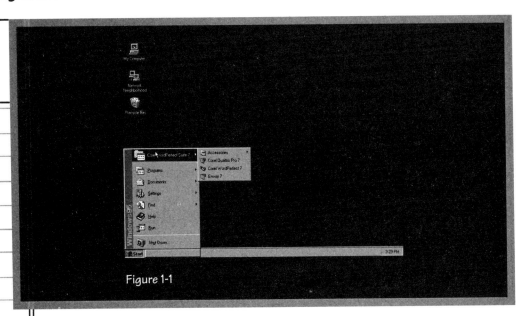

Figure 1-1

4 **Move your pointer over to the next menu and to the Corel WordPerfect 7 option. Click on Corel WordPerfect 7 with the mouse.**

You need to be careful to move the pointer over to the Corel WordPerfect Suite menu — otherwise you may accidentally move the cursor to another choice on the Start menu and display a whole different submenu. If that happens, and you're not seeing the Corel WordPerfect Suite 7 applications, all you need to do is move the pointer back to the Corel WordPerfect Suite choice.

heads up

Depending on how WordPerfect was installed, you may have an icon for it on the Taskbar (the bar at the bottom of the Windows 95 Desktop — the same place you found the Start button). The WordPerfect icon looks like a pen nib, but it's so small that it's hard to recognize. To find out if you have it, move your mouse pointer along the Taskbar to any other buttons or icons. You see the name of the programs pop up when the pointer is on them. If one is WordPerfect 7, an easier way to run WordPerfect is to double-click on that icon on the Taskbar.

5 **Watch.**

You don't always have to watch, but just this once, watch the WordPerfect logo appear and give way to the WordPerfect screen you see in Figure 1-2. Isn't technology amazing?

Great! After those few simple steps, you're ready to create a document. All you really need to do now is start typing.

heads up

Now that you have WordPerfect running, we'd like to point out one thing: You're better off not turning off your PC while WordPerfect and Windows are running. In fact, you're better off exiting *all* Windows programs and then exiting Windows itself before turning off your PC. We tell you how to turn off your computer safely in Lesson 1-5. Until then — leave it running! Don't get *too* worried about this: Turning off the PC prematurely doesn't cause the disk to fall off or the screen to blow up. You just might lose some work and possibly waste some space on your hard disk.

---

exit Windows before turning off PC

☑ Progress Check

If you can do the following, you're ready to move on to the next lesson:

❑ Turn on your computer.

❑ Run Windows.

❑ Run WordPerfect.

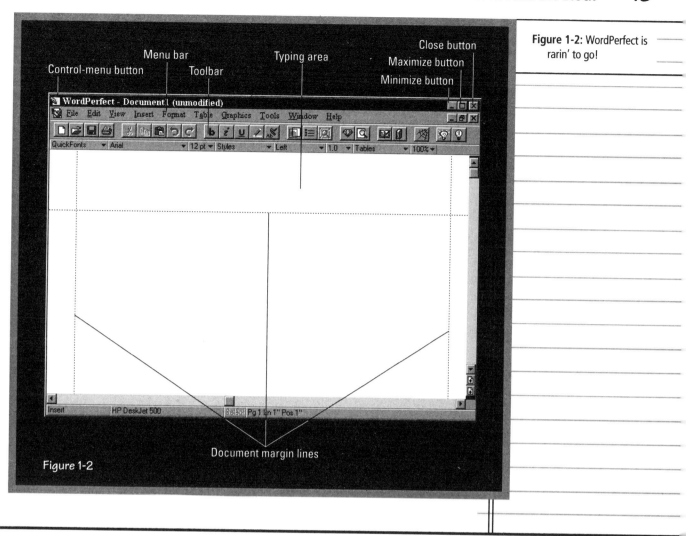

Control-menu button   Menu bar   Toolbar   Typing area   Close button   Maximize button   Minimize button

Figure 1-2

Document margin lines

Figure 1-2: WordPerfect is rarin' to go!

Typing a Letter

Are you ready to start the Great American Novel? Or the 50-page report you promised your boss? Good, because all you really need to do is start typing. In case you don't have that great opening line already in your head, we give you text to type, along with a few hints about how to use a word processor.

The first thing to know about any word processor is how to recognize the *cursor*. The cursor marks where you are — it is where text appears as you start to type or disappears from when you use the Backspace or Delete key. In WordPerfect, the cursor is (usually) a flashing thick, vertical bar. It's like your pencil point on the screen. Computer geeks sometimes call the cursor the *insertion point,* but we won't.

You may get the cursor confused with the *mouse pointer,* which is what moves when you move the mouse. The mouse pointer changes shape depending on where you point. When you point to the typing area (which is currently the big, white area in the middle of the WordPerfect window), the pointer looks like an arrow; but when text is in the typing area, the mouse pointer comes with an attached shadow cursor. When you point to the menu at the top of

Notes:

Notes:

the WordPerfect window, it still looks like a little arrow. Occasionally it turns into a hand or a funny looking *x* (like when it crosses the dotted lines in the typing area, which are your margins). You can use the mouse pointer to move the cursor simply by clicking in your document.

Most of the keys on the computer keyboard work just like their counterparts on a typewriter. In Unit 2, we talk about some of those keys that don't exist on a typewriter, like the function keys (F1 through F10 or F12), Ctrl, Alt, and Esc.

Now that you can recognize the cursor and the mouse pointer and know that the keys on the keyboard do more or less what you expect them to do, here are some hints about word processing:

- When you start a new paragraph, don't use the spacebar to indent — use tabs instead. We talk about setting tabs later (in Unit 11), so for now just use whatever tabs are set.

- After you reach the end of a line, don't press the Enter key — just keep typing. WordPerfect takes care of putting the next word on the next line. That convenience is one of the niftiest things about word processing!

- When you want to start a new line that's a new paragraph or a new item in a list, *do* press the Enter key.

- To leave a blank line, press Enter an extra time.

- When you need to type a capital letter, hold down the Shift key while you type that letter. When you need to type a bunch of capital letters, press the Caps Lock key, type the letters, and then press the Caps Lock key again so that everything else you type isn't in capitals. Caps Lock works the same as a typewriter — except that you always have to press the Shift key to use the special characters above the numbers. (If you leave Caps Lock on by mistake and want to know how to fix your text without retyping it, see Lesson 9-3.)

Typing in WordPerfect

Enough talking — the time to start typing has come. If you make mistakes, stay calm: You'll get the chance to correct them later on in this lesson. (A cool feature of WordPerfect 7 is that it underlines with a squiggly red line anything that it thinks is misspelled. Don't be surprised if the squiggly line falls under your name. Note that the squiggly red lines don't appear when you print the document. For now, just let those squiggly red lines be — we'll get back to them in a minute.)

1 **Type the letter you see in Figure 1-3. Start with your own name and address.**

Use tabs to indent the first few lines — your name and address — and press Enter at the end of each of those lines. (***Note:*** Enter may be called Return on your keyboard, or it may just have a hooked arrow on it — we always call it Enter.) Press the Tab key six times to get the name and address lines halfway across the page. Don't worry: We cover setting tabs in more detail in Lesson 11-4. For now, just approximate the way the letter looks in the figure.

2 **Type the date.**

Press Enter twice (once to finish the line you're on and once to leave a blank line) and then tab over again to type the date.

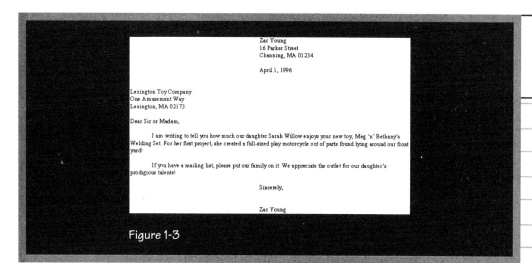

Figure 1-3

Figure 1-3: Here's a letter you might send to the maker of your kid's favorite toy.

3 Type the name and address of the addressee.

Typing this address is even easier than typing your own address, because it's *left justified* — or lined up against the left margin. When text is left justified (and most text is), you don't have to use tabs — just type and press Enter at the end of each line.

Press Enter twice after the last line of the company's address to leave the extra line.

4 Type the salutation.

Dear Sir or Madam is also left justified.

5 Now type the text of the letter.

Remember: Use Tab (rather than a bunch of spaces) to indent the first line of each paragraph and press Enter between paragraphs only.

6 Type the closing.

Remember to press Enter twice to leave a blank line and to press Tab about six times to indent *Sincerely*. Press Enter about four times before pressing Tab another six times to indent your name.

That wasn't too bad, was it? But go back and read the letter again. Did you make any mistakes?

extra credit

What's with the squiggly red lines anyway?

WordPerfect 7 has a nifty new feature — it's called Spell-As-You-Go — and on-the-fly spelling is exactly what it does. Spell-As-You-Go is like having the Spell Checker running all the time. It points out to you words that it thinks are misspelled by putting a squiggly red line under them. That mark allows you to double-check those words before you print your document or hand a disk with the document on it to your boss. The easiest way to check those words is to point to the word with the mouse pointer and click the right mouse button (*right-click* on the word). A list of possible correct spellings appears. To replace the word, just click on the correct spelling of the word in the list.

The WordPerfect dictionary isn't perfect — it doesn't have every word ever used in it, so it occasionally marks words that are spelled perfectly. You can ignore the mark or add the word to the dictionary by right-clicking on it and choosing Add.

☑ Progress Check

If you can do the following, you're ready to move on to the next lesson:

❑ Type text into WordPerfect.

❑ Use Tab and Enter correctly.

❑ Correct typos using Backspace and Delete.

Correcting mistakse

In Unit 5, we describe many ways to correct mistakes and change your mind about what you've typed. Here, we show you a couple of simple ways to correct typos.

1 **Find a typo. It will probably have a squiggly red line under it. Move your cursor to it.**

Move your cursor in one of two ways: Use the mouse to point to the mistake and click once with the left mouse button, or use the arrow keys on your keyboard to move the cursor. As you move the cursor, a little box (called a QuickSpot — it gives you quick access to paragraph formatting settings) appears in the margin next to the line that the cursor is in. This box is not a printed character — we talk more about it later.

If a squiggly red line appears under something that is correct, like your name or street address, don't worry. The squiggly line doesn't appear in your printed document.

2 **Delete the offending characters.**

Use the Backspace key to delete the character immediately before the cursor, or the Delete (or Del) key to delete the character immediately after the cursor.

3 **Type the correct characters.**

Unless you press the Insert (or Ins) key by mistake, what you type should be inserted where the cursor is. If what you type replaces what is already there, press the Insert key and try typing again (see Lesson 3-4 for information on what the Insert key does).

Backspace deletes preceding character and Delete deletes following character

on the test

Remember that the easiest way to make a small correction is to move your cursor to where the correction needs to be made, use Backspace or Delete to remove characters, and simply type in new characters.

Lesson 1-3   ## Saving a Document

Right now the letter that you typed is in a document named *Document1* (see the name at the top of the WordPerfect window?). The document doesn't exist on your hard disk, so if you turn off your computer at this point (or exit WordPerfect without saving the document), the document will evaporate into the ether, just like dew drying in the summer morning sun (hey, even we *Dummies* writers can wax poetic). But to be a little more down to earth, if you ever want to see this document again, you'd better save it. (Don't panic — it's actually not so easy to lose a document. WordPerfect will always ask you to confirm when it's trashing a file.)

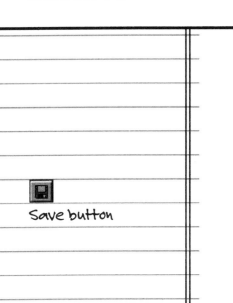
Save button

The easiest way to save a document is to use the Save button on the Toolbar. (You learned about the Toolbar in Lesson 1-1.) Unless someone has changed the way your Toolbar looks, the Save button is the third from the left. (Although it looks like a diskette, you usually use this button to save to a hard disk — it looks like a diskette because a hard disk wouldn't make such a cute button!)

When you want to save a document, you have to think of a name for it. In Windows 95, that task is pretty easy — just name it something that makes sense to you — but you might want to spend an extra second or so thinking

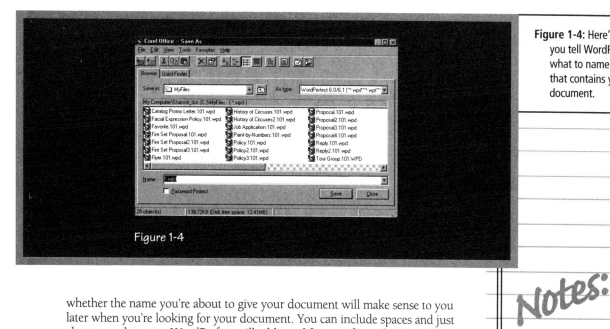

Figure 1-4

Figure 1-4: Here's where you tell WordPerfect what to name the file that contains your document.

Notes:

whether the name you're about to give your document will make sense to you later when you're looking for your document. You can include spaces and just about any character. WordPerfect will add .wpd for you if you don't specify an extension (it stands for *WordPerfect Document*, logically enough) — and we recommend that you name your file and let WordPerfect add the .wpd extension. You'll have an easier time opening the document in all the funky ways that Windows 95 provides (and we'll cover that in Unit 2).

When you installed the files from the *Dummies 101* CD, you copied the sample files for this *Dummies 101* course to your hard disk. All the sample files you use for this course have the file extension .101.wpd. This extension makes them easier to find and also ensures that they don't conflict with any files you may already have created. When you create new files, though, let WordPerfect add the extension .wpd.

You can use capital letters, small letters, or a mixture of the two when naming files — Windows doesn't pay any attention to capitalization in filenames.

Hard disks have lots of space to store files (as opposed to diskettes, which usually have less space to store files). For now, you can save to the *default directory*. WordPerfect automatically (by *default*) looks for document files in the default directory and saves them there, too. Later we'll talk about saving files to different directories and disks (Lesson 8-3) and changing the default directory (Unit 8 extra credit).

Saving your letter

The time has come to save the letter that you just wrote to the toy company:

1   Click on the Save button.

The Save button is the third from the left on the Toolbar.

The Save As dialog box appears (see Figure 1-4). Look for *.wpd in the Name box near the bottom of the dialog box. When you type the new filename in the Name box, whatever you type will replace *.wpd (which is generic for *enter a file name here*). In general, if you see something highlighted, you can type to replace whatever is highlighted with something else.

2   Type Toy Letter.

Toy Letter appears in the Name box. If you don't type an extension (the three letters of a filename after the period), WordPerfect automatically gives the file the extension *.wpd.* Using this standard extension makes the document a little easier to find later.

3 **Press Enter or click on the Save button.**

WordPerfect saves the text you typed in Lesson 1-2 in a file called Toy Letter.wpd in your default directory.

As you may have guessed, we haven't covered everything about saving documents here. But now you know a simple way to save something you've written so that you can get it back later — just use the Save button on the Toolbar and type a name for the document.

After you've given a document a name, saving it the second time is even easier: Just click on the Save button. That's it; it's saved! WordPerfect saves it with the same name it had the last time you saved it, replacing the old version of the document with the new, updated one.

Note: What if you already have a file named Toy Letter.wpd? If you do, WordPerfect asks if you want to replace it. Click on the No button, enter a different filename (how about Dummies Toy Letter?), and click on OK.

Recess

Saving your document is always a good idea, even if you're just getting up for some coffee. If you're ready to quit for now, skip to Lesson 1-5. Because you just saved the document, you don't need to save again.

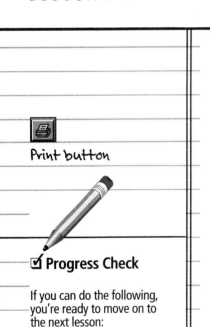

☑ Progress Check

If you can do the following, you're ready to move on to the next lesson:

❏ Use the Save button to save a document.

❏ Type a filename that WordPerfect can use when saving the document.

Lesson 1-4   # Printing a Document

Printing your document is as simple as saving it — if your printer is set up correctly. We don't cover how to troubleshoot printer problems here (that's covered in Unit 4). If your printer is connected, turned on, and — most importantly — set up correctly, printing your document is extraordinarily easy.

To print your document, click on the Print button on the WordPerfect Toolbar. The Print button is to the right of the Save button — it's usually the fourth button from the left. It looks vaguely like a printer (use your imagination).

Try printing the letter to the Lexington Toy Company:

1 **Click on the Print button.**

The Print button is the fourth button from the left on the Toolbar. After you click on it, the Print dialog box appears, and it looks something like Figure 1-5. Yikes! Look at all those buttons and tabs! Don't worry — you can ignore them all for now.

2 **Press Enter.**

Notice that the button marked Print has a somewhat darker border around it. That border indicates that pressing Enter is the same as clicking on Print. If you prefer, you can use the mouse to click on Print.

You see a message that tells you that your document is being prepared for printing, and then your printer prints the letter.

Print button

☑ Progress Check

If you can do the following, you're ready to move on to the next lesson:

❏ Identify the Print button.

❏ Print a document using the Print button.

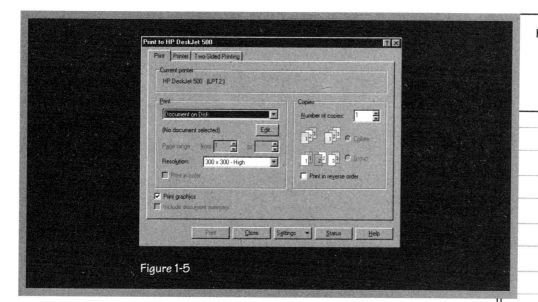

Figure 1-5

Figure 1-5: The Print dialog
box enables you to print
several copies of the
document or choose
which printer to use.

That's it — printing can be as simple as that. We cover printing in more detail
in Unit 4. If you had trouble printing, you may want to wait until Unit 4 (or
maybe even skip to it now), where we go through the mechanics and pitfalls
of printing.

Exiting WordPerfect

You should always exit both WordPerfect and Windows before turning
your computer off. It's like putting your car in park before turning off the
ignition — getting started the next time will be easier.

As with many things in Windows and WordPerfect, you have more than one
way to exit a program. We'll tell you about all of them, and you can take
your pick.

Closing the WordPerfect window

Here's how to close the WordPerfect window or, for that matter, any program
running in Windows:

1 **Click on the X button in the upper-right corner of the WordPerfect
window.**

If WordPerfect takes up your entire screen, click on the X button in the upper-
right corner of the screen. If WordPerfect appears in a window, click on the X
button in the upper-right corner of the WordPerfect window, at the far right of
the window title bar that says *WordPerfect* and the document name. The X
button is actually called the *Close button* (and we refer to it as such in the
future). It is labeled in Figure 1-2, in case you are having trouble finding it.

heads up

You may have two Close buttons, one underneath the other. We get into this
in greater detail later, but the lower one applies to your document, while the
upper one applies to the program — in this case, WordPerfect. Click on the
upper one to close WordPerfect.

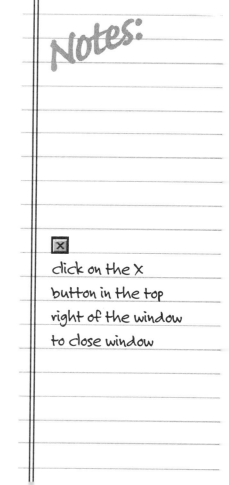

Notes:

click on the X
button in the top
right of the window
to close window

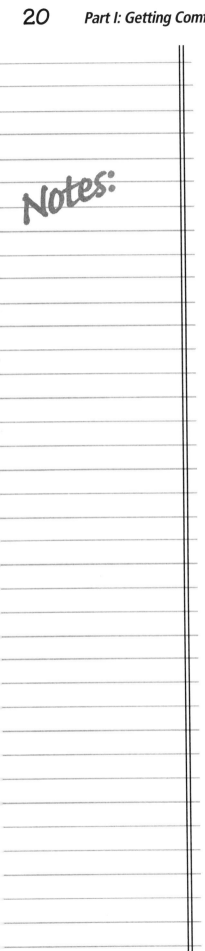

Notes:

2 **If a dialog box appears asking if you want to save your document, choose Yes or No.**

If you have made changes to your document since you last saved it, a box appears asking whether you want to save changes to your document. If you have made changes that you want to keep, click on Yes. WordPerfect saves the file and then disappears. If your three-year-old crawled into your lap sometime during the last few lessons to play with the keyboard and your document is now unrecognizable, click on No, and WordPerfect disappears *without* saving the document (you should have saved it in Lesson 1-3, and you can get it back the way it was then). Alternatively, you can click on Cancel to go back to the document and ignore the fact that you just asked to exit WordPerfect.

If you have made no changes since you last saved, WordPerfect simply disappears from the screen. You didn't lose anything — the document had been saved earlier the way that it appeared on the screen when you clicked the Close button — WordPerfect didn't need to save it again.

When closing WordPerfect, Windows, or almost any other Windows program, your alternatives to clicking on the Close button are as follows:

▶ Click on the Control-menu button (the little icon on the left of the title line) once and click on Close in the little menu that appears.

▶ Double-click on the Control-menu button.

▶ Hold down the Alt key while pressing F4 (we write *Alt+F4* in the future, to save space).

▶ Click on the word File in the menu bar (in the upper-left corner of the window), and then click on the word Exit in the menu that appears. We talk more about using the menu bar in Unit 2.

Whichever method you choose, the result will be exactly the same — WordPerfect closes, perhaps after asking you a pertinent question or two.

Closing Windows itself

If you are finished working and want to turn off your computer, you should exit Windows first. Not that you *have* to turn your computer off after you are finished working — we leave ours on most of the time. We just turn the screen and printer off, to save power. But if you have your reasons for exiting Windows, here's how:

1 **Close WordPerfect, following the steps that appeared earlier in this lesson.**

2 **Close all the Windows programs that you're using, like Solitaire, Minesweeper, or any other important, productivity-enhancing software that might be open.**

You can close any Windows program (any Windows program worth its salt, anyway) the same way that you close WordPerfect — click on the Close button or press Alt+F4.

3 **Close Windows itself by clicking on the Start button and then clicking on Sh<u>u</u>t Down. You almost definitely want to "<u>S</u>hut Down the Computer?" which is the option already chosen.**

Windows can't believe that you really want to leave — things were just getting fun! It asks you to confirm that you want to close Windows.

4 **Click on <u>Y</u>es (or press Enter).**

Windows closes any remaining programs that are running and then exits. Wait until you see a message telling you that you can safely turn off your computer before you turn everything off (my, aren't these things getting user-friendly!).

Recess

Congratulations! You've reached a great place to stop and get a snack. But don't go away for too long, because you've reached the end of the unit. The quiz and exercise that follow will tell you how much progress you've made so far!

☑ **Progress Check**

If you can do the following, you're ready to move on to the next lesson:

❑ Exit WordPerfect.

❑ Exit Windows.

❑ Tell your friends how easy WordPerfect is to use.

Unit 1 Quiz

For each of the following questions, circle the letter of the correct answer or answers. Remember, we may have included more than one right answer for each question.

1. **An easy way to start WordPerfect is . . .**

   A. Click your heels and say three times, "WordPerfect is the best."

   B. Use the Start button to find Corel WordPerfect Suite 7 and the Corel WordPerfect 7 choice.

   C. Double-click on the WordPerfect icon on the Taskbar.

   D. Find the WordPerfect program file (Wpwin.exe) in the Explorer and double-click on it.

   E. Go to the refrigerator and take out a jar of pickles.

2. **A document is . . .**

   A. A file created by WordPerfect.

   B. Anything you type and save in WordPerfect.

   C. The result of using the Save button on the Toolbar.

   D. Something you get from a lawyer.

   E. Almost any file you create with a program in Windows 95.

3. **To create a document in WordPerfect, you must . . .**

   A. Open WordPerfect and start typing.

   B. Open WordPerfect, set up margins and tabs, and change environment preferences before you can start typing.

   C. Open WordPerfect, click on every single button on the Toolbar, and see what happens.

   D. Hire a ghostwriter.

   E. Get out your parchment, quill pen, and ink, find a time machine to take you to the 16th century, and start lettering.

4. **Which button is this?**

A. Give me five.

B. Save button.

C. Insert program disk.

D. Reset button.

E. Put something on that thing in the picture.

 5. **Use this button when you want to . . .**

A. Turn your computer into the newest, hottest computer on the market, all peripherals included (modem, printer, scanner, and so on).

B. Turn your printer into a food processor.

C. Print the document that is currently displayed on-screen.

D. Display the Print dialog box.

E. Exit WordPerfect.

6. **An easy way to close WordPerfect is to . . .**

A. Double-click on the Control-menu box at the top left-hand corner of the window.

B. Press Alt+F4.

C. Click on the button that looks like an X at the top right of the WordPerfect window.

D. Wait until WordPerfect gets tired — then it will exit by itself.

E. Turn the computer off. (Hint: This is a bad idea!)

Unit 1 Exercise

1. Open WordPerfect.

2. Type a short letter to a friend.

3. Save the letter, using a filename you'll remember later (such as Letter to Karen, if you've written a letter to your friend Karen).

4. Print the letter.

5. Exit WordPerfect.

Opening, Closing, and Moving Around in Your Documents

Objectives for This Unit

✓ Controlling how much of the screen WordPerfect takes up

✓ Telling WordPerfect what to do by using commands, dialog boxes, and buttons on the Power Bar

✓ Opening documents you've already created

✓ Closing documents after you're finished with them

✓ Creating a new document

✓ Creating a new document based on one you already made

✓ Moving around in the document using the keyboard and scroll bars

Prerequisites

- ▶ Running WordPerfect for Windows (Lesson 1-1)
- ▶ The urge to learn more about WordPerfect (no lesson number, just pure desire)
- ▶ A diskette

on the CD
- ▶ Toy Letter2. 101.wpd
- ▶ Proposal.101.wpd

Typing a letter is all very well, but word processing is more than typing. This unit covers all the skills that you need to make a new document, close one when you are finished with it, and move around in it. In the course of describing how to revisit and edit a document, we also tell you about the WordPerfect screen and menus and how to see helpful information on-screen. Think of this unit as a kind of lecture session, or maybe Show and Tell! You get to use everything you learn here with more hands-on work as you go through the book.

Lesson 2-1

What's on the Screen?

Notes:

Start out by looking at all the parts of the WordPerfect window, which you see in Figure 2-1. Table 2-1 explains what all these little gizmos are called and what they do. (You don't have to read the whole table right now but do skim through it. You can always come back to find out about each part of the WordPerfect window when you need to know about it.)

Table 2-1	Parts of the WordPerfect Window
Gizmo	*What You Can Do with It*
Control-menu button for WordPerfect	Double-click on this button to close WordPerfect. Click on it once to display a menu of things you can do with the WordPerfect window. The Restore, Minimize, and Maximize commands that appear on the menu control how the WordPerfect window looks on-screen. The Close command exits WordPerfect.
Title bar	It tells you that the window contains WordPerfect (big news) and displays the name of the document. It may also tell you that the document is *unmodified* (which means that neither you nor the three-year-old who may be sitting in your lap has made changes to the document since you last saved it).
Menu bar	Click on the words in the menu bar to choose the commands that you use to control WordPerfect. We talk about commands in Lesson 2-2.
Control-menu button for the document	You use it to control how WordPerfect displays this document, not the whole program. (You can have more than one document open in WordPerfect — we get to that in Unit 3.)
Toolbar	Click on these buttons for quick shortcuts to frequently used commands, like Save and Print. You used them already in Unit 1.
Power Bar	Click on these buttons to control how your text looks. The buttons help you change the font, size, and positioning of the text where the cursor is. We talk more about buttons on the Power Bar when we discuss formatting your document in Unit 9.
Typing area	A vast expanse of white, bounded by dotted margin lines. It's just waiting for you to fill it with lucid prose (or confusing, bureaucratic nonsense — your choice).
Horizontal scroll bar	You use it for displaying parts of your document that may not fit in the window. If your document is too wide to be visible in the window, this scroll bar appears. If not, it doesn't (logical enough).
Vertical scroll bar	You use it to see more of your document when it's too long to fit in the WordPerfect window (which is almost always).
Status bar	Look at it for information about where you are and what you're doing. You can click on parts of it to change the information that you see.
Minimize button	You use it to minimize the WordPerfect window (so that it is only an item on the Taskbar).

(continued)

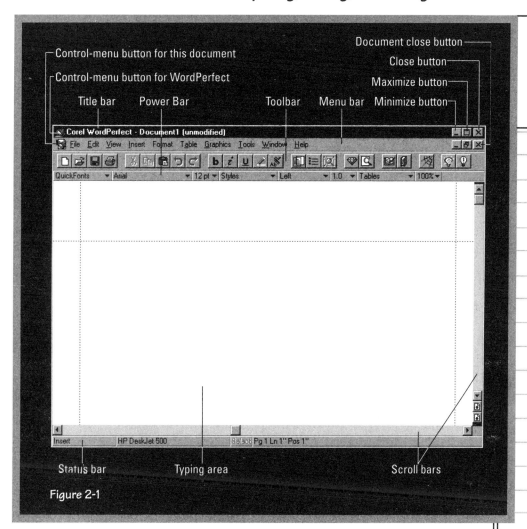

Control-menu button for this document
Control-menu button for WordPerfect
Title bar   Power Bar
Toolbar   Menu bar
Document close button
Close button
Maximize button
Minimize button

Corel WordPerfect - Document1 (unmodified)
File Edit View Insert Format Table Graphics Tools Window Help

QuickFonts ▾ Arial ▾ 12 pt ▾ Styles ▾ Left ▾ 1.0 ▾ Tables ▾ 100% ▾

Insert   HP DeskJet 500   Select Pg 1 Ln 1" Pos 1"

Status bar   Typing area   Scroll bars

Figure 2-1

Figure 2-1: The WordPerfect window has a menu bar at the top, loads of little buttons, and a great big white space where you can type.

Table 2-1	*(continued)*
Gizmo	**What You Can Do with It**
Maximize button	You use it to tell WordPerfect to expand and take up the entire screen. When WordPerfect is already in full screen mode, this button turns into the Restore button.
Close button	You use it to close WordPerfect.
Restore button	This button looks like two windows overlapping (whereas the Maximize button looks like just one window). It appears only when a window is maximized. You use it to tell WordPerfect to appear in a window, not maximized.

Using windows

Refer to Figure 2-2 to see a typical Windows 95 computer screen. Windows 95 can run more than one program at a time. It puts the programs in separate *windows* — that is, rectangular areas on the screen that display information about a program.

Figure 2-2: WordPerfect may not be the only thing on your screen.

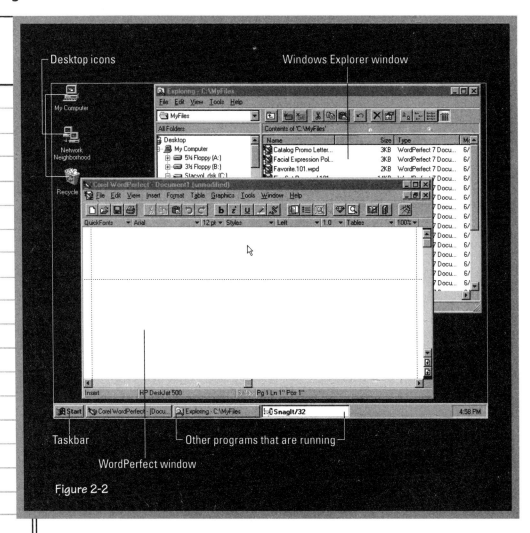

Figure 2-2

▶ The WordPerfect window, the one that says *Corel WordPerfect* at the top (the top line of the window is called the *title bar*).

▶ The Windows Explorer window, the one that says *Exploring - C:\MyFiles* at the top. It's partly covered up by the WordPerfect window.

Windows 95 is distinguished from earlier versions of Windows by the Taskbar, which in Figure 2-2 is at the bottom of the screen. The Taskbar can appear on any edge of the screen, and can also be hidden. The Taskbar has a button for any program that is running. In Figure 2-2, the Taskbar has the Start button and buttons for the programs that are running: Explorer, WordPerfect, and Snagit/32 (a program that allows us to take screen shots that the production people at IDG Books Worldwide turn into the figures in this book). At the far right of the Taskbar is the Indicators box, which contains the time and maybe some other indicators, depending on how your computer is set up (icons for Corel WordPerfect Suite programs may appear here— double-click one to start the program).

Programs running under Windows can have one of three looks:

▶ *Maximized* — they take up the whole screen

▶ *In a window* — they take up part of the screen

▶ *Minimized* — appearing only as a button on the Taskbar

When WordPerfect is running in a window, you can see the Windows 95 Desktop and possibly other programs that you may be running around the edges. If you click on another window, that window comes to the front, possibly covering up your WordPerfect window. One window is always *active* — that is, it shows the program that you're using right now. The active window has a colored border and title bar, whereas the rest of the windows have gray borders and title bars. The active window is usually *on top* — that is, it covers up other windows, not the other way around. In Figure 2-2, the WordPerfect window is active. On the Taskbar, the button for the active program will look "pushed in" and be a lighter gray than the buttons for other programs that are running.

To make the WordPerfect window active, click anywhere on it. To redisplay WordPerfect (or any other program) after it has been minimized or covered by other windows, simply click once on its button on the Taskbar. (You can also hold down the Alt key and press the Tab key until the icon for the program you want has a box around it — then let go of the keys.)

If you want to get WordPerfect off your desktop but not out of your life (that is, you want to get it out of the way, but you'll be coming back to it in the near future), click on the Minimize button, which is the first of the three buttons in the upper-right corner of the WordPerfect window (it looks like a dash — it's actually a representation of a window shrunk to a button on the Taskbar — get it?).

click on window to make it active

When you're ready to use WordPerfect again, maximize it by clicking on the WordPerfect button on the Taskbar.

click on Corel WordPerfect button on Taskbar when WordPerfect is hidden

The button immediately to the right of the Close button changes its appearance depending on whether the WordPerfect window is maximized to take up the entire screen (when the Restore button looks like two windows overlapping), or is in a window that doesn't take up the whole screen (when the Maximize button looks like just one window). You use it to tell WordPerfect whether to take up the whole screen or just part of it.

Now try some Windows basics with the WordPerfect window:

1 **If WordPerfect is taking up the whole screen, click on the Restore button at the top right corner of the screen to make your screen look more like Figure 2-2.**

This action puts WordPerfect into a window (*restoring* it, in Windows terms), which you can then move and size to suit your needs. But if all you're doing in Windows is using WordPerfect, we can't think of a good reason not to have it take the entire screen (maximized).

2 **To change the size of the WordPerfect window, click and drag the border when the window is active.**

When the WordPerfect window is active, the pointer turns into a double-headed arrow as it hits the border (on any of the four sides). After it changes, click on the left mouse button, hold it down, and move the border to a new position.

You can resize the window both horizontally and vertically if you move the pointer to a corner of the WordPerfect window, where it will turn into a diagonally pointing arrow.

3 **Move the WordPerfect window by clicking on the title bar and dragging it to a new position.**

After you've clicked, don't let go until the window is in its new position. As you move the mouse pointer, a big rectangle should move with it, showing you where the window will appear after you drop it.

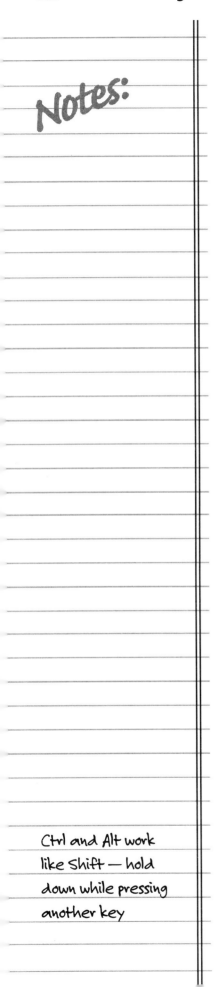

Notes:

4 **To make WordPerfect take up the whole screen again, maximize it by clicking on the Maximize button at the top right corner of the WordPerfect window.**

If you click on the Control-menu button (the pen icon) at the top left corner of the WordPerfect window, you get a menu that gives you other ways to do what you're doing in this exercise. Some items may be grayed out because they are not currently relevant (that is, you can't maximize a window when it's already maximized).

5 **Minimize the WordPerfect window by clicking on the Minimize button near the top right corner.**

This action gets WordPerfect off your desktop — it is still running, but it appears only as a button on the Taskbar.

6 **To get the WordPerfect window back, click on the WordPerfect button on the Taskbar.**

WordPerfect expands into either a window or full screen mode, depending on how it appeared just before you minimized it.

Congratulations! You have just mastered skills that you can use with any Windows-based application.

Using your keyboard

In the lessons in this unit, we tell you how to use many of the items we just listed, especially the menu bar and the Power Bar. You'll be familiar with them in no time. But first, let us introduce you to your keyboard!

Most of the keys on your keyboard do just what you expect — the H key, for example, types the letter H. But there are some computer-y keys on your keyboard, too, which you'll need to use.

The keyboard can be described in sections: function keys, the escape key, cursor control keys, regular old typewriter keys, shift and shift-type (otherwise known as *shifty* — *but only by us*) keys, and the numeric keypad. If you work on a laptop, all bets are off — your computer probably has fewer keys than the average desktop computer, and using them is probably far more complicated (although the letters, shifty, and function keys should work pretty much normally).

- The keys in the top row are *function keys*. These are the ones labeled F1 through F10 or 12 (different keyboards have different numbers of function keys). In WordPerfect, function keys are assigned to commands. We find that usually a more memorable way to use the command exists, and we always let you know what it is.

- The *Ctrl* or *Control* key is used like a Shift key: You hold it down while pressing another key. WordPerfect uses the Ctrl key to create shortcuts to commonly used commands. For example, holding down Ctrl while pressing the P key prints your document. We write such key combinations like this: Ctrl+P. Just hold down the Ctrl key with one finger and press the other key with another finger. Easy?

- The *Alt* key is another shifty key that you hold down while pressing another key. You use the Alt key mainly when you want to choose items from menus but don't feel like using the mouse. To choose a command from the menu bar, you can hold the Alt key down while

Ctrl and Alt work like Shift — hold down while pressing another key you type the underlined letter in the command. For example, Alt+F chooses the File command. You learn more about using menus in Lesson 2-2.

◗ The *Enter* key might be labeled *Return* on your keyboard, or it might just have a hooked arrow on it. When typing text, press the Enter key only at the ends of paragraphs or at the ends of headings or other lines that aren't parts of paragraphs.

◗ The *Esc* key is a kind of "Yikes!" key. Press it when you want to cancel a command or make a dialog box go away. We tell you more about when to press it as we tell you how to give commands and use dialog boxes.

◗ The cursor control keys are the arrows and the group of keys above them (Home, End, Page Up, and so on), which you can use to move the cursor.

◗ The numeric keypad is to the far right of the keyboard (not everyone has one). When Num Lock (just press the Num Lock key that should be nearby) is on, the numeric keypad is a good way to enter a great deal of numbers; when Num Lock is off, these keys work as cursor control keys.

Enough background — time to get on with how to work on your documents.

Esc key cancels commands

☑ Progress Check

If you can do the following, you're ready to move on to the next lesson:

❑ Control how big the WordPerfect window is.

❑ Shrink the WordPerfect window to an icon to get it out of the way while you run another program.

❑ Make WordPerfect take up the whole screen.

❑ Find the different kinds of keys on your keyboard.

Using Menu Commands to Open and Close Documents

Lesson 2-2

This lesson's true purpose is to tell you how to use the WordPerfect menu bar. While we're at it, we tell you how to open and close a document and how to change what your WordPerfect window displays.

The menu bar rests at the top of your WordPerfect window — it's a line of words, each with an underlined letter. To choose a command from the menu bar, click on the first word of the command. For example, if you want to use the File⇨Open command, click on the word File. Alternatively, you can skip the mouse and use the keyboard — press Alt and then press the underlined letter of the command you want to choose.

When you choose a command on the menu bar, another menu, called a *pull-down menu* (despite the fact that you haven't pulled; you've only clicked or typed) appears with yet more commands. As you move the pointer to highlight different commands, a little yellow box pops up to tell you about what the highlighted command does.

Following are the types of things that you see on a pull-down menu:

◗ **Keyboard shortcuts:** Some commands have keystrokes next to them (for example, Ctrl+O). These are *keyboard shortcuts*. The next time you want to choose this command, you may use the keystroke (if you can remember it) rather than choosing the command from the menu bar.

◗ **Triangles:** When you highlight a command with a triangle next to it, you see yet another pull-down menu.

◆ **Ellipses:** When you choose a command with an ellipsis (three periods) next to it, WordPerfect displays a dialog box.

◆ **Checks:** Some commands have checks next to them, which you can turn off and on by choosing the command. When the check mark appears, the option is turned on.

Some menu commands appear grayed-out under certain circumstances, which means that you can't use them. We'll point out some grayed-out commands as we go along, and let you know what to do to make those options valid.

If you choose a command from the menu bar and it's not the one you want, just press the Esc key a few times. Esc (which is probably at the top left corner of your keyboard) can often be used when what you mean is "No, no, that's not really what I wanted to do." It's not always foolproof, though.

In general, use your mouse to click on commands — that is, click once with your mouse and let go. Or press Alt and then type the underlined letter of the command that you want to choose. Move through the menu by moving your mouse or by typing the underlined letter of the menu choice that you want. In Windows 95, unlike earlier versions of Windows, you don't have to click to see the next level of menu or another part of the main menu — just move the pointer to the menu choice that you want to see.

Opening an existing document

Unless you're a genius or extraordinarily determined, you will probably not start and finish a document in one sitting and then never want to see it again. That's the reason diskettes and hard disks were created — to fill up with files that you might need again. You learned to save a document in Lesson 1-3. In this lesson, you learn how to retrieve a file that you or someone else has created (which could be useful if your code name is 007).

extra credit

Commanding without your mouse: using Alt key shortcuts

If you are a speed demon typist and don't want to take your hands from the keyboard to choose commands from the menu bar, you have another option. Have you wondered what all these underlined letters are about? They're for people like you! They allow you to choose commands without using your mouse.

The Alt key makes the menu bar *live* — that is, it warns WordPerfect that the next letter you type is to choose a command from the menu bar. After the menu bar is live, you can type the underlined letter of the command to choose it and display its pull-down menu. Then choose the command from the pull-down menu by pressing its letter.

For example, you can choose File⇨Close by pressing Alt (to make the menu bar live), and then F (to choose the File command), and then C (to choose the Close command).

If you press the Alt key and change your mind about choosing a command, press Alt again to make it dead (unlive?) — although hitting the Esc key a few times may be simpler and more foolproof.

(margin notes)

choose menu bar commands by clicking them

Notes:

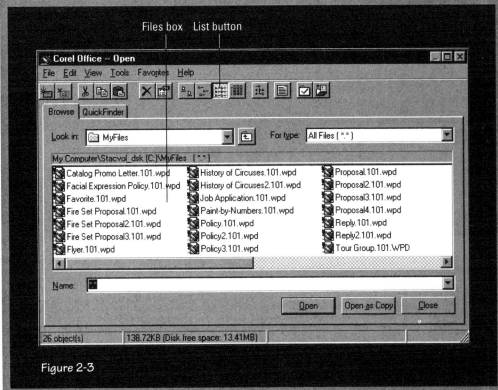

Figure 2-3

Figure 2-3: The Open dialog box lets you tell WordPerfect which file to open.

One way to open a document is by choosing File⇨Open from the menu bar. That is, choose File and then choose Open from the File pull-down menu that appears.

1 Choose File from the menu.

File is the first choice on the menu bar. Click on it with your mouse, and the File pull-down menu appears.

2 Choose Open from the pull-down menu.

Open is the second choice on the File menu — move the mouse pointer and click after it's highlighted. WordPerfect displays the Open dialog box, which you see in Figure 2-3.

Figure 2-3 shows filenames with their extensions. You may see the filenames without the extensions. Depending on how Windows 95 is set up, WordPerfect may not bother to display extensions for files of types that Windows 95 knows about. Windows 95 knows that WordPerfect documents use the extension .wpd, so it may not bother to display the extensions. But don't worry — the filename extensions are there!

3 You'll need to find the Toy Letter document in the long list of documents listed — here's the easy way to do it. Move your mouse pointer to the buttons at the top of the dialog box. Find the one that pops up a label that says "List"— the tenth button from the left on the Open dialog box Toolbar, with six tiny blue gizmos on it. Click on it.

The files were probably displayed as small icons, which gets messy looking if you use long filenames. List displays the files in easy-to-navigate columns.

File→Open opens a document

List button

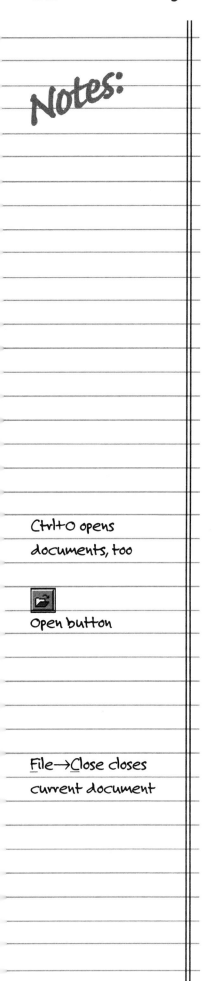

If the documents don't appear, install the files from the CD-ROM if you haven't already done so. (Read the Introduction for installation instructions.) If you have installed the files, WordPerfect probably isn't looking in the right place on your hard disk for the files. You may want to turn to Unit 8 to see how to look in different folders on your hard disk, but we suggest that you look in C:\MyFiles.

The Open dialog box is so big and fancy that it has its own menu bar and Toolbar, right below the title bar for the dialog box window. These commands and buttons control how the dialog box displays lists of files and help you find the files you need. (We talk about the Open dialog box in more detail in Unit 8.)

4 If you can see the document called Toy Letter, click on it once to select it. If you can't see the file, click on the right-pointing triangle button in the lower-right corner of the files box to see the rest of the files.

In the white box that lists filenames (which we'll refer to from now on as the files box), click on the name of the file that you want to open.

If you didn't create Toy Letter.wpd, or you have deleted it by mistake, don't panic. We have cheated on your behalf and included the letter to the toy company as a document called Toy Letter2.101.wpd. We're always thinking of you!

5 Click on Open.

WordPerfect opens the file.

Instead of clicking on the Open button, you can double-click on the file to open it.

The File pull-down menu has commands that have to do with entire files — like opening, closing, and printing them.

If you have a sharp eye, you may have noticed that File⇨Open has the keyboard shortcut Ctrl+O. (On the File pull-down menu, the notation *Ctrl+O* appears to the right of the Open command.) Any time we tell you to choose File⇨Open, you may press Ctrl+O instead.

Another shortcut for File⇨Open is the Open button on the Toolbar. The Open button has a picture of a little yellow folder.

Closing a document without closing WordPerfect

To practice using the menu, close the document using the File⇨Close command:

1 Choose File from the menu.

2 Choose Close from the File pull-down menu.

<u>C</u>lose is the third choice on the pull-down menu. After you click on it, WordPerfect checks whether you have made changes to the file. If you haven't, the document disappears, leaving you with a clean, white screen. If you have, WordPerfect asks you whether you want to save changes to the document, giving you the options <u>Y</u>es, <u>N</u>o, and Cancel. Choose either <u>Y</u>es or <u>N</u>o, depending on whether or not you want to keep the changes to the document. The document finally disappears.

<u>F</u>ile⇨<u>C</u>lose closes a document but leaves WordPerfect running. The document Close button (which is the X below the Close button for the WordPerfect window) and another shortcut, Ctrl+F4, do the same thing. Use either the command or its keyboard shortcut after you have finished with one document but still have work to do in WordPerfect.

You can use a command to exit WordPerfect, too. In Lesson 1-5, you used the Close button to exit, but <u>F</u>ile⇨E<u>x</u>it works just as well (as does Alt+F4).

You've learned a major WordPerfect skill: choosing commands from the menu bar. Pretty easy, right? The good news is that when you learn other Windows-based programs, you'll find that their menu bars usually work exactly the same way as WordPerfect's.

extra credit

What to do when you get beeps instead of text

Occasionally, you'll be trying in your humble way to type a letter, and all you'll get from an uncooperative WordPerfect are beeps. Or perhaps a pull-down menu appears. What's going on?

The problem is that you have, completely by accident, hit the Alt key. The Alt key tells WordPerfect that you want to choose a command from the menu bar, and WordPerfect is trying to do its best to execute a command. (You can choose a command from the menu bar by pressing the Alt key and then pressing the underlined letter of the command you want.) This problem isn't a bug; it's a feature — the Alt key allows you to continue using WordPerfect even if your mouse dies.

If you get beeps when you want to type, press the Esc key a few times (technically, press it until the one word on the menu is highlighted and then press it one more time to get rid of the menu). WordPerfect is now happy to accept your Pulitzer Prize-quality prose.

Recess

If you're ready to take a break, exit WordPerfect. Now that you've learned how to use commands from the menu bar, we can reveal to you a popular way to leave WordPerfect: choose <u>F</u>ile⇨E<u>x</u>it from the menu bar.

Ctrl+F4 or the document Close button closes documents

☑ **Progress Check**

If you can do the following, you're ready to move on to the next lesson:

❑ Use menu commands.

❑ Open a document using a command from the menu bar.

❑ Close a document without closing WordPerfect.

Lesson 2-3	# Using Dialog Boxes to Open or Create Documents

Notes:

Many commands display dialog boxes, which are an important way to tell WordPerfect the details about the command. For example, after you tell WordPerfect that you want to open a document, it responds by saying, "Tell me more" — it displays the Open dialog box so that you can tell it which file to open. Often, WordPerfect asks you for more information than you want to consider, or even than you know. But in most cases, you can just tell WordPerfect what you think is important, and it'll guess about the rest. Sometimes we tell you to type something in one box and ignore the rest of the dialog box.

You already used dialog boxes when you opened and printed a document. But you haven't used many of the gizmos and buttons that appear in dialog boxes. Table 2-2 describes each of the types of boxes and buttons, with instructions for using each one. Figure 2-4 shows a dialog box (the Font dialog box, the one that lets you control what the characters in your document look like) with some of its parts labeled.

Table 2-2	Ways to Use Dialog Boxes
Type of Dialog Thingy	**How to Use It**
Check boxes	If you want to turn a check box off or on, click on the check box. A check mark appears or disappears from the box. (The Appearance part of the Font dialog box in Figure 2-4 contains check boxes.) Occasionally, you may see an *X* instead of a check mark — both symbols do the same job.
Lists to choose from	Click on the file or option you want. (The Font Face is this type of setting.)
Boxes with a down arrow to their right	These are lists, with only the chosen option displayed. Click on the arrow to see the other options and click on the one you want. (The Open dialog box in Figure 2-3 contains several settings like this.)
Boxes to type in	Click on the box to put the cursor there and then type. Don't press Enter after you've finished typing — WordPerfect will think that you're finished with the whole dialog box, as though you clicked on the OK or Close button.
Boxes with numbers	You can change the number by highlighting it with the mouse (click, hold, and drag) and then typing the new number. You can also click on the up or down arrow to the right of the number with your mouse to make the number larger or smaller. (The Shading setting in the Font dialog box, shown in Figure 2-4, works this way.)

Type of Dialog Thingy	How to Use It
Buttons	Click on a button to perform an action. A button with an ellipsis opens another window, usually another dialog box. A button with a triangle displays a menu. A button with up and down arrows displays a list — click on the button and then click on the choice you want.
Icons	Occasionally, you see an icon in a dialog box. Double-click on the icon to display the next dialog box. (Choosing Edit➪Preferences brings up a box of icons.)
Menus	Dialog boxes sometimes have menus across the top of them that work just like the regular WordPerfect menu.
Radio buttons	A list of choices each with a circle next to it. A circle with a dot in it indicates that it is selected. Click on the item you want selected or the circle next to it to move the dot to that item. In the Print dialog box, Figure 1-5, Group and Collate make up a set of radio buttons. (They're named after old-fashioned radio buttons, which can be pressed only one at a time — when you press one button, the previously selected one pops out.)

on the test

Here's a valuable piece of advice: If you see a dialog box and wish it would go away, press Esc. Poof! It vanishes (the dialog box, not the Esc key). Most dialog boxes have the Close button (the X) in the upper-right corner, which provides another way to cancel a dialog box that you decide not to use. Likewise, the Cancel button (if you see one) does the same thing. A Close button near the bottom or on the right of a dialog box will probably close the box, which keeps any changes you have made; so stick with the other methods if you want to cancel your changes.

One warning about dialog boxes: Pressing Enter while you are using a dialog box is usually like clicking on the highlighted button — usually the OK or Close button. (While in a dialog box, you can tell which button will get clicked if you press Enter: One button usually has a darker border around it.) So beware of pressing Enter accidentally when typing something into a dialog box — the box may suddenly vanish because you just closed it or executed it (like clicking on the OK button in the Save As dialog box). If you need to move to another section of the dialog box, press the Tab key or use the mouse.

To sum up: In almost every lesson in the rest of this book, you use WordPerfect dialog boxes, including dialog boxes that control fonts, colors, spacing, columns, and other fancy formatting. We describe how to use the settings in each of these dialog boxes in the lessons where you meet them. Our point in this lesson is that all dialog boxes work the same way: You display the dialog box, possibly change some settings in the dialog box, and after you are finished, you click on a button labeled something such as *OK* or *Close*. If you wish you hadn't started using the dialog box, you click on the Cancel button or you press the Esc key.

The exercises in this lesson teach you some really useful stuff about opening and saving documents while teaching you how to use dialog boxes.

Notes:

Esc key cancels a dialog box

Figure 2-4: The Font dialog box has lots of settings that you can change.

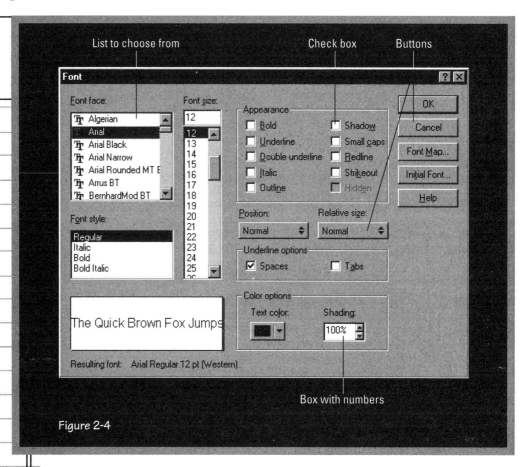

Figure 2-4

Using the Open and Save As dialog boxes to create a new document from an old one

You'll get lots of chances to practice using dialog boxes as the book progresses. We start by giving you lots of help as you open a document as Read Only. (Sounds impressive, doesn't it?)

You frequently want to use an existing document as the basis of a new document but still want to be able to use the original, unaltered document. For example, if you're a big fan of toys (or your kids are, and you like to show your appreciation to the companies that make them), you may want to send a letter similar to Toy Letter.wpd to another toy company. You can tell WordPerfect that you want to open a document as a copy — you can edit the document, but you cannot save it with the same name. Instead, WordPerfect insists that you save the document with a new name. After you have done so, you end up with two documents on disk: your original document with its original name and your new document with a new name.

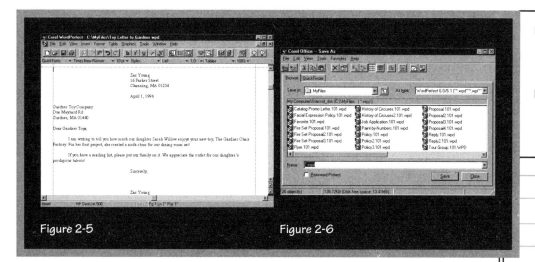

Figure 2-5

Figure 2-6

Figure 2-5: Why type a letter from scratch if you can recycle an existing letter?

Figure 2-6: The Save As dialog box enables you to give a new document a name.

To edit an existing document and save it with a new name, follow these steps:

1 Choose File⇨Open from the menu bar.

You see the Open dialog box, which appeared back in Figure 2-3.

2 Click on Toy Letter.wpd.

on the CD

If you didn't do Unit 1, click on Toy Letter2.101.wpd instead.

Only the files in one folder are displayed in the file box on the Open dialog box. If you need to open a file from another drive or folder (or both), you'll need to use the Look in setting on the Open dialog box. The Look in setting is where you select the drive and folder that you need to use — once you have the right drive, double-click on a folder name in the files box to see files in that folder. You'll learn more about moving around drives and folders in Unit 8.

3 Click on the Open as Copy button in the dialog box.

It's in the lower right part of the dialog box.

WordPerfect opens the document. In the title bar of the WordPerfect window, the words (Read Only) tell you that you can't save this document as Toy Letter2.101.wpd or Toy Letter.wpd, depending on which file you opened. To save it, you have to give it a new name.

4 Edit the document to match Figure 2-5.

Change the name and address of the toy company and edit the first paragraph of the letter.

5 Choose File⇨Save As from the menu bar.

That is, choose File from the menu bar and choose Save As from the File pull-down menu. WordPerfect displays the Save As dialog box (Figure 2-6), which is also the dialog box that appears the first time you save a document.

6 In the Name box, type the document's new name: Toy Letter to Gardner (or some other name that tickles your fancy).

When the dialog box appears, the cursor (highlight) is in the Name box, so what you type appears there. To give the file a new name, simply type **Toy Letter to Gardner**. This new filename replaces the filename that appeared originally. You don't have to add the filename extension .wpd, because WordPerfect adds it for you.

use Open As Copy button to create a copy of a document

F3 is shortcut for File→Save As

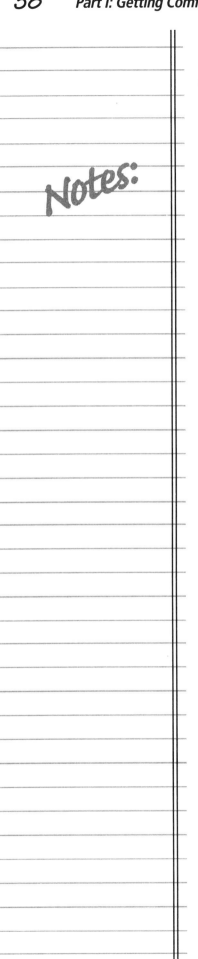

Notes:

extra credit

Dealing with documents from other word processors

You can also use the Open dialog box to open a file that was created with a different word processor. If you pick a file that isn't a WordPerfect file, an additional dialog box appears with WordPerfect's best guess about the format (the software that created the file). If it's right, just press Enter, but if it's wrong, you can change the file format by choosing the correct software that created the document.

When you save the document, WordPerfect displays a dialog box that gives you the choice of saving the file in WordPerfect format or in its original format. If you'll be giving the document back to whomever gave it to you and who personally has some other word processor, save it in the other format (and suggest that he or she step up to WordPerfect!). If you'll only be using it with WordPerfect in the future, save it in WordPerfect format. If, at some later point, you need to convert a document from WordPerfect format to a format that another word processor can read, use the As type option in the Save As dialog box (File⇨Save As).

7 **Click on Save to close the Save As dialog box and save the document with the new name, Toy Letter to Gardner.wpd.**

You used the toy letter as the basis for a new letter by opening it as a copy. You then edited the document and saved it with a new name by using the File⇨Save As command from the menu bar.

Saving a document to a diskette

What if you just wrote a fantastic report and your boss wants to edit it and make a few little changes? Or what if you want to make a backup copy of the report on a disk so that you'll have a duplicate copy just in case disaster strikes?

Making backup copies of your important documents is a good idea. If you don't have a backup scheme for backing up all the files on your hard disk, considering saving your important files to disk on a regular basis. Better safe than sorry — imagine what a drag rewriting that long report you just wrote would be!

Not a problem, as long as you've got a disk. You can use the File⇨Save As command to save a document to a diskette. You should have the Toy Letter to Gardner.wpd document on-screen. Save the file to a scratch disk (a disk that you don't need for anything important), using the name Letter to Toy Company.wpd by following these steps.

1 **Put a scratch diskette into the diskette drive.**

This lesson doesn't delete anything from the disk, but use a formatted disk that you don't need for anything else — just in case.

2 **Choose File⇨Save As from the menu bar.**

You see the Save As dialog box.

NOTE

3 Click on the **little down-arrow button at the right end of the Save in box.**

WordPerfect displays a list of your disk drives and folders.

The Open dialog box has a similar setting, called Look in, where you can tell WordPerfect where to find the file you want to open.

4 **Click on the drive that contains your disk.**

You may have to cursor up (use the up arrow) to be able to see the drive that you want. While it's highlighted, press Enter or click on it. The disk drive whirs, and WordPerfect displays a list of files on that disk in the selected folder.

5 **Click in the Name box or press Tab until the contents of the Name box are highlighted. Type the name that you want to use when saving the file.**

The box already contains the name that the document had on the hard disk. If you want to use the same name for the file when you save it to the disk, skip this step. The filename is highlighted, so when you start typing, the new name replaces the name in the box.

For this example, type **Letter to Toy Company**.

6 **Click on Save.**

WordPerfect saves the document to the disk, naming it Letter to Toy Company.wpd. The document is also still on your hard disk, under its original name.

If WordPerfect has a problem reading the disk, it will let you know by displaying an error message. The diskette may be no good, not formatted, or a Macintosh diskette in disguise. Try formatting it (as long as you need nothing on it), or try another diskette.

extra credit

Other ways to open a document

Windows 95 gives you all sorts of ways to open a document. The ways that you've been using (the Open button on the button bar and the File⇨Open command) are logical but not always the quickest way to go. But the best way depends on what you're doing. When you're already in WordPerfect, the ways you've already learned are the best ways to open an already existing document, but when you haven't opened WordPerfect yet, and you're going to work on a document that you started during another session, you do have an easier way to go.

To open a document that you've recently used, click on the Start button, move to Documents, and see if the file that you want appears on the list of documents. If it does, simply click on it to have WordPerfect run and open that document. Or when you're already in WordPerfect, recently used documents appear at the bottom of the File menu. Just click on the file you want to open.

Another way to open a document is to locate it using Explorer or My Computer and then double-click on the file. If the file has the extension .wpd, Windows 95 knows that the file is a WordPerfect document, runs WordPerfect, and opens the file.

Notes:

make backup copies of important documents

☑ Progress Check

If you can do the following, you're ready to move on to the next lesson:

❑ Use different parts of a dialog box.

❑ Open a file and save it with a different name.

❑ Save a document to a diskette.

Nice work! Dialog boxes look daunting, but they are used throughout WordPerfect and other Windows-based programs. Now you know how to display a dialog box using a command, enter information in the dialog box, change its settings, and click on buttons to finish the command. In the process, you've learned a lot of useful things about opening and saving files, and especially some of the hazards of navigating your drives and folders. You'll do these things every day that you use WordPerfect.

You're ready to spend a few minutes learning to move around in your document. As you produce longer documents, moving around will become more and more important. You'll learn to use both the mouse and the keyboard for cursor movement.

Lesson 2-4 — Moving Around in Your Document Using Keys

If the rest of this unit were a class, it would be geography class. We tell you how to get from one place in your document to another, using three methods (you may have noticed that WordPerfect never gives you only one way to do something).

on the test

Before you start moving, figuring out where you are is a good idea (after all, when you're lost, you need to know where you're starting from, or you can't use a map). One way to figure out where you are is to check out the status bar (the bottom line of the WordPerfect window). The last box of the status bar tells you where you are in your document. It tells what page you're on (Pg x), how far you are from the top of the page, including the top margin (Ln x"), and how far you are from the left side of the page, including the left margin (Pos $x.xx$"). For instance, when the cursor is at the very beginning of a document, the status bar will read Pg 1 (because it's the first page), Ln 1" (because the top margin is 1", the cursor is 1" from the top of the page), and Pos 1" (because the left margin is also 1", the cursor is 1" from the left edge of the page).

If you're going somewhere you can see, you have two easy ways to move your cursor there:

> ▶ Use the mouse to move the pointer there and click once to move the cursor to that spot.

> ▶ Use the arrow keys on your keyboard.

Using the mouse may be the best way to go — WordPerfect has added some nifty new features that make it easy. When you move the mouse pointer, WordPerfect attaches a ghost cursor (the vertical bar that tells you where you are in the document) so that you can see exactly where in the text the cursor will be after you click on the mouse button. WordPerfect also puts a block in the left margin next to the paragraph the pointer is pointing to, making figuring out where you are easier.

The arrow keys can move you anywhere in your document, but if your document is long, this process can take forever. Following are a few things we should tell you about moving around in a larger document:

use mouse or arrow keys to move around document

♦ Your document may extend farther than you can see (think of it as a scroll, extending up and down off your screen).

♦ The cursor has to stay on text — it can't hang out in margins (the mouse pointer, however, can go anywhere on the screen).

♦ Your cursor will do its darnedest to move where you ask it. So if you press the right arrow when you're at the end of a line, the cursor moves to the next character, which is at the beginning of the next line. If it's on the last line in the window and you press the down arrow, WordPerfect moves the text up a little to show you the next line.

on the test

Table 2-3 shows some keys that you can use for moving around in your documents.

Table 2-3	Cursor Control Keys
Keystroke(s)	**Where It Gets You**
Arrow key	One line or character in the direction indicated
Ctrl+up arrow	To the beginning of the current paragraph or, if you are at the beginning of the paragraph, to the beginning of the previous paragraph
Ctrl+down arrow	To the beginning of the next paragraph
Ctrl+left or right arrow	Left or right one word
Home	To the beginning of the line
End	To the end of the line
PgUp (Page Up) or PgDn (Page Down)	To the top or bottom of the screen, or up or down one full screen
Ctrl+Home	To the beginning of the document
Ctrl+End	To the end of the document

extra credit

When arrows are numbers

You may have noticed that you have two sets of arrows on your keyboard (not all keyboards do, but most do). This design is in the interest of repetition, which with the introduction of Windows has made great strides in the computer world. (Try spending some time in a third world country — then you won't sneeze at having more than one way to do something!)

The cursor control keys on the far right of your keyboard make up the *numeric keypad* and have both arrows and numbers on them. These keys can be used as numbers (when you are in *Num Lock mode)* or arrows (when you're not). To switch to or from Num Lock mode, press the aptly named Num Lock key. Most keyboards have a Num Lock light, too. If the Num Lock light is on, the numeric keypad types numbers. When the light is off, the keys move the cursor.

Notes:

Figure 2-7:
Proposal.101.wpd
is ready for you to
explore.

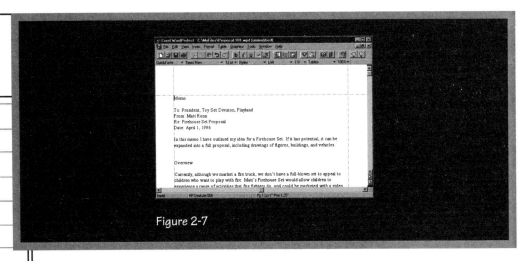

Figure 2-7

PgUp and PgDn move
one screenful at a
time

Ctrl+Home and
Ctrl+End move to
beginning and end
of document

☑ Progress Check

If you can do the following,
you're ready to move on to
the next lesson:

❏ Find the cursor control
keys.

❏ Use Ctrl+Home and
Ctrl+End to move to the
beginning and end of a
document.

❏ Use the PgUp and PgDn
keys to move through a
document one screenful
at a time.

Moving around using your keyboard

Here's how to move around in a longer document, using the keys rather than
the mouse:

on the CD

**1 Open Proposal.101.wpd, which you copied to your hard disk when
you installed the CD from the back of the book. (If you don't have
it installed, read the Introduction for instructions on how to install
it.) Use the File⇨Open command, press Ctrl+O, or click on the
Open button on the Toolbar.**

Your choice! They all do the same thing — the Proposal.101.wpd document
appears on-screen. (You can see it in Figure 2-7.)

**2 Move to the end of the document one screen at a time by pressing
the PgDn key several times.**

The first time you press PgDn, it moves the cursor to the bottom of the current
screen. The next time you press it, it moves the cursor down a full screen (it
displays the next part of the document that fits on the screen).

3 Move back to the top of the document by using Ctrl+Home.

4 Move to the end using Ctrl+End.

You've just practiced moving aimlessly around the document using keystrokes
from Table 2-3 rather than using the mouse and arrow keys. Although we'll
believe you sometimes when you say, "I needed to check to see where that
section was and what came between it and the section I'm working on," we
also know that this moving around is a great way to waste time. After all, we're
writers, too!

Recess

If you would like to take a break now (maybe all that moving has given you
ideas about how your furniture should be arranged), exit WordPerfect using
Alt+F4. You haven't made any changes, so you shouldn't need to save the
document. When you're ready to learn more about moving around documents, start up WordPerfect by double-clicking on its icon.

Moving Around in Long Documents by Using Scroll Bars

Lesson 2-5

The gray stripe along the right edge of the WordPerfect window is called the *vertical scroll bar* (you can see it in Figure 2-1). If WordPerfect can't show you the whole width of your document, the *horizontal scroll bar* appears along the bottom of the window, just above the status bar. Flip back to Figure 2-1 if you're having any trouble identifying the scroll bars. Both scroll bars work the same way, but we talk mostly about the vertical scroll bar because documents are much more commonly long than wide.

Most Windows-based programs use scroll bars to help you find your way around something that is too big to fit on-screen. Scroll bars don't move your cursor, but they change what part of the document WordPerfect displays in the WordPerfect window. (This can be tricky.)

Each scroll bar has three parts: arrows on the end, a gray area between the arrows, and the scroll box somewhere in the gray area. The WordPerfect vertical scroll bar has an extra part: two buttons below the down arrow that allow you to move up and down page by page instead of just a screenful at a time.

The *scroll box* tells you approximately what part of the document you are viewing. If the box is at the top, you're looking at the top of your document, and if it's about a quarter of the way down, you're looking at a section of the document about three-quarters of the way from the end.

heads up

The scroll bar does *not* tell you where your cursor is, a fact that can be a tad confusing. If your cursor is at the beginning of a document, you can use the scroll bars to view the end of the document — but your cursor is still sitting at the beginning of the document. If you type something, what you type appears where the cursor is, and if the cursor is off the top or bottom of the screen, WordPerfect hurriedly displays the part of the document where the cursor is so that you can see what you're typing. A quick click with the mouse puts the cursor in the text that you're looking at.

You can use a scroll bar in three ways to display different parts of a document:

> ◆ Move the display one line at a time by clicking on the arrows at the ends of the scroll bar.

> ◆ Move the display one screenful at a time by clicking between the arrow and the scroll box. If you click between the top of the scroll bar and the scroll box, you move up. If you click between the scroll box and the bottom of the scroll bar, you move down.

> ◆ Move the scroll box to reflect the part of the document you want to see. That is, click on the scroll box, hold down the mouse button, and drag it along the scroll bar to where you want it to be. Your view of the document changes to match the new position of the scroll box after you let go of the mouse button.

At the bottom of the vertical scroll bar are two buttons: They look like pieces of paper with arrows on them. The first takes you to the top of the previous page and the second takes you to the top of the next page.

heads up

Tip: If you want to move your cursor to some text that you see on-screen, just click on the text. It doesn't matter where the cursor used to be — now it's where you just clicked.

use vertical scroll bar to move forward and backward through document

Tip: A quick way to display the part of the document where the cursor is located is to press one of the arrow keys on the keyboard.

heads up

Moving up and down in the document using the vertical scroll bar

Scroll bars give you an easy way to move up or down one screenful at a time. To move down one screen, simply click on the scroll bar somewhere between the scroll box and the bottom of the scroll bar.

For this exercise, open Proposal.101.wpd if it's not already on-screen.

on the CD

1 **Move to the end of the document one screen at a time by clicking on the vertical scroll bar between the box and the down arrow.**

Your cursor stays where it is, and WordPerfect displays the last screenful of the document.

2 **Move back to the top of the document by clicking on the box and dragging it to the tippy-top of the vertical scroll bar.**

Remember to click, hold, and drag.

You moved one screenful at a time by clicking on the scroll bar between the scroll box and the ends of the scroll bar — on the elevator shaft that the scroll box moves along. You also moved around the document by dragging the scroll box to a new location on the scroll bar.

Remember that you can easily display the part of the document where the cursor is by pressing an arrow key.

Looking at the left and right edges of your document

Your document may be too wide to fit across the WordPerfect window, unless you maximize the window. Use the horizontal scroll bar to see the edges of your document.

For this exercise, run WordPerfect in a window. If WordPerfect is running maximized (taking up the whole screen), click on the Restore button (which looks like overlapping windows) near the upper-right corner of the screen.

1 **To see the right side of your document, click and drag the scroll box to the right end of the horizontal scroll bar.**

Now you can see all the way to the right edge of the paper (the virtual paper, that is — because you're looking at a picture of what will print on paper).

2 **To see the left side of your document, click between the scroll box and the left end of the horizontal scroll bar.**

WordPerfect scrolls the document to the right.

3 **Click on the arrows at the left and right ends of the horizontal scroll bar until your document is approximately centered in the WordPerfect window.**

You don't need to see your left and right margins all the time — they're blank anyway!

Margin notes:

click on above/below scroll box to move up/down one screen

use horizontal scroll bar to see sides of wide documents

Restore button

You'll find that the scroll bars often help you figure out your relative location in the document (like the locations of your relatives, your location in a document varies). You can also use it to move around, as you've just done. However, when you're typing away, it may be too much of a pain to pick up your hands, figure out where the mouse pointer is, and play with the scroll bar (unless you're into procrastination); using the cursor movement keys described in the previous lesson is frequently more convenient.

Now you know a bunch of ways to move around in your documents! If you're through with lessons for a while, close WordPerfect by pressing Alt+F4.

Recess

If you're ready to take a break, you can exit WordPerfect by choosing File⊃Exit. But wait! You're ready to take the Unit 2 Quiz!

☑ **Progress Check**

If you can do the following, you're ready to move on to the next unit:

❑ Identify the vertical scroll bar, the horizontal scroll bar, and the scroll boxes.

❑ Use the vertical scroll bar arrows to move one line at a time.

❑ Use the vertical scroll bar to move up and down one screenful at a time.

❑ Use the horizontal scroll bar to see the edges of your document.

❑ Cruise through your document using the scroll box.

Unit 2 Quiz

For each of the following questions, circle the letter of the correct answer or answers. Remember, we may give you more than one right answer for each question.

1. **The row of little buttons just below the menu bar is called . . .**

   A. The Toolbar.

   B. The status bar.

   C. The scroll bar.

   D. The sand bar.

   E. Joe's Bar and Grill.

2. **A scroll bar is . . .**

   A. Something of great historical significance found near the Dead Sea.

   B. An odd feature unique to WordPerfect.

   C. The gray bar on the right (and sometimes the bottom) of the WordPerfect window.

   D. Where a scroll goes when it's thirsty.

   E. A tool of document navigation.

3. **Pressing the Home key . . .**

   A. Has the same effect as clicking the heels of your ruby slippers.

   B. Starts that automatic map thing that some cars have nowadays.

   C. Takes you to the beginning of the line where your cursor is.

   D. Takes you to the top of the document.

   E. Displays the Taskbar.

4. **In general, using the Ctrl key with cursor control keys . . .**

   A. Confuses the computer.

   B. Takes you farther in the same direction than using the key alone does.

   C. Makes the cursor disappear from sight.

   D. Reboots the computer.

   E. Means that you really know what you're doing.

5. **If you want to know where you are in a document, the best thing to do is . . .**

   A. Press PgUp as many times as it takes you to get to the top of the document and then use PgDn to go back to where you were.

   B. Stare at the document until you can remember its entire contents and then figure out where you are.

   C. Check out the last box in the status line.

   D. Walk away — maybe you'll remember.

   E. Look where the scroll box is on the vertical scroll bar.

Unit 2 Exercise

on the CD

1. Open Toy Letter.wpd or Toy Letter2.101.wpd as a copy.

2. Save the file with the name Hated Your Toy.wpd.

3. Rewrite the letter to say that a toy you bought was lousy (you can use our example, or not).

4. Save the document (still with the name Hated Your Toy.wpd).

> Zac Young
> 16 Parker Street
> Channing, MA 01234
>
> April 1, 1996
>
> Gardner Toy Company
> One Maynard Rd.
> Gardner, MA 01440
>
> Dear Gardner Toys,
>
> I am writing to say that our family was very disappointed in your line of Rough Stuff plastic toys. The toys have not proved to be as rugged as your adds claim. For example, our daughter Sarah Willow was easily able to melt your Rough Stuff Truck into a puddle of molten plastic using only her child-sized flame-thrower.
>
> Sincerely,
>
> Zac Young

Cool Word-Processing Moves

Prerequisites
- Opening an existing document (Lesson 2-2)
- Moving around using your keyboard (Lesson 2-4)

Objectives for This Unit

✓ Using Enter and Ctrl+Enter to end paragraphs and pages

✓ Splitting and combining paragraphs

✓ Inserting characters versus overwriting what you've typed

✓ Undoing mistakes and redoing things

✓ Displaying a ruler across the top of the typing area

✓ Displaying WordPerfect's online help screens

on the CD
- Reply.101.wpd
- Reply2.101.wpd
- Proposal.101.wpd
- Facial Expression Policy.101.wpd

Unlike your old electric typewriter, WordPerfect has a clue about what you're writing. No, it can't understand the words, but it knows what a sentence is, what a paragraph is, and when you're getting close to the bottom of the page. As much as possible, you probably want to let WordPerfect handle the things that it knows how to do, like figuring out how much text will fit across each line and how many lines will fill up a page. Later, when you find out how to number pages automatically (in Lesson 12-2), the same principle will apply: Let WordPerfect handle putting page numbers on each page because it will be able to do so more consistently than you can.

This unit introduces you to a number of topics that can make you into a savvy word processor — unembarrassed when an old computer pro (or a young one, as the computer pros so often tend to be) looks over your shoulder. We tell you how to set up your WordPerfect window so that it contains the things that you actually want to see and how to type documents so that they're easy to edit later.

Lesson 3-1

Starting New Paragraphs and New Pages

In Unit 1, you did a little typing to create a document. Now we give you some how-to's and a warning about how to type when you're using WordPerfect (or any other word processor, for that matter).

Pressing Enter tells WordPerfect that you want to start a new line. It types an invisible carriage return character into your document. Here's the warning: Making the mistake of using too many Enters and spaces (instead of tabs) not only will mark you as a word processing beginner but will also make your documents considerably more difficult to edit. So make your life a little easier and learn to use Enter as we describe in this lesson!

Word processors do a wonderful thing called *word wrap*, which means that when you reach the end of a line, WordPerfect automatically puts the next word on the next line. Why is this feature useful? Well, it means that you don't have to press Enter at the end of each line, and when you change margins or the size of the letters, WordPerfect moves the words around (keeping them in order, of course) so that they still fill out the lines perfectly! If you press Enter at the end of every line, you have to delete the carriage returns (which are inserted when you press Enter) to have full lines when you change the margins or font size. So rule number one is: Only press Enter at the end of a paragraph.

You may also be tempted to press Enter enough times to get to the bottom of the page when you want to start a new page. But if you change the format of your document, the number of lines you inserted may no longer be the correct number of lines needed to finish the page. Rule number two is: Use Ctrl+Enter to start a new page (you can also choose Insert⇨Page Break from the menu).

WordPerfect is smart enough to automatically start a new page after you've typed too much text for one page. The only time you need to use Ctrl+Enter is when you want to force WordPerfect to start a new page in that place — for example, for the bibliography at the end of a term paper or a list of funny quotes that you want to enclose with a letter. Otherwise, just keep typing and let WordPerfect decide where each new page starts.

press Enter for new paragraph and new lines in a list <u>only</u>

press Ctrl+Enter for new page

Starting a new paragraph

on the CD

For this exercise, add a new paragraph to the letter that the toy company sent to you. Open the document Reply.101.wpd, which you see in Figure 3-1. Lesson 2-1 describes how to open an existing document.

1 **Move the cursor to the beginning of the third paragraph of the letter, which says *We've also included.***

This point is where you will insert a new paragraph. Use your mouse or the arrow keys to move the cursor. If you use the mouse, notice the shadow cursor in the text where the mouse is pointing — but you have to click to actually move the cursor to the same place as that shadow cursor — until then, it's just a convenience, not the actual cursor.

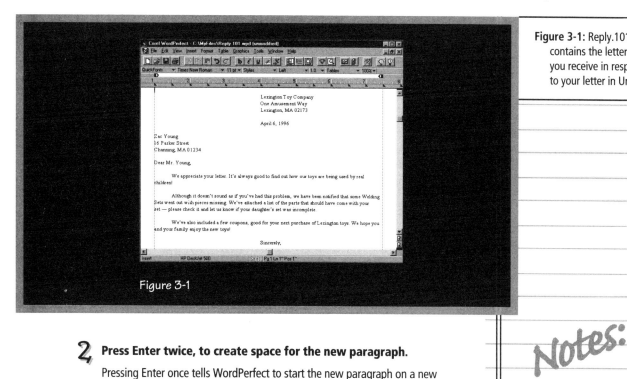

Figure 3-1

Figure 3-1: Reply.101.wpd contains the letter that you receive in response to your letter in Unit 1.

2 **Press Enter twice, to create space for the new paragraph.**

Pressing Enter once tells WordPerfect to start the new paragraph on a new line. Pressing it again leaves an empty line between your new paragraph and the existing second paragraph of the letter.

3 **Move up two lines by pressing the up arrow twice.**

This is the line on which your new paragraph begins.

4 **Start it with a tab to indent. Type a new paragraph.**

We suggest writing a paragraph that gives some excuse about why parts are missing from some of the welding sets — perhaps because of international industrial espionage, or other toys that got loose and used the welding sets.

Always start new paragraphs with the Enter key. In Lesson 11-1, we talk about how to get WordPerfect to automatically add space between paragraphs.

Combining two paragraphs

Deciding where to break a paragraph can be hard. Your fourth-grade English teacher probably had a rule of thumb — at least ours did, but we can't remember it. Anyway, if you decide that your paragraphs are too short and choppy, you can remove the space between two paragraphs, combining them. Here's how:

1 **Move your cursor to the end of the first of the two paragraphs that you want to combine.**

In the Reply.101.wpd letter, try combining the first two paragraphs of the letter: Move the cursor to the end of the first paragraph.

Notes:

Notes:

After your cursor is on the last line of the first paragraph, you can use the End key to get to the end of the line.

2 Press Delete.

This action deletes the carriage return (Enter) at the end of the paragraph. If no blank line appeared between the two paragraphs, the beginning of the second paragraph leaps up to continue where the first paragraph leaves off, and you're finished.

3 If the second paragraph still starts on a new line, press Delete again.

After you have deleted all the carriage returns between the end of the first paragraph and the beginning of the second, the second will start on the same line as the end of the first one.

4 If the second paragraph started with a tab character to indent its first line, you must press Delete yet again to delete the tab.

If the second paragraph started with a tab, you may see an unsightly gap between the end of the first paragraph and the beginning of the second one, created by the tab. Whether or not you see a large gap, delete the tab (a gap could show up later, depending on where in the line the tab is).

5 You may need to insert a space between the end of the last sentence in the first paragraph and the beginning of the first sentence in the second paragraph.

After you have deleted the carriage returns and tabs that separated the two paragraphs, you may need to stick in a space to separate the sentences. (By the way, you can forget about typing two spaces after a period, the way your typing teacher taught you. In the modern world of word processing, one space is enough.)

Conversely, you can split a paragraph into two paragraphs by moving your cursor to where the second paragraph should start and pressing Enter twice (once to start the new paragraph on a new line and a second time to leave a blank line between paragraphs). You may then need to add a tab and/or delete spaces, depending on the format you use.

extra credit

Gizmos at the ends of your lines

You know that carriage returns are littered all over your document, telling WordPerfect where your paragraphs end. But how can you tell *exactly* where they are?

Well, WordPerfect is happy to show them to you. Choose View⇨Show ¶ from the menu bar. Poof! Your document is suddenly filled with strange characters!

After you choose this command, WordPerfect displays right-pointing arrows wherever you have pressed Tab, paragraph signs where your carriage returns are, and dots in place of your spaces (they float a little above the line, so they don't look like periods). Don't worry—none of these strange symbols appear when you print the document. They just give you some inside information about how your document is formatted.

To make these symbols go back to where they came from, choose the command again—View⇨Show ¶.

☑ **Progress Check**

If you can do the following, you're ready to move on to the next lesson:

❑ Start a new paragraph by using Enter.

❑ Combine two paragraphs by deleting the carriage returns that separate them.

❑ Split a paragraph in two.

❑ Start a new page by using Ctrl+Enter.

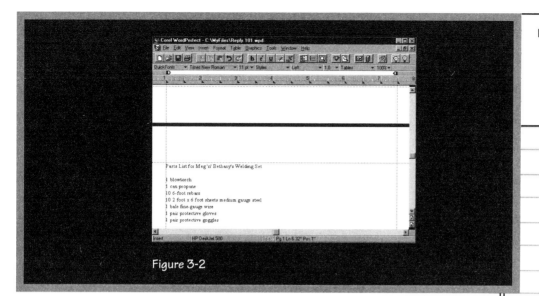

Figure 3-2

Figure 3-2: Reply.101.wpd now lists the parts on a separate page — the big white space and the black bar show the page break.

Starting a new page

Now put a list at the bottom of the Reply.101.wpd letter on a separate page. (If the document isn't already on-screen, open it, following the steps in Lesson 2-1 for opening an existing document.)

Ctrl+Enter starts new page

1 **Put your cursor where you want the new page to begin.**

Start the new page at the end of the letter, with your cursor at the beginning of the line that says "Parts List for Meg 'n' Bethany's Welding Set."

2 **Press Ctrl+Enter to start a new page.**

WordPerfect inserts a page break, which looks like a large gap between the end of one page and the beginning of the next. You see it almost as it will be printed — the rest of the empty page, with the dotted lines that indicate the margins, and the black bar that indicates the end of one page and the beginning of the next. (The dotted margin lines don't actually print.) You can see how your page should look in Figure 3-2. (If you are in Draft view, described in Lesson 4-1, you see a double line across the whole WordPerfect window.)

3 **Save your work by clicking on the Save button.**

Always use Ctrl+Enter to start a new page.

Inserting New Characters versus Typing Over What's There

Lesson 3-2

WordPerfect has two typing modes: *Insert* and *Typeover*. The way to tell the difference is to look at the status bar — so we're going to take a short detour by the status bar to show you what it's all about before we move on to typing modes.

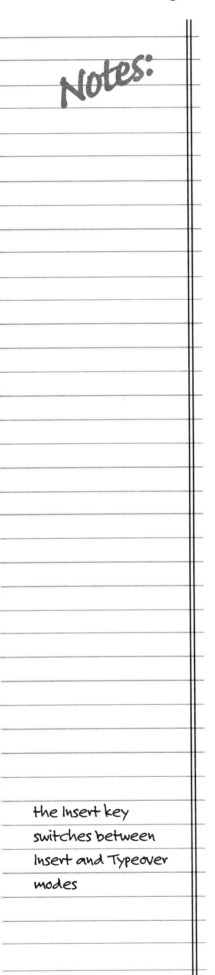

Introducing the status bar

The status bar can tell you a lot of cool things. And it doesn't just sit there, either. You can actually click on the status bar to make things happen. For instance, in the next section you will learn that you can double-click on the General Status indicator (the first part of the status bar) to change the typing mode from Insert to Typeover. You can find out more about any part of the status bar by putting the mouse pointer on it — a little box will pop up (just like the menu commands and buttons) to tell you about it. You can also read Table 3-1.

Table 3-1	What's That Stuff on the Status Bar?
Stuff	**What It Means**
General Status	Usually Insert or Typeover, which tells you whether WordPerfect is in Insert or Typeover mode. This box displays different types of status, depending on what you're doing. Double-click to change the status from Insert to Typeover, or vice versa.
Printer	What kind of printer WordPerfect thinks you have. See Unit 4. Double-click to display the dialog box where you can change the printer.
Select	This word appears in such a pale gray that you can't read it most of the time. It tells you whether you have selected some text (see Unit 5). Double-click to turn on select mode.
Combined Position	Looks like Pg *x* Ln *x.xx*" Pos *x*". Tells you the position of the cursor, including the page you're on, the line *(Ln)* measured in inches from the top of the printed page, and the position *(Pos)* from the left edge of the printed page, also measured in inches.

Changing typing mode

on the test

We prefer Insert mode — most people do. Typeover mode is startling — each character you type replaces the character to the right of the cursor. You can delete (type right over) a sentence or two before you notice what's going on. Insert mode, which is the way WordPerfect usually starts out, inserts the text where the cursor is and pushes the text that follows to the right to make room for the new next.

You can tell whether you're in Insert or Typeover mode by looking at the status bar (the last line of the WordPerfect window — see Table 3-1). The first word on the status bar is either *Insert* or *Typeover*. To change the mode, press the Insert (or Ins) key. This mode is what computer nerds call a *toggle setting* — whatever the current mode is, pressing the Insert key changes it to the other mode. You can also double-click on the box on the status bar that reads either *Insert* or *Typeover* to change it to the other setting.

on the CD

To practice using these two modes, open the Reply.101.wpd document if it's not already on-screen. If you didn't do Lesson 3-1, open Reply2.101.wpd (see Lesson 2-1 for how to open an existing file).

the Insert key switches between Insert and Typeover modes

1 **Press the Insert key until the General Status part of the status bar says *Typeover*.**

Remember, the Insert/Typeover setting is a toggle setting. If it already says *Typeover*, pressing Insert twice changes it to *Insert* and then back to *Typeover*. If you're in Insert mode, press the Insert key once to change the mode to Typeover. Or double-click on the part of the status bar that says *Insert*.

2 **Put your cursor on the first letter of *We* in the last sentence of the letter.**

3 **Type The Engineer Corps G. I. Joes have been especially well received.**

Notice that as you type each letter, it replaces a letter from the sentence that follows. Also notice that letters don't replace carriage returns — after you run out of letters to type over, WordPerfect acts like it would in Insert mode.

Incidentally, if you type very carefully, or just wait until after the next exercise to fix any errors in this sentence, the next exercise will go more smoothly.

heads up

4 **Press the Insert key until the General Status part of the status bar says *Insert* again.**

5 **Save your document by clicking the Save button on the Toolbar.**

You always want to save early and often. You never know when the power is going to burp, and it always improves computer users' moods to know that they have a recently saved copy of whatever they were working on.

Typeover mode is occasionally useful, or it may be what you're used to. But what you need to know is this: If WordPerfect is replacing text that is already there as you type, and you don't want it to, press the Insert key.

Now don't change a thing before you go on to the next lesson — you'll retrieve that sentence you just deleted.

☑ **Progress Check**

If you can do the following, you're ready to move on to the next lesson:

❏ Change the typing mode from Insert to Typeover and back again.

❏ Think of a situation in which Typeover mode would be useful.

Undeleting and Undoing   Lesson 3-3

Possibly the best excuse for not using a word processor (and one used by Winona Ryder's character in *How to Make an American Quilt* on why, in the 90s, she won't write her thesis using a computer), is that they lose things. Unfortunately, we may have more than one way to lose text we write, but the most popular is to delete it ourselves, by mistake or by Freudian slip. WordPerfect has two features that allow you to undo mistakes (and get rid of excuses for not using a computer): Undelete and Undo. They work slightly differently, so pay attention.

We start with the Undelete feature. WordPerfect remembers the last three chunks of stuff you deleted — anything beyond that goes to where things go when they are truly lost (our vote is for Newark, New Jersey). "Chunks of stuff" is defined as:

- a single character, if that is all you deleted
- contiguous characters, deleted by repeatedly pressing the Delete or Backspace key and not doing anything else in between
- a block of text replaced by typing over it in Typeover mode
- a block of text deleted all at once

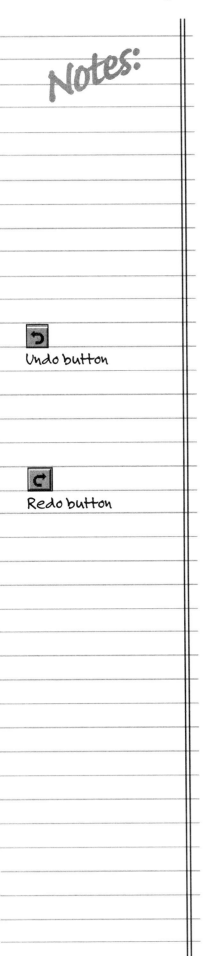

heads up

Undo button

Redo button

Most writers need this feature at one point or another — maybe you deleted a crucial paragraph, page, or table, and would do anything to get it back. Well, don't go to extremes, because all you need to do is one of the following:

▶ Choose Edit⇨Undelete from the menu bar.

▶ Press Ctrl+Shift+Z.

An added feature of the Undelete function is that the text is restored to *where the cursor is* — not necessarily to where it was originally. This ability to specify where the undeleted text should be put in the document can be useful, but it can also be confusing. Just remember to put your cursor where the formerly deleted text should go before using the Undelete command.

Undo is useful when your mistake is different from deleting something you shouldn't have. Maybe you moved something that you wished you hadn't, or formatted text until it was really ugly. Maybe you have no idea what you did, and you'd rather not try to untangle the results. Then the Undo command is ready and waiting for you, to fix what might otherwise be unfixable. (Undo also undeletes, but it puts the text back where it was, not where the cursor is.) Undo something by doing one of the following:

▶ Choosing Edit⇨Undo from the menu bar

▶ Clicking the Undo button

▶ Pressing Ctrl+Z

You can undelete by undoing, but only if deleting was the last thing you did.

Undo's twin is Redo, the button next to it pointing the other direction. Redo undoes what Undo just did. Redo something by doing one of the following:

▶ Choosing Edit⇨Redo from the menu bar

▶ Clicking the Redo button

▶ Pressing Ctrl+Shift+R

Undeleting text

You can easily start typing along, adding a sentence or a couple of words, and suddenly realize that you're in Typeover instead of Insert mode. Fortunately, you can get back the text you overwrote by using undelete. For this exercise, use the same document you used in the last lesson. If you've exited WordPerfect since then, open Reply.101.wpd or Reply2.101.wpd, change to Typeover mode, and type something somewhere in the text.

1 Put the cursor immediately after the first sentence in the last paragraph.

You're going to get back that sentence that you just deleted by typing over it.

2 To get back the text that you deleted, press Ctrl+Shift+Z or choose Edit⇨Undelete from the menu.

Two things happen — the Undelete dialog box appears, and the last thing you deleted appears, selected (which probably means that it has white letters on black background, but it depends on your personal color settings), where the cursor is.

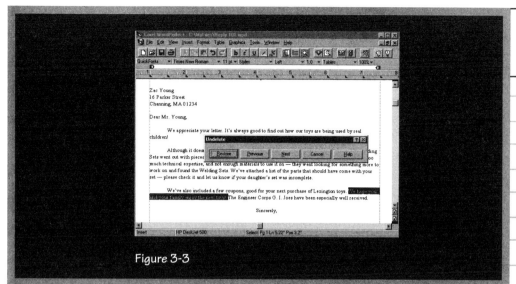

Figure 3-3

Figure 3-3: WordPerfect asks what you want to undelete.

The Undelete dialog box allows you to Restore the text that was deleted, look at the Previous text that was deleted, the Next text that was deleted, or cancel the undelete completely.

With luck, your screen now looks something like Figure 3-3. If it doesn't, keep reading.

3 If you didn't get back the sentence you typed over, click on the Previous button.

The last three things you deleted are saved, and clicking the Previous or Next buttons will cycle through them. So click on Previous until you see the sentence that you deleted.

(If you deleted too many times and you can't get the sentence back, you may want to try deleting something else now, and then going back to the beginning of this exercise.)

4 Click on Restore to get back the text that you want.

The restored text is inserted where the cursor is.

The Undelete command is the perfect solution to accidentally deleted text.

Undoing and redoing

If you make a change to your document and wish you hadn't, you can usually tell WordPerfect to undo the change by clicking the Undo button or pressing Ctrl+Z. Redo, which is the button to the right of the Undo button, allows you to redo the last action that you undid.

1 In the Reply.101.wpd or Reply2.101.wpd document (one of which should already be on your screen), move your cursor anywhere in the first paragraph.

2 Press Shift+F7, as if by mistake.

You don't know yet what the Shift+F7 command does (it centers the text after the cursor), and with your cursor in the middle of a paragraph, it makes a strange-looking mess. Yikes!

☑ Progress Check

If you can do the following, you're ready to move on the next lesson:

❑ Undelete text by pressing Ctrl+Shift+Z or choosing Edit⇨Undelete.

❑ Use the WordPerfect Undo and Redo buttons.

3 **Click on the Undo button on the Toolbar or press Ctrl+Z.**

Whew! Your paragraph looks normal again.

4 **Save and close the document, because you are finished with it for now.**

Use Undo after giving a command you wish you hadn't given.

Lesson 3-4

Controlling What's on the Screen

WordPerfect sure clutters up the screen with a lot of information, mainly in the form of bars — the menu bar, Toolbar, Power Bar, and status bar, to name a few. You may want to banish some of these bars so that you have more space on the screen for typing. Or you may want to see another bar, the ruler bar, so you can tell how far your lines of text extend across the paper.

You'll need to refer to this lesson if any of your regular WordPerfect bars vanish mysteriously — this is where you'll learn how to get them back.

Displaying the ruler bar

WordPerfect can display a ruler on-screen so that you can see your tabs and margins. You'll use the ruler bar later, in Unit 11, when you find out how to fool with margins and tabs. For now, here's how to turn on the ruler bar so that you can get an idea of how wide your lines of text are.

View menu controls window's appearance

1 **Choose View from the menu bar.**

The View pull-down menu appears, displaying some options about how your document should appear.

2 **Choose Toolbars/Ruler.**

The pull-down menu disappears, and the Toolbars dialog box appears. The four bars that you can display are listed with boxes next to them. If the box has an X in it, that means the bar is displayed. If your WordPerfect is set up in the standard way, you probably see Xs next to the WordPerfect 7 Toolbar, Power Bar, and status bar.

We've found that, at least in real life, one bar at a time is enough — but in WordPerfect, we like to see all of them. Unless you or someone else has turned it on, the ruler bar does not have an X in its box.

3 **Click on ruler bar to display an X.**

4 **Then click on OK to make the dialog box go away and the ruler bar appear.**

Interesting! A ruler appears across the WordPerfect window, just above the typing area. It's useful for seeing how far across the page your text extends, as well as where your left margin, right margin, and tab stops are. You learn how to change your margins and tab stops in Unit 11.

In the same way that you told WordPerfect to display the ruler bar, you can tell it whether or not to display the Toolbar, Power Bar, and status bar. You'd be crazy to turn off the Toolbar, because the buttons on it are really convenient, but you may want to get rid of the other two bars, at least temporarily. You can always turn them back on.

If you want to remove the ruler bar from your screen — it does take up valuable screen real estate — go through the preceding steps again. And while the Toolbar dialog box is displayed, you can get rid of any of the bars that you don't think you will use. Be warned, though, that we refer to all of them during the course of this book.

As you use WordPerfect more, you'll see which buttons and bars you use the most. Then you can decide which ones WordPerfect should display on your screen.

Recess

All this talk of bars must be making you thirsty! Take a break and come back soon to finish the unit.

☑ Progress Check

If you can do the following, you're ready to move on to the next lesson:

❑ Display the ruler bar.

❑ Turn the Toolbar, Power Bar, and status bar on and off, based on which ones you think are useful to you right now.

Opening More Than One Document

Lesson 3-5

Talking about windows starts to get confusing. You should already know that Windows lets you run more than one software application at a time — you can have a document open in WordPerfect while you're working on a spreadsheet in Quattro or Excel. You can also have more than one document open in WordPerfect. In fact, you can have up to *nine* documents open at the same time! In fact, you may have already had more than one document at a time open in WordPerfect. But the fact that you've done so doesn't mean that you know how to use this feature to your advantage — and that topic is what we tell you about in this lesson.

Notes:

extra credit

Whoa! All the bars have disappeared!

You can make *all* the bars disappear from the WordPerfect window, even the menu bar. Unlike the usual WordPerfect window, the typing area takes up the full screen when you do so, with no menus, bars, or buttons in view. This setup gives you lots of space to type, but how to return to the regular WordPerfect window or how to give a command is not obvious.

To hide all the bars, choose View⇨Hide Bars. WordPerfect displays a dialog box warning you that *everything* is going to disappear except your typing area. Click on OK. Poof! Everything vanishes.

If you want to return to the usual WordPerfect window, you have two choices:

- Press Esc.

- Press Alt+V. The View pull-down menu appears, even though you still can't see the menu bar. A check mark appears next to Hide Bars — select it (click on it) to make the check mark disappear, and the bars reappear.

You're back in business.

Figure 3-4: This
WordPerfect window
contains two open
documents displayed in
Cascaded style. A little
confusing, but very
useful.

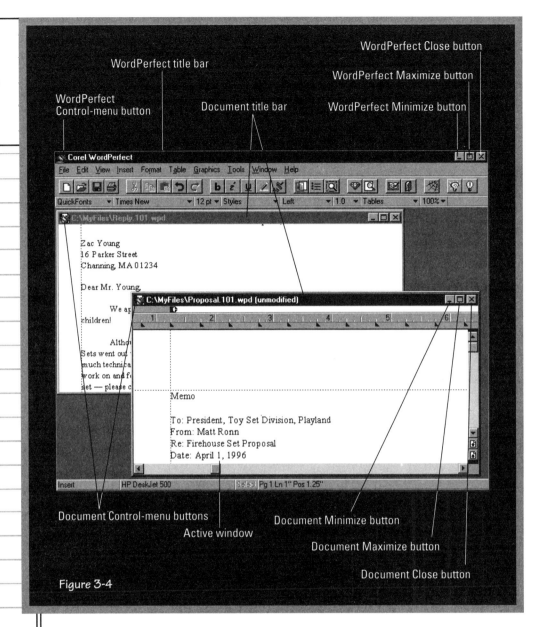

Figure 3-4

Opening more than one document at a time can be useful when you want to refer to something else you've written or maybe borrow a terrific passage that you wrote yesterday. After you learn how to move and copy text, you can do that sharing between two open documents.

When you view multiple documents in WordPerfect, you still have only one menu bar, one Toolbar and one Power Bar. So how do you know which document you're viewing? The answer is that one document is *active*, while the others aren't. You can tell the active window because the document title window is the same color as the WordPerfect title bar. You can see one active and one inactive document in Figure 3-4. Each open document has its own window, document Control-menu, and Minimize, Maximize/Restore, and Close buttons.

If one document is maximized, you may not be able to see any other open documents. Fortunately, you still have a way to get to them! Use the <u>W</u>indow menu to choose the document you want to see. Read Table 3-2 to learn everything else you need to know about managing multiple documents, and you'll get some practice in the next two exercises.

Table 3-2	Managing Multiple Documents
Things to Do with Them	**How to Do Them**
View another open document	Choose <u>W</u>indow and choose the document you want
Rotate through open documents	Ctrl+F6 or Ctrl+Shift+F6
See all open documents in the WordPerfect window	Use <u>W</u>indow⇨Cascade, <u>W</u>indow⇨<u>T</u>ile Top to Bottom, or <u>W</u>indow⇨Tile <u>S</u>ide by Side
Make another document active	Click on it
Create a new document when one is already open	Use <u>F</u>ile⇨<u>N</u>ew or the New Blank Document button
Close one document	Click on the document's Close button in the upper-right corner of the document window, or make it active, and then press Ctrl+F4, choose <u>F</u>ile⇨<u>C</u>lose, or double-click on the document Control-menu box (upper-left corner of document window)
View documents in windows	Click on the document Restore button in the upper-right corner of the WordPerfect window (it looks like overlapping windows)
View document full-screen	Click on the document Maximize button in the upper-right corner of the document window (it looks like a single window)
Move a document window	Click and drag the title bar
Size a document window	Click and drag the edge of the document window
Turn a document window into a button	Click on the document Minimize button in the upper-right corner of the document window (it looks like an underscore — or a minimized program or document)
Turn a document button back into a document	Double-click on the icon or choose the document from the <u>W</u>indow menu

Opening another document

Opening two documents is simple:

on the CD

1 Open Reply.101.wpd if it isn't already open.

You see the toy company's reply to your letter.

on the CD

2 Then open Proposal.101.wpd.

The proposal for the Firehouse Set replaces the earlier letter on the screen.

Notes:

Figure 3-5: The Window menu lists the open documents and different ways to arrange them.

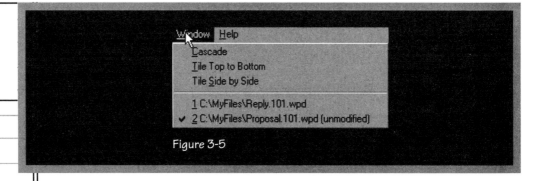

Figure 3-5

to switch among open documents, choose Window from the menu bar and then choose the document name

use Window commands to arrange the document windows

3 **To see the letter again, choose Window from the menu and then pick Reply.101.wpd from the submenu.**

The file will be listed with its full *path* (the full name of a file), including where it's saved. Just look at the end of the name to find Reply.101.wpd.

You can also press Ctrl+F6 to get to the next window. In the next exercise, you'll view these documents in windows, rather than full-screen like you're used to.

All you need to do to have more than one document open at a time is open them!

Arranging documents on the screen

Often the point of having more than one document open at a time is so you can see them both. But the current setup doesn't really let you do so — you still have to switch back and forth using either a window command or Ctrl+F6.

You have three options for viewing multiple windows, all found in the Window menu in Figure 3-5 — you can cascade the documents or tile them top to bottom or side by side. All three options put each document into its own little window, which you can then size and move (within the confines of the typing area in WordPerfect). Cascading puts documents in overlapping windows; tiling puts them in nonoverlapping windows that take up all of the available space. Tiling top to bottom puts one document in the top part of the space, while tiling side by side puts one document on the left and the other on the right. If you have more than three documents open, WordPerfect ignores the vertical and horizontal requests and tiles the documents however they'll fit.

After you have documents in windows, you can then fiddle with the size and location of the windows so that they suit your needs. Having documents overlap slightly means that you have more working space for the document you're working on, but you can see the other document — and click on it to make it active. Move document windows by clicking and dragging the title bar; size them by clicking and dragging the edge of the window. You can move documents so that you can't see the whole document window — WordPerfect then gives you two more scroll bars so that you can scroll around the view area.

You should already have Reply.101.wpd and Proposal.101.wpd open. If not, do so now. You should be looking at Proposal.101.wpd in full-screen mode.

1 **Put the proposal in a document window by clicking the document Restore button (the overlapping windows button near the top right of the WordPerfect window).**

You can also choose <u>R</u>estore from the document Control-menu by clicking the WordPerfect-nib Control-menu button just to the left of the word File on the menu bar and then choosing Restore from the Control-menu that appears.

The two documents now appear in cascaded windows — you could have also gotten here by choosing <u>W</u>indow⇨<u>C</u>ascade, but that route is not necessarily intuitive.

2 **Now tile the windows top to bottom by choosing <u>W</u>indow⇨<u>T</u>ile Top to Bottom.**

The documents now each appear in a window, with one window on top of the other. Notice that the proposal is still the active document — you can tell because the title bar is the same color as the WordPerfect title bar.

3 **Make the letter the active document by clicking on it.**

The color of the title bar changes, and if you have the ruler bar displayed, it now appears at the top of the letter.

4 **Now resize the active window: Click and drag the top border of the window and drag it so that the two documents overlap by about an inch.**

The pointer turns into a double-headed arrow when it's right on the border — you should click when you see that arrow. Sometimes the easiest way to resize the window is to click and drag the corner — that way you can change the width and height in one step.

You can move a document window by clicking and dragging its title bar. Let go of the mouse button when you're happy with the new position.

5 **To see the letter in full-screen mode again, click on the Maximize button (which now looks like a single window) at the top right corner of the document window.**

6 **Close both documents that are open by clicking the Close button in the upper-right corner of each document window. WordPerfect can't stand to be without a document, so if you close all the documents, WordPerfect creates a new blank one named Document 1.**

Manipulate multiple windows by using the <u>W</u>indows submenu and the funny-looking boxes at the corners of the WordPerfect and document windows.

heads up

While fooling around with windows management you may accidentally minimize WordPerfect — if you click on the WordPerfect Minimize button. To get WordPerfect back, click on the WordPerfect button that appears somewhere on the Taskbar, or hold down Alt and press Tab until the box is around the WordPerfect icon — then let go of both keys.

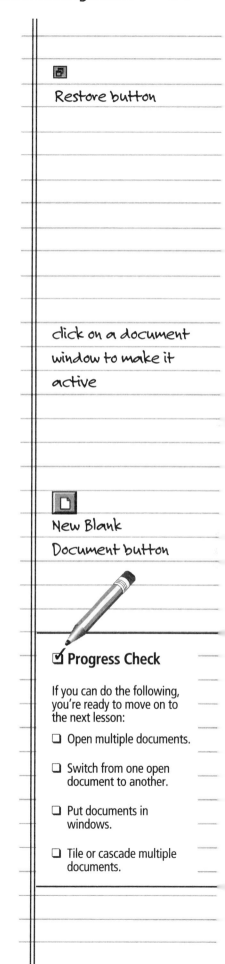

Restore button

click on a document window to make it active

New Blank Document button

☑ **Progress Check**

If you can do the following, you're ready to move on to the next lesson:

❑ Open multiple documents.

❑ Switch from one open document to another.

❑ Put documents in windows.

❑ Tile or cascade multiple documents.

Figure 3-6: This window is what you usually see when you press F1 to get help. The tabs at the top are clickable and give you different kinds of help.

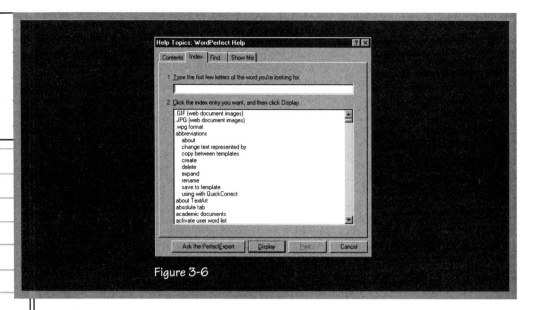

Figure 3-6

extra credit

What's new?

You can easily create a new blank document without disturbing the document or documents that are open. Just click on the New Blank Document button on the Toolbar. It's the leftmost button on the Toolbar. After you click on it, WordPerfect creates a new blank document — no wonder they named the button that!

Now you've got more than one document open — see Lesson 3-5 for how to use multiple documents.

Lesson 3-6   Getting Help

You may have realized that you have a lot to remember, or you may already have questions about WordPerfect. Therefore, we've decided to introduce WordPerfect Help to you here. The more intrepid of you may use Help to take off and learn about arcane features that aren't even covered in this book. Even if that possibility doesn't appeal to you, the help system is a good place to go when you've forgotten how to do something or you want a little more information about a command.

We don't give you a guided tour of the help system — that could take the whole book! Instead, we give you a sneak preview and show you how much Help can do for you. To start the help system, press F1 or choose Help from the menu. (We prefer F1 — using the menu forces you to decide what kind of help you want, and sometimes you just don't know.)

F1 is the Help key

You can also get help about menu commands by pressing F1 when you're in the middle of giving a command. A help screen with information about the highlighted command appears (this is called *context-sensitive* help).

If you press F1 to get help when you aren't in the middle of a menu command, you see something like Figure 3-6.

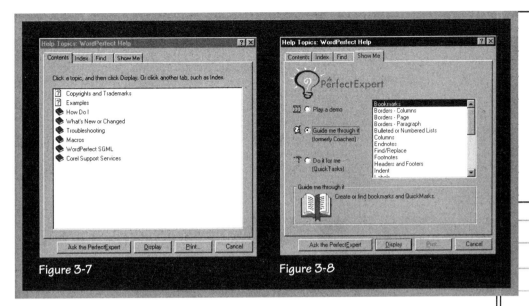

Figure 3-7

Figure 3-8

Notes:

When WordPerfect Help is displayed, it appears in its own window on-screen. (In fact, it's a separate program, with its own button on the Taskbar.) Two kinds of Help windows exist: One is the Help Topics window that you see in Figures 3-6, 3-7, and 3-8 that helps you find the kind of help that you need. The other is the Help window with a yellow background that *has* the help that you need. We start with the Help Topics window.

The Help Topics window has four buttons and four clickable tabs. The buttons are: Ask the PerfectExpert, Display, Print, and Cancel. Ask the PerfectExpert displays a screen where you can ask your question in English, and the PerfectExpert will search for an answer. You will then have to pick among the possibilities by clicking the item and then clicking Display (you can also just double-click on the item). Display opens help on the selected item, Print sends the help on the selected item to your printer without displaying it, and Cancel makes the WordPerfect help system go away.

The tabs help you find what you need in different ways:

- **Contents** displays the expandable table of contents that you see in Figure 3-7. Double-click on an item to expand it to display more items in outline form. Any item with a book in front of it is an expandable topic. An item with a question mark displays a help screen about that topic.

- **Index** displays an alphabetical index of help topics (you saw it in Figure 3-6). To find help on a particular topic, type the first few letters of the topic in the top box — the index entry will shift to show you items starting with those letters. You can then select one and click on Display to see the Help window on that topic.

- **Find** gives you a powerful full-text search option. Before you can use it to search, you have to create the database that Find will search — just follow the directions in the window. If you're not sure what to do, pick the recommended option. After the database is built, use it in the same way you use the Index.

- **Show Me** will guide you through how to do something, or even do it for you (you can see it in Figure 3-8). It has limitations — it can only do the tasks listed, but it can still be a very useful feature.

The Help screens (the ones that contain the actual help) also have some features you should know about. Each Help screen has three buttons: Help Topics (which takes you back to the Help Topics window), Back (which takes you to the previous help screen), and Options (which we let you explore on your own). Help screens also have *links* that you can click on to see another help screen on a related topic. You also often see a small representation of a bookshelf on a help screen with Related Topics next to it, or an open book that links to a definition, or a box that leads to step-by-step instructions. When the mouse pointer gets near any link, it turns into a hand, indicating that this is a link, and clicking it will take you to another help screen.

Using F1 to get help

Say that you just have to know how to double-space the paper you're writing for English class and you can't wait until Lesson 11-1, where we show you how to do it. What do you do? Get help.

1 Press F1.

You see the WordPerfect Help Topics window.

2 Click on the Contents tab.

A short list of the Help Topics contents appears.

3 Double-click on How Do I.

The book next to How Do I now looks open, and an indented list of topics appears under it.

4 Double-click on the fourth item under How Do I, which is Arrange Text on the Page (Format).

Another indented list appears, and the first item is Change Tabs, Margins, and Spacing, which sounds like exactly what you're looking for.

5 Double-click on Change Tabs, Margins, and Spacing.

Another level of outline appears, but this time instead of each item having a little book in front of it, you see little boxes with question marks. These mean that you're finally close to getting help! Change Line Spacing is fourth from the bottom.

6 Double-click on Change Line Spacing.

You now get a screen with a description and step-by-step instructions. At the bottom of the screen is one link: *Related Topics*. This is a link that you can click to get more information. A different kind of link is in the middle of the page — *line height* is in a different color and underlined with a dotted line. Click on it to get a pop-up definition (you won't lose the current help screen).

Use F1 to get into the help system. The How Do I index gives you easy access to step-by-step instructions on commonly needed WordPerfect features. Use it liberally. To get back to the Help Topics screen, click on the Help Topics button at the top of the WordPerfect Help screen.

One last thing that may be of help — when you get to a screen that tells you how to do something, you may want to keep it on top of the WordPerfect window so that you can see it as you follow the steps. Just click the Options button, choose Keep Help on Top, and then choose On Top. After you're finished with the help window, click on the window's Close button.

☑ **Progress Check**

If you can do the following, you're ready to move on to the next lesson:

❏ Get help about a feature you've used.

❏ Get help about a feature you haven't used.

Recess

If you're ready to take a break, choose File⇨Exit to exit WordPerfect. But come back soon to take the Unit 3 Quiz.

Unit 3 Quiz

For each of the following questions, circle the letter of the correct answer or answers. Remember, we may have included more than one right answer for each question.

1. **The best way to start a new paragraph is . . .**

    A. Click on the button with the paragraph sign.

    B. Press Enter.

    C. Type **code=start new paragraph**.

    D. Talk to WordPerfect. Tell it gently that you would like to start a new paragraph now.

    E. Press the spacebar until the cursor is at the beginning of the next line.

2. **The best way to start a new page is . . .**

    A Press Enter until WordPerfect gets to the next page.

    B. Type until the page is filled and WordPerfect starts a new page for you.

    C. Type gibberish to fill up the current page. ("Jabberwocky" from *Alice in Wonderland* is a good example of this technique.)

    D. Press Ctrl+Enter to insert a page break.

    E. Choose Insert⇨Page Break from the menu bar.

3. **When you need help with WordPerfect . . .**

    A. Press the F1 key.

    B. Shout a lot — maybe your coworker will hear you and come to tell you how to do whatever it is.

    C. Use the index of this book to find what you need.

    D. Buy *WordPerfect 7 For Dummies* (from IDG Books Worldwide) to get help on topics that aren't covered in this book. (And guess who wrote it?)

    E. Choose Help from the menu bar.

Notes:

4. **If you want to combine two paragraphs . . .**

    A. Print the document. Then, with tape and scissors, put the two paragraphs together.

    B. Delete the carriage return(s) between the two paragraphs.

    C. Move your cursor to the end of the first paragraph, retype the text in the second paragraph, and delete the second version of the text that you just retyped.

    D. Use the move feature to move the text.

    E. Type **code=join paragraphs.**

5. **Insert mode . . .**

    A. Is better than Typeover mode.

    B. Gets turned off and on by the Insert key.

    C. Means that the text you type is inserted into the document instead of replacing what's already there.

    D. Means that your computer is ready to accept carrots for food processing.

    E. We're sorry, but this is a family-oriented book and we can't talk about that here.

Unit 3 Exercise

on the CD

1. Open Facial Expression Policy.101.wpd, a file that came on the CD.

> The Lexington Toy Company
> Human Resources Department
>
> Quality Assurance Requirements for the Doll Face Painting Staff
>
> Effective immediately, Lexington Toys' quality standards have been expanded to include standards for the painting of facial features on our line of "Baby Sarah" dolls. Facial expressions on all of our dolls must be:
>
> * clearly drawn
> * artistic
> * pleasant and cheerful
>
> It has come to our attention that several dolls have been shipped to customers with sad, surly, or downright menacing facial expressions. Non-standard facial expressions will not be tolerated. Exception: Dolls for use within the building, or those for use by the families of our staff, may be painted with any desired expressions, as long as the faces are not painted to resemble specific members of management.
>
> Circulation:
> Director of Doll Manufacturing
> Manager of Doll Cranial Assemblies
> Director of Human Resources
> Director of Quality Assurance

2. Split the last paragraph into two before the word *Exception.*

3. Put the circulation list on a separate page.

4. Save the document with the name Final Facial Expression Policy.101.wpd (using the File⇨Save As command).

Unit 4

• • • • • • • • • •

Printing Your Document

Objectives for This Unit

✓ Using print preview to see how a document will look printed

✓ Printing some pages of a document

✓ Printing extra copies

✓ Canceling a print job

✓ Printing an envelope

✓ Faxing directly from WordPerfect (optional, and only if you have a fax modem and software to use it)

Printing is usually the ultimate goal of word processing. Few people buy WordPerfect just to see the words on a screen — usually the computer, the word-processing software, and the printer together substitute for (and improve on) a typewriter.

In Unit 1, you learned how to print a document by using the Print button on the Toolbar. In this unit, we cover printing in finer detail, using the Print dialog box to make some refinements.

First things first — before you print, your printer needs to be both on and online. *On* means that it's getting power from the socket in the wall, whereas *online* means that it's ready to receive information from your computer. You should see both a power switch and an online button (or at least a light) on your printer. You should also check that a cable leads from your computer to the printer. (If you're in a networked office, finding it may just be too difficult — but you should identify whom to bribe in case of problems, because networking can cause printing problems that are beyond the scope of this book.)

After you're sure that your printer has input (power from the plug and a cable that brings info from the computer), make sure that it has what it needs to produce printouts — whatever kind of ink and paper your printer uses.

Prerequisites

▶ Opening an existing document (Lesson 2-2)

▶ Using dialog boxes (Lesson 2-3)

on the CD

▶ Proposal.101.wpd
▶ Toy Letter2. 101.wpd
▶ Reply.101.wpd

Notes:

heads up

The last thing is probably the most important: When Windows was installed on your computer, it should have been told what printer (or printers) you use. Windows then shared that information with WordPerfect. If Windows (and therefore WordPerfect) does not know about your printer, you may have to tell Windows which printer you have. Use the Printers folder in My Computer or find an expert to help you.

But very possibly, you are one of the lucky ones — all you need to do is tell WordPerfect to spit out that paper!

How many ways are there?

As we have already told you and as you will probably continue to notice, WordPerfect nearly always offers more than one way to do any task. Although we always make the effort to tell you at least two ways to do anything, we may not tell you every way you can do it every time. We have our favorites, and we expect that you will, too. We can't think of a good reason for you to remember three different ways to do something — choose your favorite and stick with that for a while.

Displaying the Print dialog box is no exception to the rule of multiple methods. WordPerfect gives you at least four ways to leave your lover, er, to see the Print dialog box:

- Select File⇨Print from the menu bar.
- Click on the Print button on the Toolbar.
- Press Ctrl+P.
- Press F5.

All of these do exactly the same thing: display the Print dialog box.

Throughout this chapter, we tell you to print by either clicking on the Print button on the Toolbar or pressing Ctrl+P (you may prefer keystroke methods to mousing around, or vice versa). Selecting File⇨Print from the menu bar takes two mouse clicks instead of just one, so we don't mention it repeatedly — but if you prefer it, go ahead and use it every time you need to use the Print dialog box.

Lesson 4-1

Seeing How Your Printed Document Will Look

View menu controls
how documents look
on-screen

The document on the WordPerfect screen looks pretty close to what the document will look like on paper, but you may want to see how the whole page looks (even if you can't read it) rather than just the part that fits readably on the screen. WordPerfect lets you.

If you click on View on the menu bar, the View pull-down menu appears. You see that WordPerfect has three ways of looking at your document: Draft, Page, and Two Page. Here's what these views are:

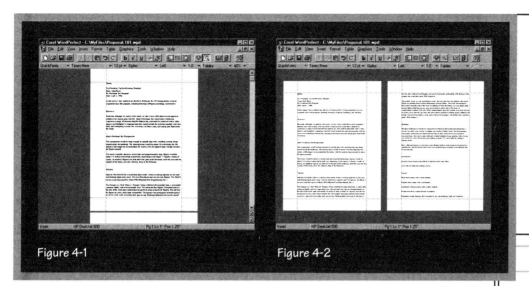

Figure 4-1

Figure 4-2

Figure 4-1: Page view with Full Page zoom shows you your entire page so that you can get a general idea of your page layout.

Figure 4-2: Two Page view enables you to see facing pages of your document, but you can't read normal-sized text unless you have a magnifying glass.

◆ Draft view is imitation WYSIWYG (What You See Is What You Get — pronounced *whizziwig*). Most of the document looks more or less the way it will look on paper, but certain parts of the printed page, such as headers, footers, and watermarks, do not appear on-screen. Each page break is displayed as a line that extends across the typing area — a forced page break (when you press Ctrl+Enter) appears as a double line, and a natural page break (after you've typed too much to fit on one page) appears as a single line.

◆ Page view (in Figure 4-1) is full WYSIWYG. It is also probably what you have been using (except you probably haven't had it zoomed like the figure does) You see everything that will be printed on the page, including headers and footers. Page breaks are displayed as they would be on paper — white space to the end of the page, followed by a break and the top margin of the next page.

◆ Two Page view (in Figure 4-2) is just what it sounds like — it displays two pages side by side as they will look printed. You can't read the words on the pages (unless you used a very large font), but you can get an overall look at your page layout.

We use Page view until we just *have* to know how each whole page will look on paper, and then we briefly switch to Full page view or use zoom to check it out (don't worry — we'll show you how to use both of these methods in a bit). Page view is what WordPerfect shows you to begin with, so why not stick with it? If you prefer to get the most text on-screen that you can, without all that white space for top and bottom margins, you will probably prefer Draft view. The choice doesn't involve a big philosophical debate; it's just a matter of personal preference.

Using the Page/Zoom Full button

The folks who make WordPerfect aren't stupid — they know that you will want to see how your document will look before you actually print it. So they put a button on the Toolbar for just that purpose.

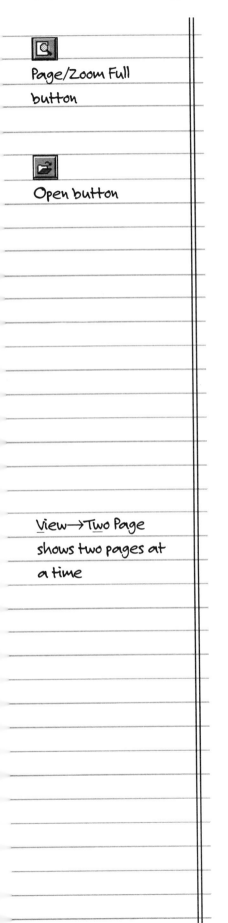

Page/Zoom Full button

Open button

The Page/Zoom Full button is a toggle button — it lets you easily switch back and forth between the way your screen looks normally (when you are typing and you need to be able to read the text) and Full page view, which shows you the whole page as it will be printed, as in Figure 4-1.

Give it a try:

on the CD

1 Open Proposal.101.wpd.

Use the Open button on the Toolbar to open Proposal.101.wpd. You see the proposal that you've seen before.

2 Click on the Page/Zoom Full button.

The Page/Zoom Full button appears pressed in after you click it.

WordPerfect displays the document in Full page view — you can see how much of the page the text takes and how the margins look.

3 To see the next page, press Page Down twice.

The first Page Down moves the cursor to the bottom of the first page. When you press Page Down the second time, WordPerfect displays the second page of the letter.

4 Return to the view you're used to by clicking on the Page/Zoom Full button again.

The Page/Zoom Full button pops back out when you click it.

WordPerfect zooms in to give you a view where you can actually read the text.

The easiest way to preview how a document will look when it's printed is to click on the Page/Zoom Full button on the Toolbar.

Previewing a printed document using Two Page view

Another way to preview page layout is to use Two Page view.

on the CD

1 If Proposal.101.wpd isn't already open, open it now.

2 Choose View⇨Two Page from the menu bar.

The typing area changes to display two sheets of paper, side by side, with your text on them in itty-bitty letters that you couldn't possibly read.

You can move around in Two Page view by using the regular cursor control keys. PgUp and PgDn move you through the pages. You can even type in this view, but we sure wouldn't want to risk it.

3 When you're ready to go back to doing real work, choose View⇨Page or View⇨Draft from the menu.

This command takes you back to a view where letters can be seen and text written.

Another way to see what your document will look like on paper is to select View⇨Two Page from the menu.

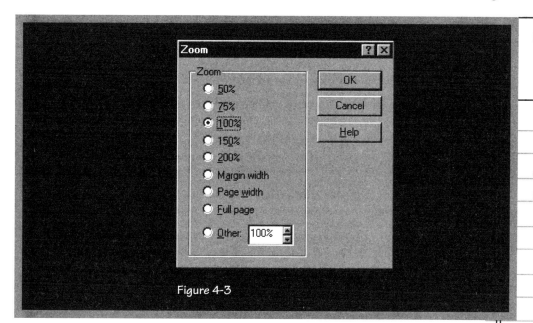

Figure 4-3

Figure 4-3: The Zoom dialog box enables you to decide how large your document appears on-screen.

Notes:

View→Zoom works
like a camera zoom
lens

Previewing a printed document using Zoom

The way that WordPerfect usually shows you your documents (Page view) is really another way to preview a document. Page view shows you everything that will be on the printed page, including margins and the edges of the paper (although it shows you the margins as dotted blue lines that don't actually print). It's also the default, which means that if you don't tell WordPerfect to show you something different, you see your documents in Page view. To see the overall page layout, you may also want to scale the view of the document so that you can see the whole page — scaling your view is like using the zoom lens on a camera. In WordPerfect, you can zoom in and out by using the View⇨Zoom command on the menu bar. Try it out now, with these steps.

on the CD

If you don't have Proposal.101.wpd on-screen, open it now.

1 **Make sure that you're in Page view. Choose View from the menu bar. If the Page command has a check by it, press Esc twice to cancel the command. Otherwise, choose the Page command.**

You see the Page view of the document.

2 **From the menu bar, choose View⇨Zoom.**

You see the Zoom dialog box in Figure 4-3. You can also use the Zoom button on the far right of the Power Bar (which is uncharted territory in this book so far). Depending on the size of the WordPerfect window, the Zoom button may be invisible off the right edge of the window — if so, use the View⇨Zoom command instead (or maximize your WordPerfect window so that you can see the whole Power Bar).

3 **Choose Full page from the Zoom dialog box and click on OK.**

You see one whole page of your document with margins on all sides in the WordPerfect window (the size of your page depends on the size of the WordPerfect window). In Page view, you see the whole sheet of paper as it will be printed — with margins, headers, and footers. If you think this view makes your screen look a lot like it did when you clicked the Page/Zoom Full button, you're right — it's exactly the same. But with zoom, you have more choices.

When you're in Draft view, the text shrinks so that you see a page worth of text on-screen. You still don't see margins, and page breaks appear as single or double lines across the screen. You must be in Page view to see a preview of how your printed document will look.

You can use PgUp and PgDn to move around the document, just as you do in Two Page view.

 After you have seen how the document looks, select View⇨Zoom again and choose 100% to go back to working on your document.

100% shows the document at approximately actual size.

What you just did is the same as using the Page/Zoom Full button. Using the View⇨Zoom command is another way to view your document before printing. In fact, you may find that you use the Zoom feature at other times — making your text bigger to make it easier to read, or smaller to see more of the page. Using the zoom dialog box, you can specify from 25 percent to 400 percent zoom — the larger the percentage, the bigger the text looks. Play with it to see what you like. As with Two Page view, you can actually work on your document while it is zoomed to Full Page, but working with text that you cannot read could make a mess of your document. You can also display the Zoom dialog box by double-clicking on the Zoom button on the Power Bar, or clicking on the Zoom button once and then choosing Other from the drop-down menu.

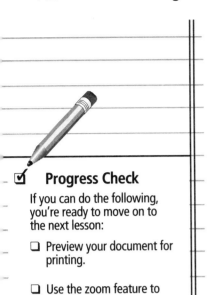

Progress Check

If you can do the following, you're ready to move on to the next lesson:

❏ Preview your document for printing.

❏ Use the zoom feature to change the size of your document on-screen.

Lesson 4-2

Printing Just What You Want

print the whole document by clicking on the Print button and then clicking on another print button (on the Print dialog box)

Most of the time, you want to print your whole document. You learned, back in Lesson 1-4, that printing your whole document is as easy as clicking on the Print button and then clicking on the Print button on the Print dialog box.

At times, you may not want to print the whole document. Perhaps you only want to print certain pages or certain blocks of text. This may happen when you notice a typo on the fifth page of your ten-page essay, or when you want to print section 100 of your 207-section welfare reform proposal. Whatever the occasion, learn how to print just what you need and save some trees.

The settings on the Print dialog box are grouped into sections. On the left side, a box labeled Print surrounds a number of settings. The first of those is a setting that we call the Print Selection setting. It's the setting that usually reads *Full Document,* but it can be changed to print only specific parts of your document. We refer to the Print Selection setting frequently during the rest of this unit, so have a look at Figure 4-4 now so that you can be sure that you know what we're talking about.

Another useful setting here is the Print in reverse order check box. Some printers spit out the pages so that they have to be collated to be in the right order — putting a check mark in this setting (by clicking on the box) takes care of that inconvenience for you.

We can't guarantee this little trick will work (it's undocumented), but if you press Ctrl+Shift+P, your document should go straight to the printer — you do not pass go, you do not collect $200, and you do not have to mess with the Print dialog box!

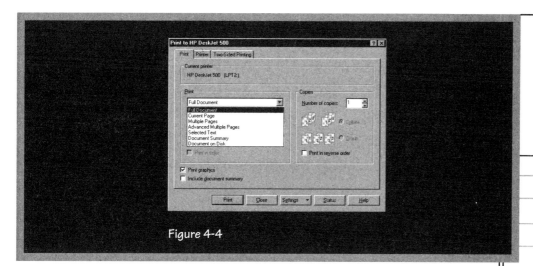

Figure 4-4

Figure 4-4: The Print dialog box lets you choose which pages and how many copies to print using the list setting displayed here (click on the down arrow on the box to see it).

Notes:

Printing one page

on the CD

Printing the page that the cursor is in is easy. In this exercise, you change one word on the second page of Proposal.101.wpd and print just that page. If Proposal.101.wpd isn't already open, open it now.

1 On the second page of Proposal.101.wpd, change *horn* to *whistle*.

The change occurs in the paragraph that starts with Playland Firehouse.

Find the reference to the horn in the tower of the fire house, and change the word to whistle.

Because you made a change on the second page of the document, you know that the cursor is on that page. You're ready to print just the current page.

heads up

In general, before you print the current page, you should always double-check that the cursor is actually on the page that you want to print. Just because the page is on-screen doesn't mean that your cursor is on that page — when you use the scroll bar to view a certain page, you don't move your cursor. If you're not sure where your cursor is, click once with the mouse somewhere on the page that you want to print.

2 Click on the Print button or press Ctrl+P.

You see the Print dialog box.

3 The setting that you want to change is the box that currently reads `Full Document`. **Click on the arrow on the right side of the box and choose Current Page.**

This setting gives you the option to print less than your whole document.

4 Click on Print.

WordPerfect tells you that the document is being prepared for printing, and the specified page then prints.

The Current Page option in the Print dialog box lets you print just the page where your cursor is.

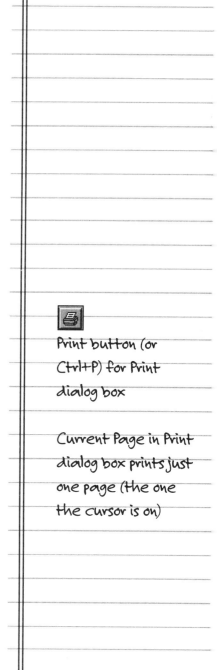

Print button (or Ctrl+P) for Print dialog box

Current Page in Print dialog box prints just one page (the one the cursor is on)

Notes:

Printing selected pages

on the CD

Follow these steps to print pages 1 and 2 of Proposal.101.wpd:

1 **Click on the Print button or press Ctrl+P.**

You see the Print dialog box.

2 **Click on the to box of the Page Range setting. Type** 2.

The from box should already say 1 — if it doesn't, change it to 1. When you use either of the Page Range boxes, WordPerfect, in its quiet way, changes the setting above from Full Document to Multiple Pages.

3 **Click on the Print button.**

WordPerfect tells you that the document is being prepared for printing. The specified pages should soon appear in the printer.

4 **Close Proposal.101.wpd and save your changes. You'll practice printing with a shorter document in the next lesson!**

You just used the Page Range setting to print two contiguous pages of Proposal.101.wpd.

Multiple Pages in
Print dialog box
prints combination
of pages

extra credit

Other ways to save trees

You can print multiple pages even if they're not contiguous. Just change the Full Document setting to Advanced Multiple Pages. WordPerfect adds an Edit button to the dialog box right below the Print Selection Setting. (If you're the type of person who enjoys this sort of thing, you can change the print selection option from Full Document to Advanced Multiple Pages and back again and watch the button appear and disappear.) Click on the Edit button to display the Advanced Multiple Pages dialog box. You can ignore all the settings in this dialog box, except the one that you need to print multiple pages: Page(s)/label(s). The other settings are for truly long documents. Input the pages you want in the Page(s)/label(s) setting using the rules below, and then click on the OK button to return to the Print dialog box. Click on the Print button to actually print the pages you specified on the Advanced Multiple Pages dialog box.

Here are ways you can specify which pages you want:

- Specify one page number (for example, **3**) to print that page.

- Specify more than one page number, separated by commas or spaces (for example, **3, 5** or **3 5**), to print those pages but not the pages in between (WordPerfect prints pages 3 and 5 but not page 4).

- Specify a range (for example, **3-5**) to print all the pages in that range.

- Specify a page to start, followed by a dash (for example, **3-**) to start printing on that page and continue printing to the end of the document.

- Type a dash followed by a page to end (for example, **-5**) to print from the beginning of the document through the end of that page.

- Use a combination of the above (for example, **1, 3-5** to print pages 1, 3, 4, and 5). The pages must be specified in order.

You can also print a chunk of text by selecting it (you'll learn lots about selecting text in Unit 5) and then clicking on the Print button. WordPerfect then assumes that you want to print just the selection — in fact, if you want to print the whole document, you need to make sure to change the setting. The Selection choice only appears when text is selected, so don't be surprised if you haven't seen it yet.

Printing on both sides

WordPerfect understands environmentalism and the new features of some printers — it provides you with a place to see all the settings that allow you to print on two sides of the page, whether or not your printer knows how to print on both sides of a piece of paper. The Print dialog box has tabs at the top — click on the tab labeled Two-Sided Printing to see these settings.

This dialog box has the settings to use if your printer supports two-sided printing — just change the setting to Flip on long edge or Flip on short edge (if you're printing regular stuff — portrait style — you want to Flip on long edge).

If your printer doesn't know how to print on both sides, you can still do so using the Manual settings near the bottom of the first column of settings. Using these, you can print all the Front, or odd pages, and then put the paper back in the printer, and change the setting on this dialog box to print the Back, or even pages. Voilà! Two-sided printing!

Recess

If all that work with the Print dialog box gave you a headache, exit WordPerfect (use Alt+F4) and go take a rest. Don't save your document (you made only one teeny, tiny unimportant change).

If this stuff is all fun and games for you, please continue!

☑ **Progress Check**

If you can do the following, you're ready to move on to the next lesson:

❏ Print the entire document that's on-screen.

❏ Print the page where the cursor is.

❏ Print just a few pages of your document.

Printing More Than One Copy

Lesson 4-3

If you want more than one copy of your document and you'd rather print them than wander down the hall to the photocopier, you can tell WordPerfect to print copies.

All you need to do to print multiple copies is play with the Print dialog box again!

1 Open Reply.101.wpd.

2 Click on the Print button on the Toolbar or press Ctrl+P.

You see the Print dialog box.

3 Change the Number of copies from 1 to 2.

The easiest way is to click on the up arrow next to the number. If you're printing an obscene number of copies — say 15 — you may not want to click on the up arrow 14 times; in that case, you can select the number in the box (click and drag the mouse over the number) and type the new number in its place.

4 Choose Print.

Away goes the printer — a piece of cake!

Number of copies in Print dialog box prints duplicate copies

☑ **Progress Check**

If you can do the following, you're ready to move on to the next lesson:

❏ Print more than one copy of whatever you want to print.

❏ Plant a tree to make up for all the paper that you'll be using now that you can print lots of copies of your WordPerfect documents.

The <u>N</u>umber of copies option in the Print dialog box allows you to tell WordPerfect to print more than one copy of your document. You can also use this option with the Print Selection setting to print more than one copy of the current page or multiple pages.

Lesson 4-4   Canceling a Print Job

Canceling a print job is relatively simple if your computer is hooked up directly to a printer, but probably not so easy if you print through a network. If you regularly use a networked printer, you should talk to your network administrator (who, in our cases, are our sweeties — just what does that say about us?) to find out how to cancel a print job. If you don't have a network, read on for the gory details.

When you send a document to be printed, WordPerfect formats it and sends it off to the printer. You can only stop it for as long as it is in WordPerfect's court. After it goes to the printer, it's out of our hands (you may still be able to stop it, but not by using WordPerfect — so stopping it is beyond the scope of this book).

heads up

You might think that the best way to cancel a print job is to turn off the printer. Unfortunately, this approach usually doesn't work and just complicates matters. Your computer and Windows notice when you turn off the printer and complain about it until you turn it back on. Try the steps in this lesson instead!

on the CD

If you want to try this procedure, use Proposal.101.wpd. It's long, giving you a little extra time to try to stop it. Also, read the steps through before you begin printing. WordPerfect and printers are so quick these days that WordPerfect could have finished sending the document to the printer before you get far enough in the steps to stop it!

After you've sent a print job to a local printer (one attached directly to your computer, not through a network), you can cancel it in the following way:

1 **Click on the Print button or press Ctrl+P.**

You see the Print dialog box.

2 **Click on the <u>S</u>tatus button.**

You see the Print Status and History dialog box, which appears in Figure 4-5. It gives you a lot of information about your current and past print jobs that you'll probably never need to know.

The current print job appears at the top of the list. If the Status column says something other than Complete, you're in luck.

3 **To stop the print job, choose <u>D</u>ocument⇨Cancel Printing from the menu at the top of the window.**

The status changes to Canceled. The printer may print some of the document anyway (whatever was sent to the printer before you canceled the job), but you should have succeeded in canceling some of the print job.

☑ Progress Check

If you can do the following, you're ready to move on to the next lesson:

❑ Change your mind about printing a document.

❑ Cancel printing a document by using the Print Status and History window.

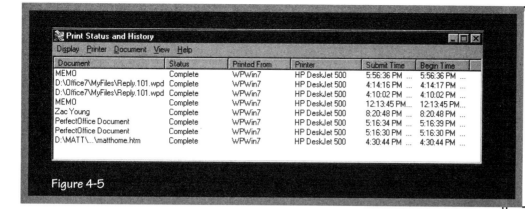

Figure 4-5

Figure 4-5: The WordPerfect Print Status and History dialog box shows the current status of the document that WordPerfect is printing and a list of other things that you have printed. It's where you can check on your print job and cancel it if it's still in WordPerfect's court.

 Close the Print Status and History window by clicking on the X in the upper-right corner.

The Print Status and History window is not really a dialog box — it's more like a separate program that comes with WordPerfect. If you like, you can leave it open so that you can switch to it easily to check on the status of your print jobs.

on the test

Don't waste paper if you realize that you don't want to print your document after all — you can also stop a print job by using the Status button on the Print dialog box and then choosing Document⇨Cancel Printing.

Printing an Envelope   Lesson 4-5

Not all printers can print envelopes, but if yours does, learn to use the envelope feature — it sure beats going back to the typewriter to make a good-looking envelope. Many printers require you to feed envelopes to them one by one. So each time you print an envelope, you have to feed your printer a size 10 envelope, assuming that it's hungry.

The first step is to figure out how to feed envelopes into your printer. Some printers have little diagrams of how to feed in an envelope. If yours doesn't, you may have to resort to reading the manual.

WordPerfect tries to make printing addresses on envelopes easy. Under certain circumstances, WordPerfect can even find the address on a letter and automatically print it on the envelope.

Creating an envelope for a letter

on the CD

Following is the easiest way to get an address onto an envelope, using the letter you wrote in Unit 1 to the Lexington Toy company or the letter you created in Unit 2 to the Gardner Toy Company. Before starting this exercise, open one of these letters. If you didn't write either of these letters, open Toy Letter2.101.wpd.

Figure 4-6: You can tell WordPerfect what to print on your envelope.

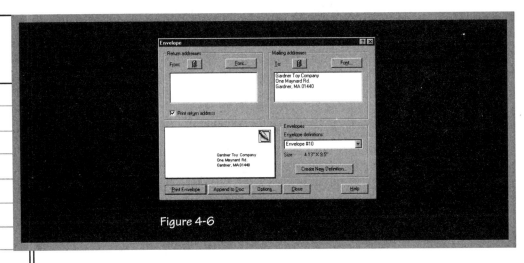

Figure 4-6

1 Choose Format⇨Envelope from the menu bar.

You see the Envelope dialog box, which appears in Figure 4-6. The mailing address appears in the Mailing addresses box at the top right of the dialog box, and on the preview envelope at the bottom left of the dialog box (WordPerfect makes it easy, doesn't it?).

If WordPerfect doesn't find the address, you can exit the dialog box, select the address, and display the Envelope dialog box again. The address will be there this time.

2 Click in the Return addresses box and type your return name and address there.

After you've put your name and address (the return address) in once, you won't have to do it again (you can press Enter to start each new line of the address, despite our warnings about pressing Enter in a dialog box). WordPerfect will remember it (still enabling you, of course, to put in a different name and address if you want to).

3 Click on Print Envelope.

Now you need to feed an envelope to your printer. Depending on what kind of printer you have, you may see a message on-screen asking you to insert an envelope, or your printer may wait for you to insert an envelope before printing. (Another possibility is that your printer can't print envelopes — get a new printer!)

The Format⇨Envelope command lets you tell WordPerfect what you want on your envelope. WordPerfect takes over from there, printing the addresses in the correct places on the envelope.

Recess

If you don't have a fax modem, you can skip the next lesson and go right to the Unit 4 Quiz. If you want to take a break, exit WordPerfect first by pressing Alt+F4 or choosing File⇨Exit from the menu bar.

☑ **Progress Check**

If you can do the following, you're ready to move on to the next lesson:

❑ Print an envelope.

❑ Think of someone to write a letter to, just so that you can practice printing envelopes. If you'd like to tell us what you think of this book, write to Alison Barrows and Margy Levine Young, c/o IDG Books Worldwide, 919 E. Hillsdale Blvd., Suite 400, Foster City, CA 94404 (USA).

Faxing Using a Fax Modem   Lesson 4-6

Faxing is just like printing a document — except that rather than printing it on a piece of paper in your office, you're sending it to a fax modem, which prints it on a piece of paper in someone else's office (unless the person at the other end also has a fax modem, in which case they may simply look at it on their screen).

The key is to have fax modem software installed that works as a Windows printer driver. If you do have a fax modem printer driver, it appears as a printer option. To send a fax, you simply specify the fax modem software as the printer and print normally (so in this lesson you're also learning how to change the printer to which WordPerfect prints). You will then be asked to specify the fax phone number and other cover sheet information.

If you don't have both a fax modem and fax software that works as a Windows printer driver, the instructions in this lesson won't work. Skip right to the Unit 4 Quiz.

To send a fax, you need a fax number. Get the fax number of a friend, use WordPerfect to write a quick note to tell your pal how quickly you are getting up to speed with your computer, and follow these steps to fax the note:

1 **Click on the Print button on the Toolbar or press Ctrl+P.**

You see the Print dialog box with the three tabs at the top.

2 **Click on the middle tab labeled Printer.**

You see the current printer settings on the Print dialog box, which appears in Figure 4-7. It allows you to choose a printer. Make a note (mental or pen-and-paper) of what is selected right now so that you can put the settings back this way after you're finished faxing.

3 **Click on the little down arrow to the right of the Name box to see the printer options that are available.**

Now you can tell WordPerfect *which* specific printer you want to use. Instead of choosing a real printer, you'll choose the printer driver software that sends your text as a fax.

WordPerfect displays a list of the printers that your copy of Windows knows. Somewhere in that list should be your fax modem software, if it's been installed correctly. For example, if you use WinFax PRO fax software, you might see WINFAX on COM2, which means that the document will be faxed using the WinFax PRO printer driver and a fax modem connected to the COM2 port of your computer.

If you don't see an entry for your fax software, it was not installed correctly. Refer to the manual for your fax software or get some help!

4 **Pick your fax modem software from the list.**

When you click on the fax modem printer driver, it appears in the Name box.

5 **Click on the Print button.**

Your fax modem software takes over and asks you to supply the phone number and name of the person to whom you're sending the fax. Type that information and then click on Send Fax or OK (whichever your fax software requires). Different fax modem packages work differently — you may need to look at the documentation of yours for more specifics.

Notes:

Figure 4-7: You can tell WordPerfect to print to your fax modem rather than to your printer.

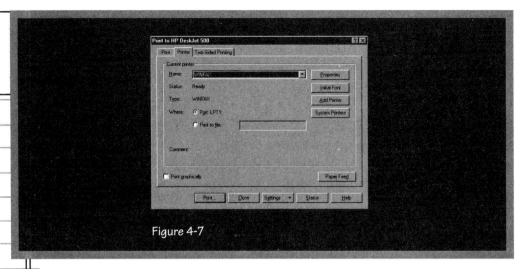

Figure 4-7

 Progress Check

If you can do the following, you're ready to move on to the next lesson:

❑ Know whether you have a fax modem installed.

❑ Print your document to someone else's fax machine rather than to your printer.

❑ Switch your printing setting back to your regular printer.

6 **After the fax has been sent, click on the Print button on the Toolbar or press Ctrl+P again.**

You need to select your regular printer again. Otherwise, your next printout will want to be faxed, too.

7 **In the Print dialog box, click on the Printer tab.**

8 **Choose the same settings that were in place before you chose your fax modem.**

You should have noted them in Step 2.

9 **Click on Close to close the Print dialog box without printing anything.**

Isn't technology amazing — your WordPerfect document went zinging across the phone wires in the form of a fax, only to get printed at the far end in someone else's office. Happy faxing!

Unit 4 Quiz

For each of the following questions, circle the letter of the correct answer or answers. Remember, we may include more than one right answer for each question!

1. What does this button do?

   A. Turns your printer into a typewriter — for when you need to do envelopes

   B. Same thing as Ctrl+P

   C. Same thing as F5

   D. Same thing as File⇨Print

   E. Displays the Print dialog box

2. **The best way to see how a document will look after it's printed is to . . .**

   A. Print it.

   B. Use <u>V</u>iew⇨T<u>w</u>o Page.

   C. Use the Page/Zoom Full button on the Toolbar (the button with a picture of a magnifying glass).

   D. Hold a thin sheet of paper up to the screen.

   E. Fax it to someone and have that person tell you how it looks.

3. **In <u>D</u>raft view, you see . . .**

   A. What the document would have looked like if you'd typed it.

   B. What the document would have looked like if you'd handwritten it.

   C. What the document looked like before it was finished.

   D. Just the text of the body of the document — no margins, headers, footers, and so on.

   E. Whatever your spouse will let you see.

4. **To fax a letter from WordPerfect, you need . . .**

   A. A fax modem.

   B. Fax modem software that's set up to work with your fax modem.

   C. A second phone line.

   D. A fax machine.

   E. A printer.

5. **The best way to address an envelope is to . . .**

   A. Print the to and from addresses on separate sheets of paper, cut them out, and paste them onto an envelope.

   B. Get a good pen and write the address neatly.

   C. Hire a calligrapher.

   D. Use the Fo<u>r</u>mat⇨En<u>v</u>elope command.

   E. Faxing is really much easier. Besides, you won't need a stamp!

Notes:

Unit 4 Exercise

1. Close the document that you are working on so that you see a nice, blank document in WordPerfect.

2. Type a letter to thank someone you know for doing something nice for you. (If no one you know did anything nice for you recently, write us a letter c/o IDG Books telling us what you think of this book! IDG's address is in the margin at the end of Lesson 4-5.)

3. Save the document so that your valuable opinion isn't lost, using the name Thank You.wpd.

4. View the document in Page view to make sure it looks right.

5. Print two copies of the letter — one for you and one to send.

6. Print an envelope using your own return address.

7. Mail the letter. (Don't forget the stamp!)

Part I Review

Unit 1 Summary

- **Starting WordPerfect for Windows:** Click on the Start button, choose Corel WordPerfect Suite 7, and then click on Corel WordPerfect 7.

- **Making the WordPerfect window active:** Click anywhere in the window to make it active.

- **Typing text in a document:** Move the cursor to the point where you want the text to appear and start typing.

- **Pressing Enter:** Don't press Enter at the end of each line — only at the ends of paragraphs.

- **Deleting characters:** Use the Backspace key to delete the character immediately before the cursor, or use the Delete (or Del) key to delete the character immediately after the cursor.

- **Saving a File:** To save a file, click on the Save button on the Toolbar. (Or press Ctrl+S or choose File⇨Save from the menu bar.)

- **Printing:** To print a file, click on the Print button on the Toolbar and then press Enter when you see the Print dialog box. (You can also display the Print dialog box by pressing Ctrl+P or choosing File⇨Print from the menu bar.)

- **Exiting WordPerfect:** Exit from WordPerfect by clicking on the Close button in the top right corner of the window — the button with an X in it. Or you can click on the Control-menu box and choose Close (or press Alt+F4 or choose File⇨Exit from the menu bar).

Unit 2 Summary

- **Opening a document:** To open an existing document, choose File⇨Open from the menu bar, click on the Open button on the Toolbar, or press Ctrl+O.

- **Closing a document:** To close a document, choose File⇨Close from the menu bar, click on the document close button, or press Ctrl+F4. If you made changes to the document and didn't save them, WordPerfect asks if you want to do so.

- **Opening a document as a copy:** To create a new document based on an existing one (why start from scratch?), choose File⇨Open from the menu bar and then choose the Open as Copy button on the dialog box. Make changes to the document and save the document giving it a new name.

- **Opening a document on disk:** To open a document that is stored on a diskette, choose File⇨Open from the menu bar; then change the Look in setting on the Open dialog box to show files on the diskette drive.

- **Moving around the document:** Use the mouse or arrow keys to move the cursor around the document.

- **Moving around a long document:** To move the cursor around a long document, use the vertical scroll bar. Or use the Page Up or Page Down keys to move up or down one screenful at a time and the Ctrl+Home or Ctrl+End keys to move to the beginning or end of the document. Or use Go To by pressing Ctrl+G.

Part I Review

Unit 3 Summary

▶ **Starting a new paragraph:** To start a new paragraph, press Enter.

▶ **Starting a new page:** To start a new page, press Ctrl+Enter.

▶ **Using the Insert key:** To replace text with new text, switch to Typeover mode by pressing the Insert key. Press Insert again to switch back to Insert mode.

▶ **Displaying bars at the top of the window:** Choose which bars to display at the top of the WordPerfect window by choosing View⇨Toolbars/Ruler from the menu bar.

▶ **Getting help:** To see online help, press F1, choose Help from the menu bar, or click on the Help button if one is displayed.

Unit 4 Summary

▶ **Using the View menu:** To see how your document will look when printed, choose View⇨Page from the menu bar or choose View⇨Two Page to see two facing pages.

▶ **Using the Page/Zoom Full feature:** To see one full page of your document on the screen, click on the Page/Zoom Full button on the Toolbar.

▶ **Printing a document:** To print your document, click on the Print button on the Toolbar, or press Ctrl+P, or choose File⇨Print from the menu bar. When you see the Print dialog box, click on the Print button.

▶ **Printing one page:** To print only one page, move the cursor to that page, click on the Print button on the Toolbar to display the Print dialog box, choose Current Page, and click on Print.

▶ **Printing a range of pages:** To print a range of pages, click on the Print button on the Toolbar to display the Print dialog box, choose Multiple Pages, type the range of page numbers in the Page Range boxes, and click on Print.

▶ **Printing more than one copy:** To print more than one copy of a document, click on the Print button on the Toolbar to display the Print dialog box, change the Number of copies setting, and click on Print.

▶ **Stopping a document from printing:** If you decide that you want to stop a document from printing, click on the Print button on the Toolbar to display the Print dialog box and click on the Status button. Select the print job to be deleted and press Del.

▶ **Printing envelopes:** If your printer can print on envelopes, choose Format⇨Envelope from the menu bar and click on Print Envelope to print an envelope with the address listed in the letter that you're working on.

Part I Test

The questions on this test cover all of the material presented in Part I, Units 1-4.

True   False

T   F   1. You can save a file without giving it a name.

T   F   2. As soon as WordPerfect is open, you can start typing a document.

T   F   3. WordPerfect gives you an electric shock if you type something that is not perfect.

T   F   4. To choose a command from a menu, click on the command or hold Alt while you press the underlined letter of the command.

T   F   5. WordPerfect is an excellent tool for writing postcards.

T   F   6. A dialog box is the balloon in a comic strip that contains what the character is saying or thinking.

T   F   7. Press the F1 key to get help anytime.

T   F   8. You can use the View⇨Zoom command to access WordPerfect's flight simulator feature.

T   F   9. You can move around your document by telekinesis.

T   F   10. To start a new paragraph, press Enter.

Multiple Choice

For each of the following questions, circle the correct answer or answers. Remember, there may be more than one right answer for each question!

11. **Is turning off the computer without exiting from WordPerfect a good idea?**

   A. No.

   B. Yes.

   C. Sure, if you don't mind losing the document that you're working on.

   D. It's fine if you don't mind a confused computer.

   E. This is a good way to discharge negative feelings about WordPerfect.

12. **Which of the following do not appear in the WordPerfect window?**

   A. The strip joint.

   B. The Candy Bar.

   C. The Milk Bar.

   D. The menu bar.

   E. The Toolbox.

13. **Snoopy's sparrow friend is named:**

   A. Tweety.

   B. Woodstock.

   C. Burlington.

   D. Toto.

   E. Chirpie.

14. **How do you save a document?**

   A. Press Ctrl+S.

   B. Choose File⇨Save from the menu bar.

   C. Click on the Save button on the Toolbar.

   D. Press Esc a lot.

   E. Throw it a life preserver.

Part I Test

15. What happens when you press the Del key?

A. The calories in the cookies that you are eating disappear (similar to crumbling the cookie before eating it).

B. The character to the left of the cursor disappears.

C. The character to the right of the cursor disappears.

D. The entire document disappears.

E. The computer disappears.

16. How do you run WordPerfect?

A. Ask it politely.

B. Choose it from the Corel WordPerfect Suite 7 part of the Start menu.

C. Double-click on the filename Wpwin.exe in Windows Explorer.

D. Select the WordPerfect icon on the Taskbar.

E. Reinstall WordPerfect from diskettes (all 12 of them).

Matching

19. Match the following buttons with what they do when you click on them:

A.

B.

C.

D.

E.

1. Closes WordPerfect (when you double-click on it).

2. Displays the Open File dialog box.

3. Saves the document on the disk.

4. Shrinks the WordPerfect window to a little, tiny icon.

5. Displays the Print dialog box.

17. What happens when you press Ctrl+End?

A. The end of the world.

B. WordPerfect automatically adds a closing to your letter.

C. The cursor moves to the end of the line.

D. The cursor moves to the end of paragraph.

E. The cursor moves to the end of the document.

18. What's the name of the TV game show where the host gives you the answer and you have to give the question?

A. *Wheel of Fortune.*

B. *Good Morning, America.*

C. *Star Trek.*

D. *Jeopardy.*

E. *What's My Line?*

20. Match the following keys with what they do:

A. Home

B. Del (Delete)

C. Esc

D. Backspace

E. Ins (Insert)

1. Cancels a dialog box or the last menu command that you chose.

2. Deletes the character to the left of the cursor.

3. Deletes the character to the right of the cursor.

4. Switches between Insert and Typeover modes.

5. Moves the cursor to the beginning of the line.

Part I Lab Assignment

This is the first of several lab assignments that appear at the end of each part of the book. These lab problems are designed to allow you to apply the skills that you learned while studying the lessons in realistic situations. (Well, almost realistic, anyway. Your real-life word-processing chores probably won't be as fun as these.)

These lab assignments aren't quite as directed as the exercises that appear in the lessons. For example, you aren't told exactly which keys to press and which buttons to click. Instead, you're given more general tasks to complete — such as "save the document with the name Hire Designer.wpd" — and you are left to your own devices to figure out how best to accomplish the task. In case you're not sure how to accomplish a task, look back at the Part I Review to see where the task is described.

In this lab assignment, you, the Manager of Product Testing of the Lexington Toy Company, will write a letter to a product designer telling him that he is hired.

Step 1: Type the letter

Create a new document that is formatted as a letter. Type the address of the Lexington Toy Company (you can use your own address), at the top of the letter. Then type the date and the name and address of the person you are hiring. For the text of the letter, you can use the text shown in the figure here, or make up your own letter. Make it friendly and enthusiastic.

Henry Thoreau
Lexington Toy Company
One Amusement Way
Lexington, MA 02173

April 1, 1997

Mr. Harold Houdini
1 Way Out
Appleton, Wisconsin 87654

Dear Harry,

As per our discussion earlier today, I am thrilled to be able to offer you a position as a product designer for our new line of toys for budding magicians, starting immediately. We have an exciting new line of toys planned, and your background as a stage magician and escape artist indicates that you will be a valuable member of the design team. We look forward to your knowledge and flair making Lexington Toys even more fun and exciting than they already are.

The salary is as we discussed last week at your interview. If you have any questions, call our personnel director, Peter Pratfall. Please report to work on April 16, at 8 a.m. Attached is a list of meetings you will need to attend on your first day to acquaint you with Lexington Toys and the company with you.

One point: we have discussed your proposed tricks with our insurance agent, who insists that tricks that involve instructing children to get locked into boxes, whether or not they are underwater, would not be covered under our regular liability insurance.

We look forward to your joining our happy community!

Sincerely,

Henry

Lexington Toys

At the end of the letter, close with your own name. Save the letter using the filename Hire Designer.wpd.

Step 2: Edit and format the letter

Append a list of meetings that the new employee will have to attend on his first day at work, as shown in the following figure. Insert a page break so that this list appears on page two.

Please attend the following meetings on April 16th.

8:30 a.m.   Peter Pratfall, Director of Personnel
10:00 a.m.   Rosie Spinner, V.P. of Product Planning
11:00 a.m.   Matt Ronn, Product Liability Manager

The first planning meeting will be at 3:00 p.m. — ask Rosie where it will be held. At 5:00 p.m., there will be a party in the staff lounge to welcome you to the company.

Step 3: Print the letter

Print one copy of the letter.

Step 4: Close WordPerfect

Save the document again and exit from WordPerfect.

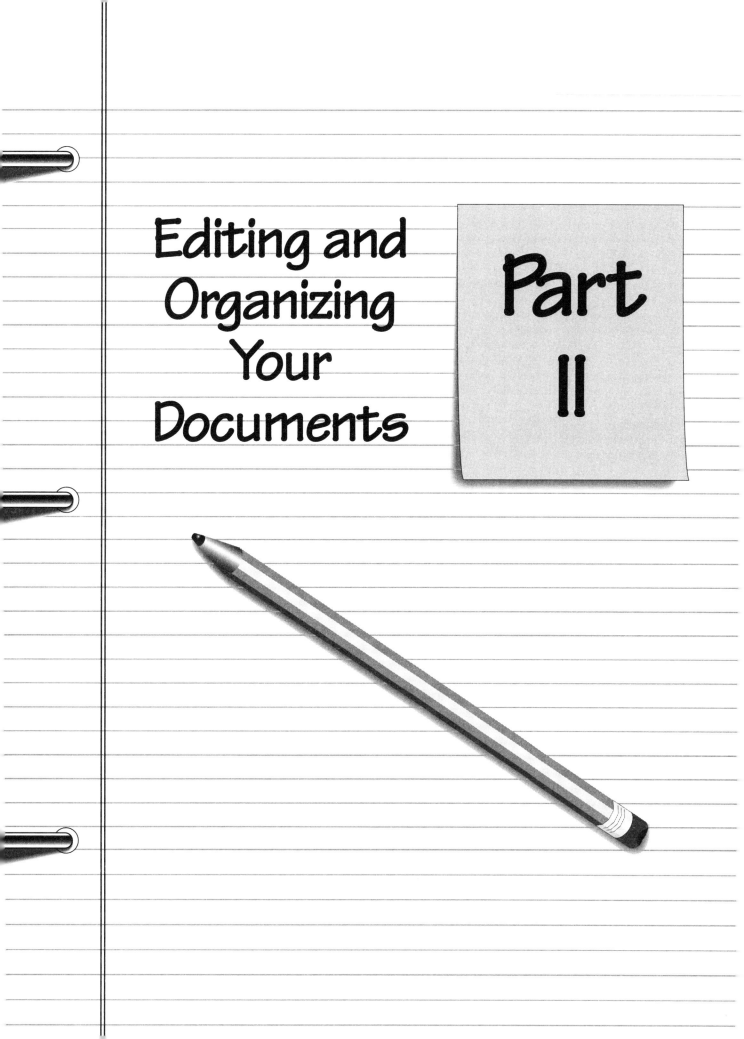

Editing and Organizing Your Documents

Part II

In this part . . .

No one gets it all right the first time. At least, no one *we* know does. This part of the book concentrates on editing — getting rid of text you regret having written, moving things around to make more sense, searching for stuff that you're sure you must have written somewhere, and keeping track of the documents that you've saved all your changes in.

Luckily, WordPerfect 7 makes editing a breeze. The lessons in this part of the book teach you how to use the WordPerfect cut-and-paste commands to move text and the find-and-replace commands to fix errors throughout a document. You also learn how to check your spelling, word choice, and even your grammar — try doing *that* with your old typewriter!

Selecting, Moving, Copying, and Deleting Text

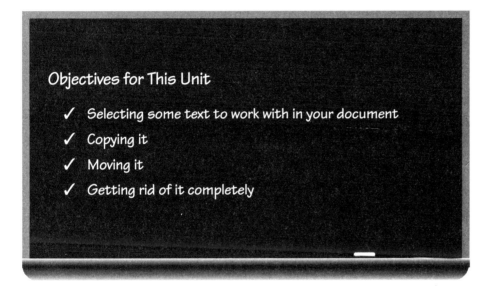

Objectives for This Unit

✓ Selecting some text to work with in your document

✓ Copying it

✓ Moving it

✓ Getting rid of it completely

Prerequisites

▶ Opening a document (Lesson 2-2)

▶ Moving around your document using keys (Lesson 2-4)

on the CD

▶ Tour Reservation. 101.wpd

▶ Favorite.101.wpd

W hat's the point in using a word processor if you're not going to stir the words around a bit, or even slice and dice them? When you peruse the first draft of an important letter, you frequently see things that can get moved around. That introductory paragraph, for example, might go better at the end of the letter as a wrap-up.

In this unit, you learn how to select text for slicing and dicing. Then you learn some things that you can do with selected text, including moving it to another location in your document, deleting it completely, or making one copy or more of it. You even learn how to move the text to another program completely — for example, to an electronic mail program so that you can include some of your gorgeously crafted prose in an e-mail message.

on the test

You can select text in at least three ways:

▶ Hold down the mouse button while you move from the beginning to the end of the text.

▶ Hold down the Shift key while you use the cursor-movement keys (otherwise known as *arrow keys*) to move from the beginning to the end of the text (see Table 5-1).

▶ Double-, triple-, and (believe it or not) quadruple-click to select a word, sentence, or paragraph (respectively) — see Table 5-2.

WordPerfect displays the selected text in *reverse video,* which is a fancy computer-geek phrase that means you see white letters on a black background.

Notes:

Table 5-1 Ways to Select Text with the Keyboard

To Select This Much Text	Press This
Character to the right of the cursor	Shift+→
Character to the left of the cursor	Shift+←
From the cursor to the beginning of the next word	Shift+Ctrl+→
From the cursor to the beginning of the current word	Shift+Ctrl+←
From the cursor to the same position all the way on the next line	Shift+↓
From the cursor to the same position up one line	Shift+↑
From the cursor to the end of the line	Shift+End
From the cursor to the beginning of the line	Shift+Home
From the cursor to the beginning of the next paragraph	Shift+Ctrl+↓
From the cursor to the beginning of the current paragraph	Shift+Ctrl+↑
From the cursor to the end of the document	Shift+Ctrl+End
From the cursor to the beginning of the document	Shift+Ctrl+Home
From the cursor to the bottom of the screen	Shift+PgDn
From the cursor to the top of the screen	Shift+PgUp

Table 5-2 How to Select Text with the Mouse

When You Want to Select This	Do This
Word	Double-click with the mouse pointer anywhere on the word.
Multiple words	Double-click on the first or last word. Hold down the mouse button on the second click and move to the other end of the selection. The text is selected word by word, rather than character by character.
Sentence	Triple-click on the sentence or click once in the margin to the left of the sentence.
Multiple sentences	Select a sentence, using one of the methods in this table. Hold down the mouse button on the last click and move the pointer to the other end of the selection.
Paragraph	Quadruple-click on the paragraph or double-click to the left of the paragraph.
Multiple paragraphs	Select a paragraph, using one of the methods in this table. Hold down the mouse button on the last click and move the pointer to the other end of the selection.
From the cursor to the mouse pointer	Shift+click

After you've selected text, you can do something to it by pressing keys, clicking on buttons, or choosing commands from menus. You can do lots of things with selected text — moving, copying, and deleting it is just the start. In later units, you find out how to make selected text bold or italicized, change its size, check its spelling, or even change its capitalization. Feeling confident about selecting text is important — most of the whiz-bang features of word processing require that you know how to select text. Fortunately, it's not difficult.

One useful thing that you can do is copy the selected text to the *Windows Clipboard*. The Windows Clipboard is a usually invisible parking space for information (although you can look at it if you want to — choose Programs⇨Accessories⇨Clipboard Viewer from the Windows 95 Start menu). After you copy or move some information to the Clipboard, you can copy it from the Clipboard back into your document or into any other Windows-based application.

Following are a few key facts about the way that the Windows Clipboard works:

> ▸ You can *move* information from your document to the Clipboard. This action is called *cutting*. You do it by selecting the information to move and then choosing the Edit⇨Cut command, pressing Ctrl+X, or clicking on the Cut button on the Toolbar.

> ▸ You can *copy* information from your document to the Clipboard. This action, quite reasonably, is called *copying*. You do it by selecting the information to copy and choosing the Edit⇨Copy command, pressing Ctrl+C, or clicking on the Copy button on the Toolbar.

> ▸ You can copy information from the Clipboard back into your document. This action is called *pasting*. You do it by choosing the Edit⇨Paste command, pressing Ctrl+V, or clicking on the Paste button on the Toolbar.

> ▸ Using the Clipboard is frequently called *cutting and pasting*.

> ▸ The information on the Clipboard stays there until you replace it with something else — that is, until you cut or copy something else to the Clipboard. After you cut or copy something new, the previous contents of the Clipboard vanish.

> ▸ You can paste the information from the Clipboard into your document more than once. In fact, you can paste it as many times as you want. This feature is a convenient way to make a bunch of copies of some text; just copy it to the Clipboard and then paste it a bunch of times.

> ▸ You can cut or copy information from one program onto the Clipboard and then paste it into another program. The Windows Clipboard works for almost all Windows-based programs, and almost all programs use the same commands and keystrokes (Ctrl+X, Ctrl+C, and Ctrl+V) for cutting and pasting.

The Clipboard holds only one chunk of information, although it can be pretty huge. But after you cut or copy something else, it replaces whatever was in the Clipboard.

Cut button

Copy button

Paste button

Ctrl+X to cut
Ctrl+C to copy
Ctrl+V to paste

Lesson 5-1

Selecting and Deleting Some Text

The easiest thing to do with a bunch of text is to delete it, plain and simple. So why not start there? While we're at it, we'll explore several ways of selecting text.

on the CD

To give you something to delete, open the Tour Reservation.101.wpd document supplied with this book (see Figure 5-1). Tour Reservation.101.wpd is a letter from a school to the Lexington Toy Company, reserving tickets for a school trip.

Blowing text away

Hmm. . . . The last sentence in the first paragraph of the letter has got to go — it's a little too candid! Use the keyboard to select the sentence:

1 Move the cursor to the beginning of the last sentence of the first paragraph of the letter.

This sentence reads *In fact, it may have been the only educational thing we did!*

You can use the mouse or arrow keys to move the cursor just to the left of the *I* in *In fact.*

2 Hold down the Shift key while you use the arrow keys to move to the exclamation point at the end of the sentence, highlighting the whole sentence, including the finishing punctuation.

When you press the Shift key, WordPerfect *extends the selection.* That is, it stretches the highlighted area to include the text up to the cursor. You can press the right arrow to move to the end of the sentence, character by character. Or press the down arrow just once.

Either way, the entire last sentence of the paragraph should be selected, as it is in Figure 5-1, and should appear in white letters on a black background.

If you need to deselect the text (maybe because you started in the wrong place), move the cursor without holding down the Shift key.

3 Press the Delete (or Del) key.

The sentence goes up in smoke. (Just kidding — deleting text is not a fire hazard!)

To select text with the keyboard, hold down Shift while you move the cursor. To delete selected text, press Delete. Easy enough!

Selecting text by using the mouse

Select some more text to delete, this time by using the mouse. The last sentence in the first paragraph (that is, the *new* last sentence, now that you've deleted the original last sentence) doesn't sound right.

---

to select text, hold down Shift while moving cursor

to deselect text, just move cursor using arrows

Delete key deletes selected text

to select, hold mouse button down while dragging mouse pointer across text

to deselect, click anywhere in text

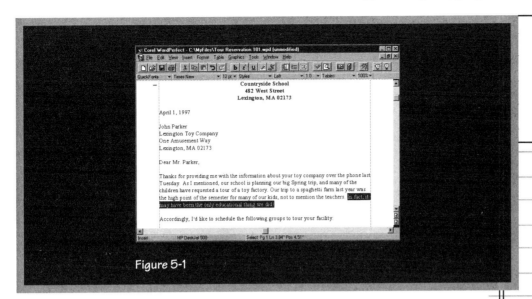

Figure 5-1

Figure 5-1: Tour Reservation.101.wpd contains a letter from a school arranging a trip to the Toy Company. In the figure, one sentence is highlighted.

Notes:

1 Move your mouse pointer to the last sentence of the first paragraph, placing it just before the comma.

Right now the last sentence reads *Our trip to a spaghetti farm last year was the high point of the semester for many of our kids, not to mention the teachers.*

Put the mouse pointer just before the comma that separates the last phrase from the rest of the sentence.

2 Hold down the mouse button and move the mouse pointer to the end of the sentence, just before the period. Release the mouse button after you've selected the phrase to delete.

As you move the mouse, WordPerfect selects (and highlights) the text, starting with the place where the mouse pointer was when you pressed the mouse button. Select the phrase *, not to mention the teachers* — be sure to include the comma at the beginning of the phrase but not the period at the end. (The idea is not to delete the period, because you still need it at the end of the sentence.)

If you miss and want to try again, just start over. If you already deleted it and want it back, click on the Undo button. If you've selected text and want to deselect it, click the mouse pointer once anywhere in your text.

3 Press Delete.

Shazam! The phrase disappears, and the period moves over to end the sentence.

If you deleted the period by mistake or didn't delete the comma, just use Backspace and Delete to clean up your sentence and then retype the period.

Tip: When you select multiple lines of text with the mouse, you can move the pointer in a straight line from the first character that you want to select to the last. You don't have to select the text line by line.

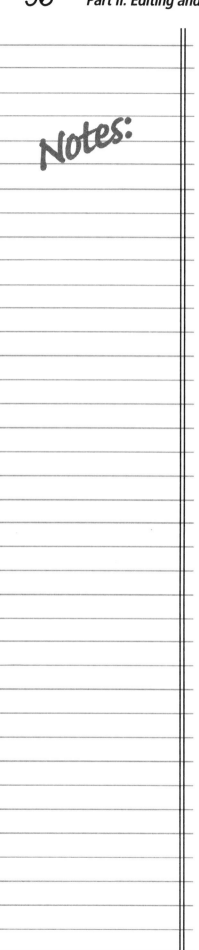

WordPerfect mouse tricks

WordPerfect makes using the mouse to select complete words easy — it assumes that you want whole words and jumps the selection to include each full word. When you want just part of a word, you can select just that, too. If, however, you find the feature annoying, you can turn it off:

- ▶ Choose Edit⇨Preferences.
- ▶ Double-click on the Environment icon.
- ▶ Click on the check box next to Automatically select words so that it doesn't have a check in it (it's at the bottom).
- ▶ Click on OK to return to the document.

This action turns off the word-selecting feature permanently (or until you turn it on again).

Selecting text by doing lots of clicking

Did you really see something about quadruple-clicking back in the introduction to this unit? Yes, you did. Unbelievable, but true. If you have the manual dexterity to click two, three, or four times in quick succession, you can select a word, sentence, or paragraph with the mouse. If Tour Reservation.101.wpd isn't open, open it now and follow these steps:

1 Move to the end of the letter so that you can see the last paragraph.

Press PgDn or use the scroll bar.

You decide that the word *Phooey* detracts from the businesslike tone of the letter.

2 Double-click on the word *Phooey*.

WordPerfect selects just the word, not the exclamation point after it.

3 Press Delete to delete the word.

WordPerfect deletes the word and the space before it, which it figures you don't want anymore. But that extra exclamation point is still there.

4 Press Delete again to delete the extra exclamation point.

Looks good. Hmm, on second thought, perhaps the whole sentence in parentheses should be cut.

5 Click in the margin next to the sentence in parentheses.

You have to click next to the second line of the paragraph. If you click in the margin next to the first line of the paragraph, WordPerfect selects the first sentence.

Or you can go another route — triple-click on the sentence.

6 Press Delete to delete the sentence.

Kablooey — it's gone.

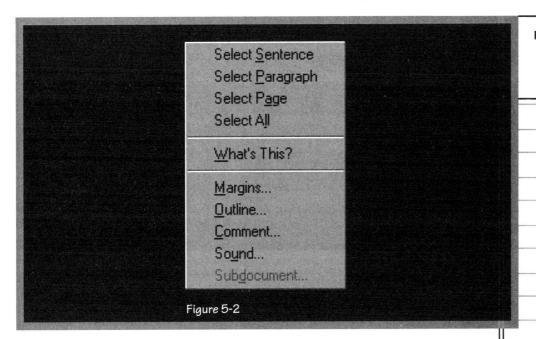

Figure 5-2

Figure 5-2: Surprise! A QuickMenu appears if you click the right mouse button.

If you can get your fingers to click fast enough, double-clicking selects a word, triple-clicking selects a sentence, and quadruple-clicking selects a paragraph. But as you will find is usual in WordPerfect, if you can't manage this method, WordPerfect always provides another way (just have another look at the tables at the beginning of this unit to find one). In particular, you may find the click-in-the-margin technique a little less clicky and somewhat more useful.

extra credit

Using QuickMenus

WordPerfect 7 has a set of menus that you have not yet used. They're called *QuickMenus*, and they appear when you click the right mouse button. Which QuickMenu appears depends on where the mouse pointer is and what you're doing. QuickMenus offer yet another way to choose commands.

If you click the right mouse button when the mouse pointer is in the typing area, you see a QuickMenu that is relevant to formatting characters. If you click the right mouse button when the mouse pointer is in the left margin, you get a QuickMenu that allows you to select various portions of text (using the cursor as the reference point, not the mouse pointer). Figure 5-2 shows the Select Text QuickMenu.

Other QuickMenus appear when you click other parts of the screen. Clicking with the right mouse button on the status bar, scroll bars, Power Bar, or Toolbar displays different QuickMenus with options that are related to that part of WordPerfect. When you can use a QuickMenu to choose a command, we tell you about it.

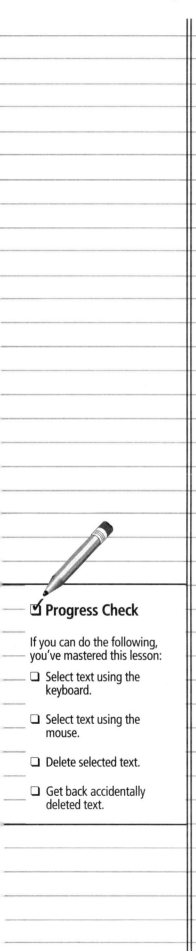

extra credit

More ways to select text and extend a selection

You may think that you know plenty of ways to select text, and you do. But whether you like it or not, WordPerfect 7 has even more ways to select text — and they are:

▶ **Selecting text with menus:** To get the QuickMenu you see in Figure 5-2, click the right mouse button when the pointer is in the left margin. This menu allows you to select the Sentence, Paragraph, Page or document (All) where your cursor is.

You can use the regular menu to get the same choices — it just takes longer. Choose Edit⇨Select and choose Sentence, Paragraph, Page, or All. (So the letters aren't very consistent. Who uses the underlined letters anyway!)

▶ **Using F8 or double-clicking Select on the status bar:** WordPerfect has a Select mode that you can turn on. When Select mode is on, you can select text with the keyboard without using the Shift key — so, for example, pressing the End key selects the text from the cursor to the end of the line. Turn Select mode on and off by pressing the F8 key or double-clicking *Select* in the status bar.

If you have made a selection only to discover that you really should have selected more, never fear. WordPerfect has a relatively simple method to extend a selection — or rather several methods (Higher Being forbid that WordPerfect have only one way to do something).

If you need to extend a selection, try one of the following:

▶ Press Shift and click on the point to which you would like the selection extended.

▶ Press Shift and use the arrow keys or other selection keyboard key combinations.

Oops! Getting deleted text back

on the test

What if you delete something by accident? Not a problem, as long as you notice it quickly. Choose Edit⇨Undelete from the menu bar or press Ctrl+Shift+Z, which is the keyboard shortcut. The deleted text reappears — it may not appear exactly where you deleted it from, though — it reappears where the cursor is. Click on Restore to undelete the text. You may need to give the command again to get back more deleted text, if you deleted it in two steps. Undelete works even when you've done other things with your document since mistakenly deleting text.

If deleting text was the last thing you did, you can use Edit⇨Undo, or just click on the Undo button, to get it back.

Always remember to save your document often, especially before you make drastic changes.

☑ **Progress Check**

If you can do the following, you've mastered this lesson:

❑ Select text using the keyboard.

❑ Select text using the mouse.

❑ Delete selected text.

❑ Get back accidentally deleted text.

Copying Text

WordPerfect 7 makes copying text easy. All you need to do is select the text that you want to copy, use Ctrl+C or the Copy button on the Toolbar to tell WordPerfect to store the text on the Windows Clipboard for later use, move the cursor to the position where the text should be copied, and use Ctrl+V or the Paste button to insert the selection there. (You can also find the Copy and Paste commands in the Edit menu.)

Copying a selection

on the CD

If you haven't already opened the Tour Reservation.101.wpd document, open it now. Reading the letter, you notice that on May 12, a total of 142 children are going to the toy factory. You decide to send some of those kids the next day, so you need to add an extra line to the letter and change some of the numbers. Follow these steps:

1 Select the line that starts *May 12*.

Use your favorite method — the easiest may be to click once in the margin to the left of the line.

The entire line is highlighted.

2 Copy the selection to the Clipboard by pressing Ctrl+C or by clicking on the Copy button.

The selection is copied to the Clipboard without anything noticeable happening to your letter.

3 Move the cursor to the beginning of the next line.

This is where you want to add a copy of the line.

4 Copy the selection by pressing Ctrl+V or clicking the Paste button.

WordPerfect inserts a copy of the line from the Clipboard to the line where the cursor is. Your cursor is at the end of the line.

5 Press Enter to add a carriage return.

This step adds a blank line below the line that you just inserted.

6 Edit the line, changing the date to the 13th, the number of kids to 70, and the number of adults to 4.

To be consistent, change the information for the 12th so that the number of kids is 72 and the number of adults is 4. If WordPerfect has deleted the tab at the beginning of the line, stick it back in.

7 Save the document.

Click on the Save button on the Toolbar.

Copying is simply cutting and pasting, using the keystroke commands or buttons.

Notes:

☑ **Progress Check**

If you can do the following, you've mastered this lesson:

❑ Copy text to the Windows Clipboard.

❑ Paste copies of text from the Clipboard into your document.

Recess

If it's time to feed the chickens, save your file and exit WordPerfect by choosing File➪Exit from the menu bar or pressing Alt+F4. (Your chickens would probably love the crust of that Danish you didn't get around to finishing!)

When you're ready to come back and finish the unit, open WordPerfect and open Tour Reservation.101.wpd.

Lesson 5-3

Moving Text

WordPerfect has two ways to move text. You may have already figured out the first way — you can use the cut and paste features of WordPerfect to cut the text from where it is now and then paste it where you want it. The other way to move text is to select it and drag it.

Cutting and pasting

on the CD

You may still have Tour Reservation.101.wpd open. If not, open it now.

Move the paragraph that starts *We will pay for the tours* earlier in the letter, using WordPerfect's cut and paste feature:

1 Select the paragraph to move.

Use your favorite method:

- ◆ Position the cursor at the beginning of the paragraph. Hold down the Shift key as you use the arrow keys to get to the end of the paragraph (remember, you can use the down-arrow key to move down to the end of the paragraph — you don't have to press the right-arrow key forever).

- ◆ Click and drag the mouse from one corner of the paragraph to the opposite one.

- ◆ Quadruple-click anywhere in the paragraph.

- ◆ Double-click in the left margin.

2 Cut the paragraph by pressing Ctrl+X, choosing Edit➪Cut from the menu, or clicking on the Cut button.

The paragraph disappears — but don't worry: It's on the Windows Clipboard, and you can get it back easily as long as you don't cut or copy anything else.

3 Move your cursor to where the paragraph will be inserted.

In this case, move your cursor to the beginning of the paragraph that starts *Accordingly, I'd like to schedule the following groups to tour your facility.*

4 Insert the paragraph by pressing Ctrl+V, choosing Edit➪Paste from the menu, or clicking the Paste button.

The paragraph will be pulled from the Clipboard and inserted where the cursor is.

5 **If you didn't select the carriage returns at the end of the paragraph you moved, insert or delete carriage returns as needed.**

If no carriage return appears between the paragraph that you just moved and the next paragraph *(Accordingly . . .),* move your cursor there and press Enter twice.

If you see extra blank lines where the paragraph that you moved used to be, move your cursor there and delete them by pressing Delete.

on the test

One way to move text is to select it, cut it from its current position, and paste it to the new position.

Congratulations! By learning to use the cut, paste, and copy features of WordPerfect, you have learned skills that will be useful throughout Windows.

Dragging

You can move text without ever putting it on the Clipboard — as easily as selecting it and dragging it to a new location. This technique, though, can be more trouble than it's worth unless you can see both the initial position of the text that you're moving and where you want to move it on the screen without scrolling.

To try it, move two sentences to a different part of the letter:

1 **Scroll the screen so that you can see both the paragraph that begins *We will pay for the tickets in advance,* and the one that begins *We plan to arrive by bus.***

As we said above, this technique is difficult to use unless you see the text you're moving and where you're moving it on the screen at the same time.

2 **Select the sentences *We plan to bring bag lunches — let me know if this is a problem. Buying lunch in the cafeteria tends to be far too confusing (and too expensive) for this large a group!***

These sentences are at the end of the paragraph that starts *We plan to arrive by bus.* Use your favorite method to select the sentences.

3 **Click on the selected text and hold down the mouse key.**

The mouse pointer changes when the mouse is moved — a little box is now added to it to indicate that something (the selected text) is going with the mouse pointer. (Give it a second — it may not appear as quickly as you think it should.)

4 **Continue to hold down the mouse button and move the mouse pointer where you want to put the text.**

In this case, move the mouse pointer to the end of the paragraph that begins *We will pay for the tours in advance.*

As you move the mouse pointer, the insertion point moves too, indicating where the text will go when you let go of the mouse button.

5 **Let go of the mouse button.**

The text moves to the new position. Notice that it stays selected, so if it didn't land in exactly the right place, you can drag it to a new position.

drag selected text to new location

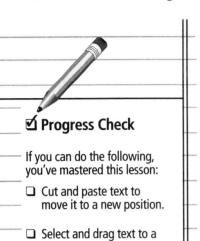

☑ Progress Check

If you can do the following, you've mastered this lesson:

❑ Cut and paste text to move it to a new position.

❑ Select and drag text to a new position.

on the test

heads up

6 **Click the mouse in the text to unselect the two sentences. Then add the missing space before the first of the two sentences you just moved.**

7 **Save your document by pressing Ctrl+S.**

The intuitive way to move text is to select it and drag it to its new position. Computer geeks call this feature *drag and drop*.

A caveat: You can move the selected text to a point that is currently off the screen — if you move the cursor a little past the top or bottom of the typing area, the document scrolls up or down. In our experience, however, it scrolls so quickly that you can have difficulty getting where you want to be. If you're moving text to a place in the document that you can't see, you may want to stick with the cut-and-paste method.

Another unit under your belt! Now you know how to perform lots of slick editing moves, including slicing and dicing your text by using the Windows cut-and-paste commands. You're ready for — you guessed it — the Unit 5 Quiz.

Unit 5 Quiz

For each of the following questions, circle the letter of the correct answer or answers. Remember, we may include more than one right answer for each question!

1. **This button . . .**
   A. Does the same thing as Ctrl+X.
   B. Does the same thing as Edit➪Cut.
   C. Uses pinking shears on your printed document.
   D. Denotes that this document is good only for children's art projects.
   E. Deletes selected text from your document and puts it in the Clipboard.

2. **This button . . .**
   A. Does the same thing as Ctrl+C.
   B. Does the same thing as Edit➪Copy.
   C. Puts a dotted line around the selected text.
   D. Changes the type in the document from black to blue.
   E. Copies selected text to the Clipboard.

3. **This button . . .**
   A. Does the same thing as Ctrl+V.
   B. Does the same thing as Edit➪Paste.
   C. Prints the document neatly so you can carry it around on your clipboard.
   D. Pastes the document to a clipboard so you don't lose it when you shake hands.
   E. Pastes text from the Clipboard to the document (starting at the cursor).

4. **The Clipboard . . .**

    A. Makes you look good at meetings.

    B. Is a place to hold text before it's copied or pasted.

    C. Is a feature of Windows that allows you to move or copy information from one Windows-based program to another.

    D. Is where text goes when you cut it from your document.

    E. Is usually invisible, but very useful.

5. **Text can be selected by . . .**

    A. Using the mouse by clicking at the beginning of the text and dragging the mouse pointer to the end of the text.

    B. Choosing Edit⇨Select from the menu bar.

    C. Using a QuickMenu — that is, right-clicking in the left margin of the document and then choosing Select Sentence, Select Paragraph, Select Page, or Select All from the QuickMenu that appears.

    D. Double-, triple-, or quadruple-clicking to select a word, sentence, or paragraph (respectively).

    E. Holding down the Shift key while pressing the cursor movement keys: ↑, ↓, →, ←, PgUp, PgDn, Home, and End.

6. **In the Mary Martin version of Peter Pan, what happens when the title character comes back for Wendy?**

    A. She happily follows him to Neverland and lives there as a child forever.

    B. She has grown up and can't go with Peter to Neverland.

    C. Wendy's daughter Jane goes with Peter Pan for an adventure.

    D. Peter challenges Wendy's brother John to an arm-wrestling match.

    E. She calls the police.

Notes:

Unit 5 Exercise

on the CD

1. Open the file Favorite.101.wpd (in Figure 5-3). It contains a list of toys.

> My favorite toys are (in this order):
>
> Dolls
> Construction equipment
> Cars
> Fire trucks (a working siren is important)
> Stuffed animals
> Cooking set
> Carpentry set
> Welding set
> Blocks
> Model trains
> Hobby horse
> Tricycle
> Puzzles

2. At the bottom of the list, add any other toys that you like (adult toys count).

3. If the list contains any toys that you don't enjoy, select and delete the items.

4. Move your favorite toy to the top of the list.

5. Save the document.

Finding and Replacing Text

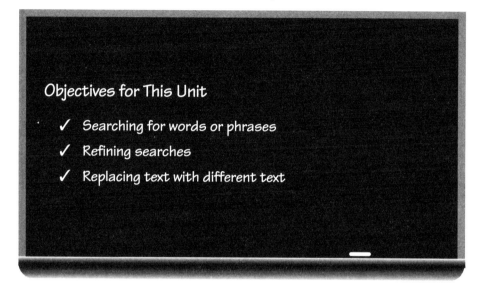

Objectives for This Unit

✓ Searching for words or phrases

✓ Refining searches

✓ Replacing text with different text

Prerequisites

▶ Using commands
(Lesson 2-2)

▶ Using dialog boxes
(Lesson 2-3)

▶ Opening documents
(Lesson 2-2)

▶ Paint-By-
Numbers.101.wpd

on the CD

If you've ever needed to replace multiple instances of a word in a document or wondered where a certain word was in a document, you need to know how to use the search feature of WordPerfect 7.

Searching for text is nearly hassle-free — however, using the replace feature can royally screw up your document if you don't do exactly what you need to do. Someone once called to tell us that she had replaced all her spaces with nothing — a serious problem. With all the spaces gone, each paragraph in the document was one long word. So be careful when replacing text and make sure that you save your document before you do a major search-and-replace job so that you can get the saved version back if you need to.

WordPerfect can also find (and even replace) formatting codes. For example, you can replace all the formatting codes that center lines with codes that right-align them. For information about finding and replacing WordPerfect's codes, see Unit 10.

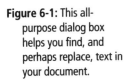

Figure 6-1: This all-purpose dialog box helps you find, and perhaps replace, text in your document.

Figure 6-2: The Paint-By-Numbers.101.wpd document.

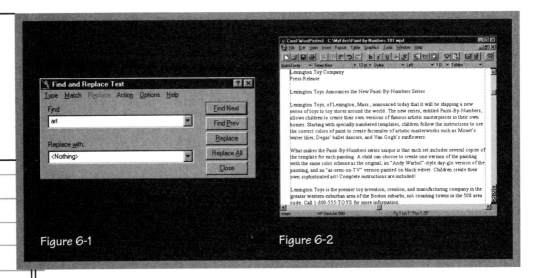

Figure 6-1

Figure 6-2

Lesson 6-1

Searching for Words or Phrases

on the test

The way to search for a word or phrase in WordPerfect is to use the Find and Replace Text dialog box. Even when you are searching for something and aren't planning on replacing it with anything, this is still the dialog box you need to use. To begin a search, display the dialog box in one of the following ways:

- Press F2.
- Press Ctrl+F.
- Choose Edit⇨Find and Replace from the menu bar.

Figure 6-1 shows the Find and Replace Text dialog box.

on the CD

You can use the document Paint-By-Numbers.101.wpd to learn how to search — see Figure 6-2. You start by searching for the first use of the word *number*.

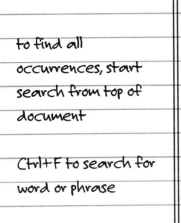

to find all occurrences, start search from top of document

Ctrl+F to search for word or phrase

1 **Open Paint-By-Numbers.101.wpd.**

2 **Make sure that your cursor is at the top of the document by pressing Ctrl+Home.**

This action insures that you find the first instance of the text that you're looking for. (If you want to find, say, the first instance on the fifth page, put the cursor at the top of page 5.)

3 **Display the Find and Replace Text dialog box by pressing Ctrl+F or F2.**

If you prefer, choose Edit⇨Find and Replace from the menu.

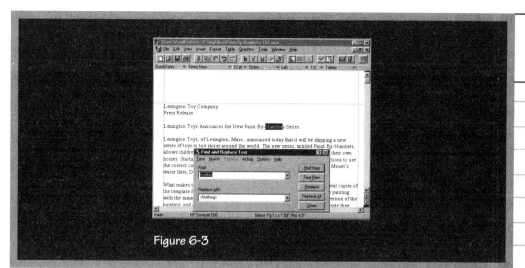

Figure 6-3

Figure 6-3: WordPerfect
found the first occurrence
of the word *number*.

Notes:

WordPerfect displays the Find and Replace Text dialog box (refer to Figure 6-1). The myriad of options may be daunting now, but they will prove to be extremely useful. For the time being, the important thing to notice is that the Find box is highlighted, ready to receive your input.

4 **Type** number **in the Find box.**

Your cursor is already in the Find box, so all you need to do is type the word.

5 **To find the word, press Enter or click on the Find Next button.**

WordPerfect highlights the first occurrence of that text in the document after the cursor (see Figure 6-3). Notice that the word that WordPerfect finds is actually *Numbers*, not just *number*. Because you didn't tell WordPerfect whether capitalization was important or whether you were looking for the whole word *number*, WordPerfect finds any occurrence of those six letters in that order. You learn how to look for specific capitalization and only the whole word in the next lesson. Right now, WordPerfect is looking for any occurrence of those six letters in that order.

The Find and Replace Text dialog box may be right on top of the word that WordPerfect found — you can move the dialog box by dragging its title bar.

6 **To keep finding *number,* keep pressing Enter or clicking on Find Next.**

Notice that WordPerfect doesn't care whether the word is capitalized.

When the last *number* in the document has been found, WordPerfect displays the message `"number" Not Found` and asks you to acknowledge that fact by clicking on OK. This message means that in the direction that WordPerfect is searching (from top to bottom, in this case), the text *number* does not appear between the cursor and the end of the document.

7 **Click on OK to acknowledge that no more *number*s exist in the document.**

You're finished searching.

8 **Click on Close to close the Find and Replace Text dialog box.**

WordPerfect takes you back to your document. Notice that the last instance of *number* is highlighted — that's where your cursor is in the document.

☑ Progress Check

If you can do the following, you've mastered this lesson:

❑ Find the first instance of a word in a document.

❑ Find all instances of a word in a document.

on the test

To find something in your document, use the Find and Replace Text dialog box — simply type the text that you're looking for in the Find box and press Enter. You can keep looking for the text by clicking on the Find Next button in the Find and Replace Text dialog box.

click on Find Next to continue search

on the test

When you display the Find and Replace Text dialog box, WordPerfect remembers what you searched for last time and suggests it again. To search for a word that you've previously searched for, click on the arrow on the right side of the box to display a list of the last few words or phrases that you searched for.

Lesson 6-2   Refining Your Search

In a long document, finding what you're looking for can take awhile. You have at least two ways to make finding what you're looking for a little easier: One is to be smart about your search, and the other is to tell WordPerfect as much as you know about what you're looking for — and that may mean using WordPerfect's find features. So what does *being smart* mean? It means:

- Not looking for something where you know you won't find it (that is, don't start looking at the beginning of a 20-page document if you know that what you're looking for is in the last section — move your cursor to the beginning of the last section and start the search there).

- Looking for the whole phrase, when you know it, and not just a word. You can even include punctuation.

- Telling WordPerfect whether capitalization is important.

- Telling WordPerfect whether the text you're looking for is a whole word or just a string of letters.

Table 6-1 lists the specifics of how to refine a search.

The Find and Replace Text dialog box has its own little menu bar at the top of the dialog box. You can choose commands from this menu bar to control how the searching works. This lesson shows you how to use some of these commands.

Table 6-1	Search Options
To Find This	*Use This Option on the Find and Replace Text Dialog Box*
A phrase	Type the whole phrase with punctuation in the Find and Replace Text dialog box.
The word, the whole word, and nothing but the word	Choose Match⇨Whole Word from the dialog box menu.
Something anywhere in the document, regardless of where the cursor is	Choose Options⇨Begin Find at Top of Document or Options⇨Wrap at Beg./End of Document.
Something above (before) your cursor	Click on the Find Prev button.
Something below (after) your cursor	Click on the Find Next button.

To Find This	Use This Option on the Search and Replace Text Dialog Box
A match with specific capitalization	Choose Match⇨Case from the dialog box menu.
The text in a specific font or in a particular text style	Choose Match⇨Font from the dialog box menu and specify the font or text style in the Match Font dialog box.

Nothing extraneous, please

You may frequently notice, especially when you're searching for a short word, that WordPerfect finds your search word within other words. If, for example, as in Lesson 6-1, you're looking for the word *number*, WordPerfect may also find that combination of letters in *number*s and *number*ed. Sometimes the results are surprising — WordPerfect will find *man* in wo*man* and *man*gy.

One way to solve this problem is to type a space before or after the word in the F*i*nd box. Searching for *man* preceded by a space, WordPerfect won't find wo*man* but will still find *man*ager and *man*gy. Searching for *man* followed by a space still doesn't work perfectly, because it finds wo*man*. And adding a space after the word causes WordPerfect to miss the word when it is followed by punctuation, such as a period or a comma.

Luckily, WordPerfect has a feature that lets you tell it to find a string of letters only when they form an entire word and not when they form part of a larger word.

on the CD

In these steps, you find *art* in Paint-By-Numbers.101.wpd only when it's a word, not when it's part of a word.

1 **Open the Paint-by-Numbers.101.wpd document if it's not still open from the preceding lesson.**

2 **Move to the top of the document by pressing Ctrl+Home.**

WordPerfect starts looking from the current location of the cursor — in this case, the top of the document.

3 **Open the Find and Replace Text dialog box by pressing F2 or Ctrl+F.**

If you prefer, you can choose *E*dit⇨*F*ind and Replace from the menu.

4 **Type art in the F*i*nd box.**

This part is the same as if you were looking for any instance of *art*.

5 **Click on *F*ind Next a few times.**

WordPerfect finds the letters *art* within the words *art*istic and st*art*ing.

6 **Click in the document to tell WordPerfect that you want to work there; then press Ctrl+Home to move back to the beginning of the document.**

The Find and Replace Text dialog box remains visible while you do this step. Moving back to the top of the document ensures that your next search includes the whole document.

Notes:

in Find and Replace Text dialog box, Match→Whole Word to find whole words only

click in the document during a search to move the cursor

7 **Choose Match⇨Whole Word from the menu bar in the dialog box.**

The phrase *Whole Word* appears under the Find box in the dialog box to let you know that WordPerfect is looking only for the word *art*.

8 **Press Enter or click on Find Next.**

WordPerfect highlights the first (and only) time that the word *art* is used in the document.

9 **Click on Close or press Esc.**

The dialog box disappears, leaving a highlight on the text that you found.

Using the Find and Replace Text dialog box menu bar lets you be more specific about what you're looking for. The Match⇨Whole Word command tells WordPerfect that you want the text in the box only when it's a whole word, not when the letters appear as part of another word.

heads up

The Whole Word setting remains in effect until you turn it off. The next time you use the Find and Replace Text dialog box, you'll see that the words *Whole Word* still appear beneath the Find text box. Turn off the Whole Word setting by choosing the Match⇨Whole Word command from the dialog box menu bar again.

Using the whole word setting is one way to specify your searches so that they go quickly. Don't forget to read Table 6-1 to find other ways.

Recess

If you need to look for something other than text — your kids, your keys, your sanity — exit WordPerfect without saving the document. When you're ready to play with toys (or documents pertaining to toys), open Paint-by-Numbers.101.wpd again.

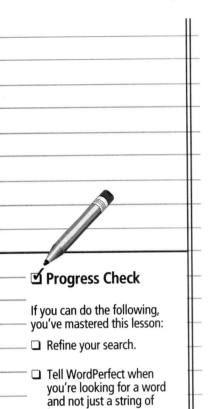

☑ Progress Check

If you can do the following, you've mastered this lesson:

❑ Refine your search.

❑ Tell WordPerfect when you're looking for a word and not just a string of letters.

Lesson 6-3

Replacing What You've Found

WordPerfect makes it easy to find all instances of a word or phrase and replace it with something else. For example, while working on your forthcoming novel, you write a magnificent chapter in which the main character eats a brownie. You then realize that in an earlier chapter, you wrote that she's allergic to chocolate. You decide to replace *brownie* with *butterscotch bar* throughout the chapter.

Replacing one word or phrase with another is called *global search and replace* in computer lingo. WordPerfect makes it a breeze, using the same Find and Replace Text dialog box that you use when searching for text. You type the text to be replaced in the Find box and the text to replace it with in the Replace with box. Then you click on the Replace button, which tells WordPerfect to find the first instance of that text and ask you whether you want to replace it with the text in the Replace with box. WordPerfect shows you each place in which it finds the Find text and lets you decide whether it should be replaced.

If you want to replace all instances of a word or phrase without WordPerfect asking about each one, you can click on the Replace <u>A</u>ll button, which takes the choice out of your hands and replaces all instances of the F<u>i</u>nd text with the Replace <u>w</u>ith text.

Although WordPerfect is trustworthy, it does *exactly* what you tell it to do, which can backfire dreadfully. So watch out when you use the Replace <u>A</u>ll button because you can easily make mistakes. For example, you may forget to use the <u>M</u>atch⇨<u>W</u>ord command when you're replacing text like *in* with, say, *inside*. You can end up with words like *Lexinsidegton, providinsideg,* and *insideformation.* As much as you may like these new words, they are probably not exactly what you had in mind.

on the test

Following are three steps to take to avoid making hash out of your document when replacing text:

- Save your document before using the Find and Replace Text dialog box to replace text. (Then if you need to get it back, close the current document *without* saving it and open the saved version.)

- Use the <u>F</u>ind Next button to find a few instances of the text that you're planning to replace, to make sure that WordPerfect finds the text you had in mind.

- Use the <u>R</u>eplace button, not the Replace <u>A</u>ll button, to do the replacement, unless you're *sure* that you know what you're doing.

The Lexington Toy Company has found out that it can't call its new product Paint-by-Numbers for copyright reasons. So instead they're going to call it Paint-by-Letters. You're going to find every instance of *Number* in the press release and replace it with *Letter.*

on the CD

1 **Open the Paint-By-Numbers.101.wpd document (if it isn't already open).**

2 **Save it immediately as Paint-By-Letters.wpd, using the <u>F</u>ile⇨Save <u>A</u>s command.**

This step insures that you won't accidentally replace the document that you've been working on with the new document that you want to create. (You could also have opened the document as Read Only.)

If you are continuing from the previous lesson and the word *art* is still selected, WordPerfect asks if you want to save just the selected text or the entire file — click on OK to save the whole file.

3 **Move the cursor to the top of the document by pressing Ctrl+Home.**

Start at the top of the document to be sure that you find all occurrences of the word or phrase that you're looking for.

4 **Open the Find and Replace Text dialog box by pressing F2.**

The last word that you looked for is still in the F<u>i</u>nd box, even though you looked for it in a different document. The contents of the F<u>i</u>nd box are highlighted, so whatever you type replaces it.

5 **Type number in the F<u>i</u>nd box and then press Tab to move to the Replace <u>w</u>ith box.**

Be sure not to type a space after the word.

6 **Make sure that Whole Word is turned off.**

If *Whole Word* appears beneath the F<u>i</u>nd box, choose <u>M</u>atch⇨Whole Word from the dialog box menu bar to turn off this setting.

Notes:

in F<u>i</u>nd box, type text to be replaced

in Replace with box, type text to replace with

Notes:

7 **In the Replace with box, type** letter.

8 **Press Enter or click on Find Next.**

WordPerfect highlights the first instance of *number,* which is on the title line.

9 **Click on the Replace button.**

WordPerfect replaces *Number* with *Letter.* The *s* at the end of *numbers* is unaffected, so it is on hand to turn *letter* into *letters.* You may be pleased and surprised to see that WordPerfect is smart enough to match capitalization when it replaces a word; that is, because *numbers* was capitalized, it capitalizes *letters.*

10 **Continue through the document, deciding whether or not to replace each instance of *number* with *letter.***

In this case, you can click to replace each time *number* is found. Replacing them all with *letter* makes sense.

When WordPerfect reports no more instances, click on OK to dismiss the message that appears.

11 **Save the completed document by pressing Ctrl+S; then close it by pressing Ctrl+F4.**

By specifying a word in the Replace with box, you can replace one word in your text with another.

You aren't limited to replacing single words. You can replace a phrase or punctuation by using the Find and Replace Text dialog box. In Unit 10, you find out how to replace formatting, too (for example, changing all bold to italics).

extra credit

Swapping two terms

Sometimes you need to search and replace in several steps. For example, if you've written an article comparing butterscotch bars and brownies and then realize that you have them mixed up and need to replace every instance of *butterscotch bars* with *brownies* and vice versa, you need to do it in three steps. If you use the search and replace feature to replace all instances of *butterscotch bars* with *brownies,* you have no way of telling the difference between the *brownies* that are supposed to get changed back to *butterscotch bars* and those that should remain *brownies.* You would have an article that was only about brownies, with no mention of butterscotch bars at all!

Instead, you need to do something like the following:

1. **Replace all instances of *brownies* with something that won't appear anywhere else in your document — something like *xbrownies.* Now the article is about xbrownies and butterscotch bars.**

2. **Replace all instances of *butterscotch bars* with *brownies.* Now the article is about xbrownies and brownies.**

3. **Replace all instances of *xbrownies* with *butterscotch bars.* Now the article is about butterscotch bars and brownies again.**

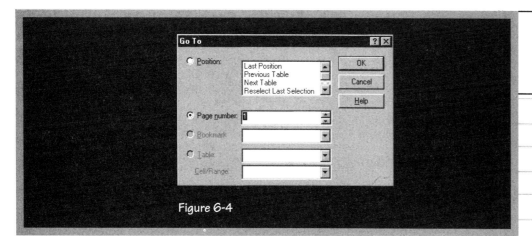

Figure 6-4

extra credit

Replacing all forms of a word with a different word

WordPerfect 7 has an ultra-cool feature: You can find and replace all forms of a word. For example, you can replace all references to *thinking* in your electronic diary to *writing* (if you think that your diary might become public, say, and you want to sound a little more active). That switch means that *thought* becomes *wrote, think* becomes *write,* and so on.

To tell WordPerfect that you want to deal with word forms, choose Type⇨Word Forms from the menu bar in the Find and Replace Text dialog box. WordPerfect displays the phrase *Word Forms* below the Find box to remind you of what you're doing.

When you're replacing word forms, confirming each replacement rather than using the Replace All button is a good idea — WordPerfect isn't smart enough not to change a noun into a verb, and you may find that your substitution makes no sense. Occasionally, WordPerfect gives you a choice of the form of the Replace with word — just pick the one that you want and click on Replace to continue.

extra credit

Finding your place in a long document

You already know about moving around in the document by using the mouse and the keyboard. But when documents get long, WordPerfect has a powerful way for you to find your way around: the Go To dialog box that you see in Figure 6-4. The Go To dialog box allows you to specify some places that you might want to be (the Bahamas is not on the list): the position you were at last, the previous or next table — but we haven't covered tables, the top or bottom of the current page, or a particular page.

You can display the Go To dialog box in any of the following ways:

- Choose Edit⇨Go To.

- Press Ctrl+G.

- Put your mouse on the scroll bar, click with the *right* mouse button, and pick Go To off the QuickMenu that appears.

(continued)

☑ Progress Check

If you can do the following, you've mastered this lesson:

❑ Replace all the occurrences of a word in a document with a different word.

❑ Replace all the occurrences of a phrase with a different phrase.

Ctrl+G for Go To dialog box

last Position in Go To
dialog box returns
cursor to previous
location

(continued)

- Double-click on the location section of the status bar (the far right of the bottom line, the part that says something like *Pg 1 Ln 1″ Pos 1″*).

The Go To dialog box lets you move either back to the last place your cursor was before it was last moved or to a particular page.

The Last Position setting in the Go To dialog box is a quick way to get your cursor back to where it was before you moved it.

The Go To dialog box is also useful for moving to a specific page in a long document: Just enter a page number in the Page <u>n</u>umber box.

extra credit

Finding where you left off

WordPerfect has a nifty feature that creates a bookmark where your cursor was when you last saved the document. It uses bookmarks, actually a special bookmark called a Quickmark, but you don't have to know anything about bookmarks to use it. Here's how to turn on the feature.

1. **Choose Edit⇨Preferences from the menu.**

   The Preferences dialog box is displayed. It has a bunch of icons in it.

2. **Double-click on the <u>E</u>nvironment icon.**

   The Environment Preferences dialog box appears (see Figure 6-5).

3. **Click on the Set <u>Q</u>uickmark on save setting to put a check in the box.**

   This step sets a bookmark, called a Quickmark, each time you save a file.

Turn the Quickmark feature on by using the Environment Preferences dialog box. You can then quickly return to that location by using Go To and finding Quickmark under the Bookmarks.

In the same dialog box is another setting that allows you to tell WordPerfect to open the same documents and put the cursor in the same place that it was when you last exited. Just change the Save Workspace setting to <u>A</u>lways or Prompt on e<u>x</u>it (which means that WordPerfect will ask you each time whether you want your workspace saved).

Unit 6 Quiz

For each of the following questions, circle the letter of the correct answer or answers. Remember, we may give you more than one right answer for each question!

1. **The Find and Replace Text dialog box is used to . . .**

   A. Find text in your document.

   B. Find text in your document and replace it with other text.

   C. Find a word or phrase.

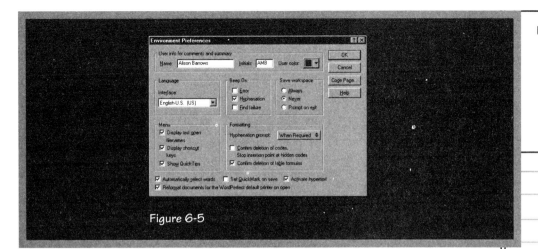

Figure 6-5

D. Find a character, such as an asterisk.

E. Replace all the occurrences of *I* in your document with *Elvis*.

2. **Global search and replace is . . .**

A. When you look all over the world for something.

B. When WordPerfect looks through a document, replacing one word or phrase with another.

C. A convenient way to fix a mistake that you've made consistently throughout a document, such as spelling someone's name wrong.

D. A dangerous command that can foul up your document if you aren't careful.

E. Something that you can do with the Find and Replace Text dialog box.

3. **Before clicking on the Replace or Replace All button on the Find and Replace dialog box, a good idea is to . . .**

A. Think twice: Are you sure that you want to make the change?

B. Save your document, just in case.

C. Check that the sentence will read correctly after the replacement is made.

D. Check whether the Whole Word setting is on.

E. Utter a brief prayer to the gods of word processing.

4. **A good way to display the Find and Replace Text dialog box is to . . .**

A. Press F2.

B. Press Ctrl+F.

C. Press Alt+E and then F. (Try it!)

D. Press and release the Alt key. Then type **ef**. (Again, try it!)

E. Position the mouse pointer on each of the buttons on the Toolbar in turn and read the description of the button that appears to see if any of them displays the Find and Replace Text dialog box. After you determine that there is no button for this command, give up and press F2.

Notes:

5. **To move your cursor to page 3 of a document . . .**

    A. Press Ctrl+Home to move to the top of the document and then press the Next Page button on the scroll bar twice.

    B. Move your cursor around in the document until you see *Pg 3* on the status bar.

    C. Press Ctrl+G to display the Go To dialog box, type **3** in the Page number box, and click on OK.

    D. Print the document, find page 3, read what it says, and use the Find and Replace Text dialog box to locate that text in the document.

    E. Click on your mouse three times, close your eyes, and say, "There's no place like page 3."

Unit 6 Exercise

Notes:

1. Write a memo to your boss (imaginary or real) proposing that your toy company come out with a revolutionary new product named Fun-O-Matic. Explain the benefits of this new product in full detail. (Make them up!)

2. Save the document as New Product.wpd.

3. Change your mind about the name of the product, deciding that Totally Awesome Thingamajig would sound more up-to-date. Use the Find and Replace Text dialog box to replace all instances of Fun-O-Matic with Totally Awesome Thingamajig.

4. Save the document again.

5. Experiment with a way to totally ruin a document with the Find and Replace Text dialog box so that you will remember not to do so to a document that's actually important. Using the Find and Replace Text dialog box, replace all the spaces in your document with nothing. (Replace the contents of the F_ind box with a single space, delete the contents of the Replace _with box, and then click on Replace _All.)

6. Wow! A document with no spaces is totally unintelligible! Close the document *without* saving it.

7. Open the New Product.wpd document, which should be the version of the memo that describes your Totally Awesome Thingamajig product, with the spaces intact.

Writing Tools to Improve Your Spelling, Grammar, and Word Choice

Prerequisites
▶ Using commands (Lesson 2-2)
▶ Using dialog boxes (Lesson 2-3)
▶ Opening documents (Lesson 2-2)

Objectives for This Unit

✓ Checking your spelling

✓ Automatically correcting common mistakes

✓ Using the Thesaurus to improve word choice

✓ Checking grammar

▶ Job Application. 101.wpd
▶ History of Circuses.101.wpd
on the CD

*O*ne reason that many people switch from a typewriter to a computer is to take advantage of a computer's smarts so that their letters, memos, reports, and other documents look slicker and more professional. This unit is the one in which you learn how to take advantage of the smart features of WordPerfect. WordPerfect can check your spelling (even without you asking!), automatically correct common mistakes as you type, list synonyms and antonyms of a word so that you can hone in on exactly the word that will get your point across, and even check your grammar. These tools are useful when finishing off your own document or editing someone else's document.

You should always use some sort of spell checker on any document before you print it. WordPerfect 7 lets you choose between Spell-As-You-Go and the more conventional Spell Checker. Both work by comparing the words in your document against a dictionary that comes with WordPerfect. If a word in your document isn't in WordPerfect's dictionary, WordPerfect flags the word as misspelled. Of course, it may just be a word that WordPerfect doesn't know, such as someone's last name or the name of your town. In this unit, you learn how to add words to the WordPerfect dictionary so that WordPerfect doesn't keep stopping for perfectly spelled words.

An even cooler feature is QuickCorrect. QuickCorrect works for you whether you know it or not — so you may as well learn to get the full power of it. As you type, QuickCorrect is on the lookout for misspelled words. As soon as you type the space or punctuation following a misspelled word, WordPerfect corrects it on the spot, without asking and without any further ado. You can control which words appear on QuickCorrect's list of misspelled words.

Many people (like us, the authors of this book) don't use the other two features — the Thesaurus and Grammatik — very often, but *you* might. Learn to use them and then see if they're useful for the word-processing work that you do.

Spell Checker, Thesaurus, and Grammatik are all tabs on the Writing Tools dialog box, so when you're editing your document, you can easily switch from one writing tool to another. The Writing Tools dialog box can appear in two different ways. It can take up half of the WordPerfect window, making the typing area smaller, but never covering any text; or it can appear as a regular dialog box, covering part of the typing area. You can change the appearance of this dialog box by clicking and dragging when the mouse pointer turns into a hand — the box outline tells you where the dialog box will be when you let go of the mouse button.

Lesson 7-1   Checking Your Spelling

When you use WordPerfect to write your documents, you don't have to be able to spell perfectly — WordPerfect's Spell Checker can check your words against its dictionary. You should be aware, however, that the speller can't check the context of a word — it may think that *there* looks fine when what you actually meant to type was *their*. The Spell Checker compares your words with words in its dictionary (a dictionary that contains no definitions). The Spell Checker is very good at finding misspellings of common words and can suggest to you what you actually meant to type. It can be tiresome, however, when you frequently use words that are not in the WordPerfect dictionary. Fortunately, you can add words to the dictionary to avoid that annoyance.

WordPerfect has two Spell Checkers — they work off the same dictionary, but one checks spelling as you type, and the other you run after you are finished. We think Spell-As-You-Go is such a nifty feature that no one should ever need the regular Spell Checker again, but you may find those little squiggly lines under your words annoying. You may also decide that checking the spelling of your whole document at once is more efficient than taking the time to fix spelling one word at a time. What it boils down to is that checking spelling is so easy with WordPerfect 7 that there's no excuse for having misspelled words in your documents. So these are your choices:

Spell Check button

- Leave Spell-As-You-Go on (it should be on if you haven't turned it off). Each time you see a word with a squiggly red line under it, right-click on the word and choose the correct spelling, add it to the dictionary, or tell WordPerfect that using that spelling in this document (Skip in Document) is all right.

- Turn Spell-As-You-Go off, and instead use the Spell Checker after you've finished writing and editing your document. Click on the Spell Check button to run the Spell Checker.

- Turn off Spell-As-You-Go, forget to use the Spell Checker, and let the world know that you are a word-processing beginner (not a problem in itself, but probably not worth broadcasting, either).

Taking advantage of Spell-As-You-Go

Spell-As-You-Go is your authors' favorite new feature. You can fix your spelling whenever you like, but you're unlikely to miss a misspelled word. Spell-As-You-Go enables you not only to fix the spelling of a misspelled word, but also to tell WordPerfect that a word is correctly spelled, either in general or just for this document. Figure 7-1 shows a Spell-As-You-Go menu, displayed by right-clicking on a misspelled word. Following are your choices on a Spell-As-You-Go menu:

- Click on the correctly spelled word to use it in place of the misspelled word in your document. After you do, the Spell-As-You-Go menu goes away.

- Sometimes, you may have the option of clicking on the More choice to see more correctly spelled words.

- Add a word to the spell check dictionary. From then on, WordPerfect will not mark that word as misspelled.

- Skip in Document. WordPerfect will never mark this word misspelled in this document, although it will continue to mark it in other documents. (It adds the word to a supplementary dictionary that is attached only to the document that you are working on.)

- Spell Check. Run the regular Spell Checker, covered in the next exercise. You may want to do so if you have a number of spelling errors — the Spell Checker might be a little quicker than right-clicking on each marked word.

You may prefer to fix your spelling as you go, in bunches, or after you're completely finished with your document. Whichever you prefer, use Spell-As-You-Go as follows:

on the CD

1 Open Job Application.101.wpd, a letter from Zac Young to the Lexington Toy Company, applying for a job.

You see it in Figure 7-2.

2 Find the word *resumee* with a squiggly red line under it.

If you don't see any squiggly red lines, Spell-As-You-Go may be turned off. Choose Tools from the menu. If you don't see a check mark next to Spell-As-You-Go, click on it once to turn it on.

3 Move your mouse to *resumee* and click with the right mouse button.

A small menu appears (see Figure 7-1) with alternative correct spellings to *resumee* at the top and some additional options at the bottom.

4 Choose one of the correct spellings — we prefer *resume* (without the accents, although that version is also correct).

WordPerfect replaces *resumee* with *resume* (or whichever spelling you choose). The squiggly red line under the word disappears.

5 Right-click on *Zac,* whose name appears at the top of the letter.

The Spell-As-You-Go menu appears.

You may not want this word in your permanent dictionary, but it is correct in this context, and not having to see the squiggly red line would be nice.

6 Click on Skip in Document.

Figure 7-1: Spell-As-You-Go is the state-of-the-art way to check your spelling — just right-click on a marked word to fix it.

Figure 7-2: The Job Application.101.wpd document.

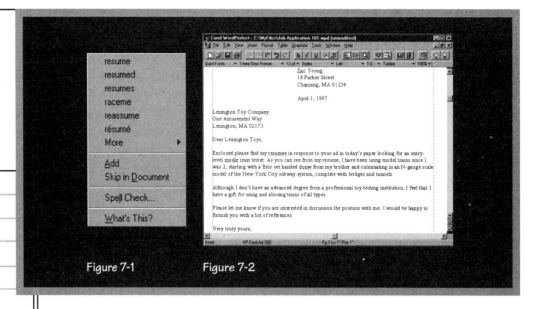

Figure 7-1   Figure 7-2

WordPerfect will take away the squiggly red line under *Zac*. If you use *Zac* in another document, WordPerfect will mark it as misspelled. If your name is Zac, you probably want to <u>A</u>dd the word to the dictionary — seeing it marked as misspelled can be a little demoralizing — it makes you feel like you don't really exist. Take a look at the end of the letter, where Zac's name appears again — no squiggly red line!

7 Close the document without saving changes.

You'll use this document again with the other, more conventional Spell Checker.

If you really don't like the Spell-As-You-Go feature, you can turn it off by choosing <u>T</u>ools from the menu. A check mark next to Spell-As-You-Go means it's on — click on it once to turn it off. Follow the same procedure to turn it back on.

Using the WordPerfect Spell Checker

If you prefer to do all your spell checking at once, use the Spell Checker. Run the Spell Checker by:

- ▶ Clicking on the Spell Check button on the Toolbar (the button that shows an open book with a red S on one page and a red check mark on the other)

- ▶ Choosing <u>T</u>ools⊏>Spell Check from the menu

- ▶ Pressing Ctrl+F1

- ▶ Choosing Spe<u>l</u>l Check from the Spell-As-You-Go menu

WordPerfect displays the Spell Checker dialog box (shown in Figure 7-3), finds the first word that it doesn't recognize, and waits for you to decide what to do with it. (Notice that you have access to the other writing tools through the tabs at the top of the dialog box.) Your options are as follows:

- ▶ **The word is spelled wrong, all right, but WordPerfect figured out the correct spelling.** Click on <u>R</u>eplace to replace the misspelled word with the correct spelling.

- ▶ **It's spelled wrong, but WordPerfect guessed wrong about the correct spelling.** Replace the misspelled word by picking a word from the list of WordPerfect suggestions — click on the word you want and

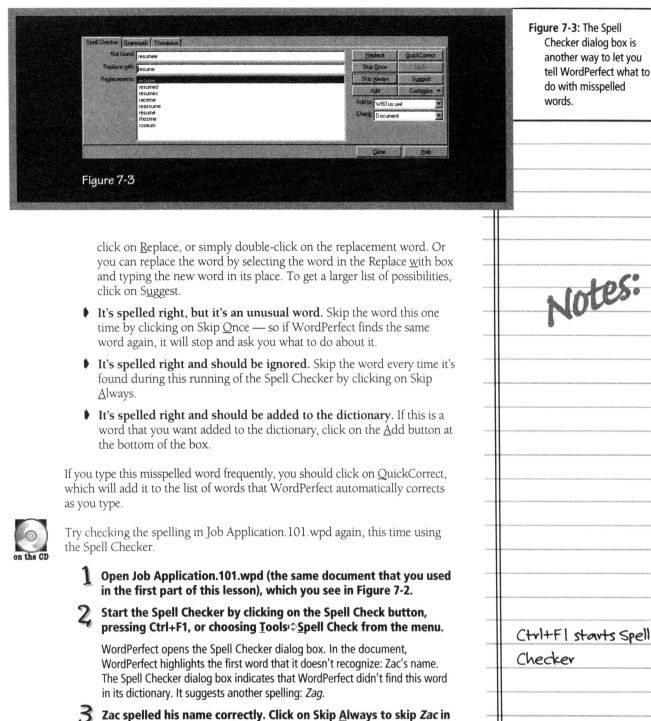

Figure 7-3

click on Replace, or simply double-click on the replacement word. Or you can replace the word by selecting the word in the Replace with box and typing the new word in its place. To get a larger list of possibilities, click on Suggest.

▶ **It's spelled right, but it's an unusual word.** Skip the word this one time by clicking on Skip Once — so if WordPerfect finds the same word again, it will stop and ask you what to do about it.

▶ **It's spelled right and should be ignored.** Skip the word every time it's found during this running of the Spell Checker by clicking on Skip Always.

▶ **It's spelled right and should be added to the dictionary.** If this is a word that you want added to the dictionary, click on the Add button at the bottom of the box.

If you type this misspelled word frequently, you should click on QuickCorrect, which will add it to the list of words that WordPerfect automatically corrects as you type.

Try checking the spelling in Job Application.101.wpd again, this time using the Spell Checker.

1 **Open Job Application.101.wpd (the same document that you used in the first part of this lesson), which you see in Figure 7-2.**

2 **Start the Spell Checker by clicking on the Spell Check button, pressing Ctrl+F1, or choosing Tools⇨Spell Check from the menu.**

WordPerfect opens the Spell Checker dialog box. In the document, WordPerfect highlights the first word that it doesn't recognize: Zac's name. The Spell Checker dialog box indicates that WordPerfect didn't find this word in its dictionary. It suggests another spelling: *Zag.*

3 **Zac spelled his name correctly. Click on Skip Always to skip *Zac* in this document.**

After you click on Skip Always, WordPerfect skips *Zac* this time and any other time that it's found in this document. (The first time the Spell Checker finds *your* name, thinking it's misspelled, you will probably want to Add it to the dictionary.) The next word that the Spell Checker finds is *resumee.* WordPerfect is already suggesting the correct spelling.

4 **To replace *resumee* with the correct spelling, *resume,* click on Replace.**

WordPerfect replaces the misspelled word with the word that appears in the Replace with box and moves to the next misspelled word: *modle.*

5 **The correct spelling of *modle* is *model,* and it appears on the list. Double-click on it to replace *modle* with the correctly spelled word.**

Ctrl+F1 starts Spell Checker

Notes:

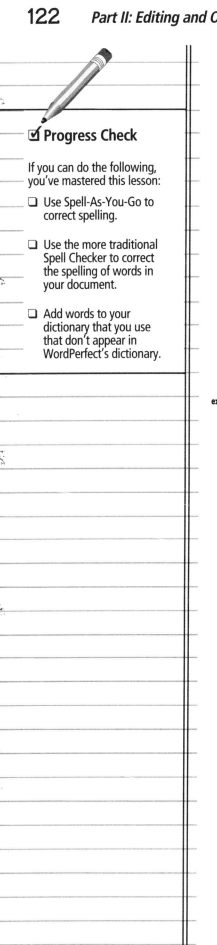

☑ Progress Check

If you can do the following, you've mastered this lesson:

❑ Use Spell-As-You-Go to correct spelling.

❑ Use the more traditional Spell Checker to correct the spelling of words in your document.

❑ Add words to your dictionary that you use that don't appear in WordPerfect's dictionary.

on the test

You could also click on *model* once and then click on the Replace button. Either method works fine: double-clicking on the word you want or clicking once to put the correct word in the Replace with box and then clicking on Replace.

6 **Instead of correcting *donw* automatically, type the correct spelling (*down*) by selecting the word in the Replace with box; then type the correct spelling, down, and click on Replace.**

Sometimes typing the right spelling is easier than trying to find it in WordPerfect's list of perfectly spelled words that resemble your misspelled one. But if you don't like typing, you can nearly always find the word you want — if WordPerfect doesn't list it on the first try, click on Suggest to list additional possibilities.

WordPerfect can't find any more misspelled words and says `Spell Check Completed. Close Spell Checker?`

7 **Click on Yes.**

After the spell checking is complete, you don't need to keep the Spell Checker dialog box open — you can work around it, but it just gets in the way.

You can close the Spell Checker at any time by clicking on Close.

extra credit

Adding and deleting words from the dictionary

You can add a word to the dictionary if you think that you're likely to use it again. Just click on the Add button in the Spell Checker dialog box or the Add option on the Spell-As-You-Go menu to add a word to the *supplemental dictionary* — that is, the list of words that are spelled correctly and that you don't want WordPerfect to flag as misspelled in any document.

You may find, however, that you're happily clicking along, adding words to the dictionary so that WordPerfect doesn't annoy you by stopping at perfectly spelled words, and then bang! You add a word that you didn't look at carefully and that was indeed misspelled. Now it's in the dictionary! What do you do?

When you add words, you're actually adding them to a supplementary dictionary, and that's where you need to delete them. Incidentally, this is the same dictionary from which QuickCorrect works. Following is how to delete words you have added to the dictionary:

1. **Run the Spell Checker.**

2. **Click on the Customize button on the Writing Tools Spell Checker dialog box menu. Choose User Word Lists from the drop-down menu.**

   The User Word List Editor dialog box appears.

3. **Click on the word list that you want to edit (probably WT61US.UWL, if it's not already highlighted).**

   The box at the bottom now displays the words in that file in alphabetical order. Words beginning with symbols come before words beginning with letters.

   Notice that instead of WT61US.UWL, you can pick the document word list to edit words that you have told WordPerfect to skip for the current document.

4. **Type the first few letters of the word in the Word/Phrase box.**

   The word you are looking for should appear in the box below. You may want to use the scroll bar or the up- and down-arrow keys to find the misspelled word.

5. **Click on the misspelled word and click on Delete Entry.**

6. **Click on Close to return to the Spell Checker dialog box.**

Check the spelling of a whole document by clicking on the Spell Check button and then deciding what to do with each word whose spelling WordPerfect doesn't like.

You're finished with this document for now — go ahead and close it, using the File➪Close command. Save it with the corrected spelling.

Recess

Now that you've checked the spelling in your document, you may want to rest a spell. Save your document and then exit WordPerfect by choosing File➪Exit from the menu bar. Just come back soon to find out how to tell WordPerfect to correct misspelled words as you type them!

Correcting Mistakes Automagically   Lesson 7-2

QuickCorrect is one of WordPerfect's snazziest features. It's a wonderful feature but, like anything automatic, can be annoying if you don't know how to make it do what you want.

QuickCorrect automagically corrects spelling errors and typos as you type. If you type two capital letters at the beginning of a word, QuickCorrect makes the second letter lowercase. You can make QuickCorrect automatically expand abbreviations to full words — for example, whenever you type **LTC**, QuickCorrect can change it to *Lexington Toy Company*. QuickCorrect can also be used to insert typographical or other symbols into your document so you don't have to use WordPerfect commands each time.

QuickCorrect is similar to WordPerfect's Spell Checker because it corrects mistakes, but they have a big difference: The Spell Checker fixes things only when you tell it to, whereas QuickCorrect works any time that you're typing. Here's how QuickCorrect works: As soon as you type the space or punctuation after a word, QuickCorrect checks whether the word is on its list of misspelled words and abbreviations. If the word you typed appears on its list, QuickCorrect replaces it with the correctly spelled word or the unabbreviated version.

WordPerfect comes with a list of commonly misspelled words already entered into QuickCorrect's list, along with the correctly spelled versions of each. You can add your own entries to the QuickCorrect list, including words that you frequently misspell and abbreviations that you want QuickCorrect to spell out for you.

QuickCorrect at work

When QuickCorrect works, it works silently and efficiently. Test it out in a new, blank document:

1 Close all the documents so that you see a new, blank document.

Adventurous readers, you can choose File➪New and click on Select instead to create a new, blank document without closing the other document(s) that you're using.

Notes:

QuickCorrect corrects spelling as you type

Notes:

2 **Type the following sentence exactly as it appears here:**

```
teh wierd aquaintance also has asma, as was aparent
on that ocasion in febuary.
```

As you type, QuickCorrect puts a capital letter on the beginning of the sentence and corrects the spelling of every incorrect word. However, it has limitations.

3 **Type the following sentence exactly as it appears here:**

```
hte strang man she's engagd to siezed the oportunity
to return when she greived about loseing him.
```

Although WordPerfect marks all the misspelled words, it only manages to make one correction: it puts a capital on the beginning of this sentence. QuickCorrect knows how to correct *sieze* and *greive*, but not when they're in the past tense. The other misspellings are simply not in QuickCorrect's list.

4 **Close the document with the nonsense sentences you just typed, without saving the document.**

All you need to do is type and make errors that QuickCorrect knows about — WordPerfect fixes those errors automatically as you type.

Making QuickCorrect work for you

QuickCorrect doesn't always correct errors that you think it should. Fortunately, you can add your favorite typos to the list so that QuickCorrect knows how to fix those, too. QuickCorrect runs whenever WordPerfect runs, so any changes that you make to QuickCorrect's word list apply to any document that you create.

Add a typo to QuickCorrect's list of words to correct by following these steps:

1 **Choose Tools⇨QuickCorrect from the menu. (You can also press Ctrl+Shift+F1, but you don't need to remember that — you're not likely to use the QuickCorrect dialog box often.)**

WordPerfect displays the QuickCorrect dialog box (Figure 7-4), showing a box with a list on the left of words that it knows how to correct and, on the right, how it corrects them.

Imagine that you frequently misspell the word *opportunity,* leaving out one of the *P*s. Why not take this opportunity to add *oportunity* to QuickCorrect's list of misspelled words?

2 **Type oportunity.**

The word appears in the small Replace box. Be sure to spell the word wrong!

3 **Press Tab to move your cursor to the small With box. Alternatively, click on the With box.**

4 **Type the correct spelling, opportunity.**

Make sure that you spell it correctly!

5 **To put the new entries in QuickCorrect's list (and on its list of corrections), press Enter or click on Add Entry.**

WordPerfect will now change *oportunity* to *opportunity* every time you type it.

6 **Click on Close to close the QuickCorrect dialog box.**

7 **Try out your new QuickCorrect entry by typing oportunity a few times.**

As soon as you type the space or punctuation after the misspelled word, WordPerfect corrects the spelling on the spot.

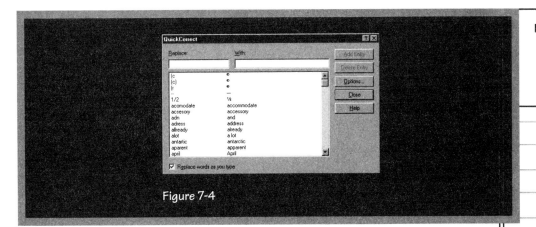

Figure 7-4

Figure 7-4: You can tell WordPerfect about your most frequent misspellings by using the QuickCorrect dialog box.

on the test

You can add a new item to the QuickCorrect list — or just check what's there already — by choosing Tools⇨QuickCorrect and putting the new words in the Replace and With boxes. You can also delete items by selecting them and clicking on Delete Entry, or you can change the way in which QuickCorrect works by clicking on Options. Options that you can change include telling QuickCorrect whether or not to capitalize the first letter of a sentence, correct a word when the first two letters are capitals, change a double space to a single space, make the spaces at the end of sentences consistent, and change the appearance of single and double quotes.

Now you know how to customize WordPerfect to respond to the typos that you tend to make. QuickCorrect is an easy way to save editing time — typos disappear before you can correct them.

While you're at it, you can also add abbreviations that you'd like to use while typing so that QuickCorrect automatically replaces them with full words. You can create abbreviations for all the long, awkward words and phrases that you have to type, including company names, addresses, phone numbers, and long boilerplate phrases. Using QuickCorrect for your own abbreviations is a great time-saver!

When you add an abbreviation to the QuickCorrect list, make sure that you plan to use the abbreviation only as an abbreviation — because if you ever try to use it in another way, QuickCorrect will replace it with whatever you told it to replace it with. For example, suppose that you decide to abbreviate *circus tent* as *ct;* when you type **CT** as an abbreviation for Connecticut in an address, WordPerfect replaces it with *CIRCUS TENT*! (QuickCorrect matches your capitalization.) So choose something a little more obscure for the abbreviation that you want WordPerfect to replace. In the same way that you add a frequent typo and its correct spelling, you can add an abbreviation and the full word(s) that you want to replace it to the QuickCorrect list.

Note: You can turn QuickCorrect off by displaying the QuickCorrect dialog box and clicking on the Replace words as you type choice so that no check mark appears in the box. However, most people like to leave QuickCorrect running all the time because it's so useful. If you occasionally find it annoying, you can play with the Options to change the way that it works or just go back and edit what QuickCorrect changed. If you don't type a whole word with a space or punctuation at the end of it, QuickCorrect won't kick in and make changes.

You're finished with the silly sentences that you used to test QuickCorrect — close the document without saving it. Don't worry — WordPerfect will remember the changes that you made in the QuickCorrect dialog box.

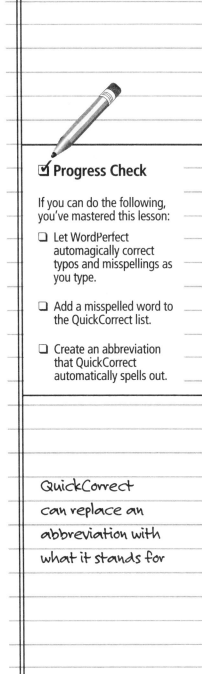

☑ Progress Check

If you can do the following, you've mastered this lesson:

❑ Let WordPerfect automagically correct typos and misspellings as you type.

❑ Add a misspelled word to the QuickCorrect list.

❑ Create an abbreviation that QuickCorrect automatically spells out.

QuickCorrect can replace an abbreviation with what it stands for

Lesson 7-3 Finding Just the Right Word

Thesaurus shows
synonyms for
selected word

on the CD

The Thesaurus — sounds like a dinosaur, doesn't it? "The mighty Thesaurus lumbered across the Jurassic plains." Well, the thesaurus in book form is becoming a dinosaur as it is replaced by the online thesaurus. WordPerfect's Thesaurus is a great online (that means that you don't have to go to your bookshelf) reference to use when you can't quite think of the word you want. You tell WordPerfect a word, and it suggests other words that have similar meanings.

To run the WordPerfect Thesaurus:

> ◆ Choose Tools⇨Thesaurus from the menu.

> ◆ Press Alt+F1.

> ◆ Click on the Thesaurus tab on the Writing Tools dialog box (that's the dialog box you see when you're using Spell Checker, Grammatik, or the Thesaurus — sometimes you can't see its name).

Give it a try using the Job Application.101.wpd document:

1 Find the word *abusing* at the end of the second paragraph.

You can move your cursor there with the mouse or cursor keys, or you can choose Edit⇨Find and Replace to find the word.

2 Select the word *abusing*.

Double-clicking on the word is a good way to do this.

3 Run the mighty Thesaurus by choosing Tools⇨Thesaurus from the menu bar or by pressing Alt+F1.

The Thesaurus dialog box opens (see Figure 7-5), and options for replacing *abusing* are listed. You have to use the scroll bar to see them all — they go on and on!

Hmmm. . . . None of the words you can see at first looks right. *Exploit* may be a move in the right direction — so you want to find other words like *exploit*.

4 To find synonyms for *exploit*, double-click on it (or click on it once and then click on Look Up).

Synonyms for *exploit* appear. Sometimes at the bottom of the list of synonyms will be a list of antonyms (opposites).

As you might guess, you can go on like this for a while, double-clicking on words to see their synonyms.

5 Continue to explore the synonyms available. After you find the word that you want to use (we like *manipulate*), click on the word to put it in the Replace With box; then click on Replace to replace the selected word in the text.

Or if you decide that your word choice was fine after all, click on Close to close the Thesaurus and keep the selected word *(abusing)* as is.

The Thesaurus lets you look for synonyms to a selected word and replace it with a word that you find.

☑ **Progress Check**

If you can do the following, you've mastered this lesson:

❑ Find synonyms for a selected word.

❑ Replace a word with a synonym.

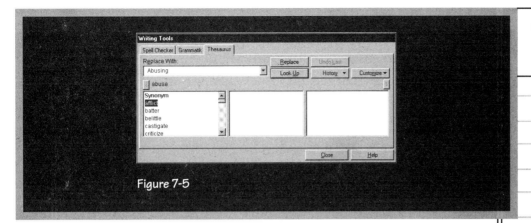

Figure 7-5: The WordPerfect Thesaurus helps you find just the right word.

Figure 7-5

Checking Your Grammar with Grammatik

Lesson 7-4

on the test

Grammatik is a grammar program that comes with WordPerfect. It's not as good as Sheila, who occasionally edits our stuff, but it gives you a way to review your document for common grammatical errors. Computers are smart, but they can only do what they're told. Grammatik follows some rules for judging grammar, and some of those can be changed to suit your style, but it doesn't catch every error.

You run Grammatik (display the Grammatik dialog box) by:

- Choosing Tools⇨Grammatik from the menu
- Pressing Alt+Shift+F1
- Clicking on the Grammatik tab on the Writing Tools dialog box

on the test

At the bottom of the Grammatik dialog box, the Checking Style box lets you tell Grammatik what type of document you're checking. If you tell Grammatik that you're writing a formal memo or letter, it applies higher standards than if you were doing a quick grammar check on something more casual.

Using Grammatik

on the CD

Find out what Grammatik thinks of the grammar in Job Application.101.wpd, the cover letter you saw back in Figure 7-2. If you just finished Lesson 7-3, it should still be open.

1 **Open Job Application.101.wpd.**

If it's already open, press Ctrl+Home to move to the top of the document.

2 **Run Grammatik by choosing Tools⇨Grammatik from the menu or by pressing Alt+Shift+F1.**

The Grammatik dialog box opens (see it in Figure 7-6) and presents you with the first problem that it finds, which it thinks is a spelling error (Zac's name again).

Ignore this for a moment — we're going to backtrack and play with some Grammatik settings.

Notes:

Tools→Grammatik
to start Grammatik

Figure 7-6: The Grammatik
dialog box.

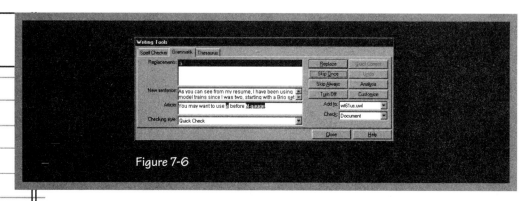

Figure 7-6

Notes:

3 **Find the Checking Style box at the bottom of the dialog box and click on the down arrow to see the choices. Normally for a cover letter, the Formal Memo or Letter rules would be the right choice. For this exercise, however, leave the setting on Quick Check.**

The first thing to do with Grammatik is tell it what type of document you're checking (and, therefore, what kinds of rules it should use). Picking the right kind of check makes Grammatik do a more useful grammar check. Because this is a cover letter for a resume and Zac wants to impress his potential employers, the rules for a formal letter are appropriate.

You can decide which of Grammatik's rules should be on or off. Click on the Customize button and select Checking styles. Edit the style by clicking on the Edit button in the Checking Styles dialog box. You may want to turn off the Spelling rule because you've already checked the spelling of this document. Click on Save to exit and then Select to exit the dialog boxes.

4 **Now that you've dealt with the checking style, you can get to dealing with the problems that Grammatik finds. The first problem, the alleged misspelling of Zac's name, is not a problem at all. Click on Skip Always.**

That action will skip Zac for the rest of this grammar check. Grammatik goes on to the next problem that it finds.

5 **Grammatik suggests replacing *2* with *two,* a good idea. Click on Replace to accept Grammatik's changes.**

The next problem Grammatik finds is *an* instead of *a* before *N-gauge.*

6 **Grammatik made a good guess, but in your authors' humble opinion, *an* is correct because *N* starts with a vowel sound. Click on Skip Once.**

7 **The last error Grammatik finds is a misused word (really a typo that is still a correctly spelled word). To fix the problem, click in your document and replace *discussion* with *discussing.***

Grammatik lets you work in your document if you need to. After you're finished fixing, click on the Resume button.

8 **Click on the Resume button.**

Grammatik finds no more grammar problems and displays a dialog box asking if you want to close Grammatik.

9 **Click on Yes to close Grammatik.**

The Grammatik dialog box fades gently into the mist. (Wordy. Consider simplifying.)

10 **Close the document, saving your changes.**

Grammatik is an easy way to edit your document — you may not always agree with its suggestions, but it may give you ideas of how to improve your text. Just remember: It's only a mindless electronic editor, but it's easily better than nothing!

Recess

Because you've already closed the document that you were using, just close WordPerfect if you have real work to do. Otherwise, go ahead and try the end-of-unit quiz.

Unit 7 Quiz

For each of the following questions, circle the letter of the correct answer or answers. Remember, we may have included more than one right answer for each question!

1. **After you click on the Spell Check button, WordPerfect . . .**

   A. Types a small red *s* in your document.

   B. Types a small red check mark in your document.

   C. Checks the spelling of your document or, if text is selected, of the selected text.

   D. Compares each word in your document with the list of words in its dictionary.

   E. Displays the Spell Checker dialog box.

Spell Check button

2. **When WordPerfect's Spell Checker finds a word that is misspelled, you can . . .**

   A. Choose the correctly spelled word from the list of suggestions and click on <u>R</u>eplace.

   B. Double-click on the correctly spelled word in the list of suggestions.

   C. Click on the <u>S</u>uggest button to see other possible spellings.

   D. Type the correct spelling in the Replace <u>w</u>ith box and click on <u>R</u>eplace.

   E. Click on the <u>C</u>lose button to forget about the whole idea of checking your spelling. Eat lunch instead.

3. **If WordPerfect thinks that a word is spelled wrong but it's not, you can . . .**

   A. Click on Skip <u>O</u>nce to ignore this word this one time. If WordPerfect finds the same word later in the document, it complains about it again.

   B. Click on Skip <u>A</u>lways to skip this word for the rest of the document. WordPerfect ignores the word for the rest of this session with the Spell Checker.

   C. Click on the A<u>d</u>d button to add this word to the dictionary so that WordPerfect considers it to be a correctly spelled word from now on.

   D. Click on the QuickCorrect button to add the misspelled word and the suggested correction in the Replace <u>w</u>ith box to QuickCorrect's list of misspelled words.

   E. Jump up and down and yell at WordPerfect because it's not as smart as it thinks it is.

4. **The WordPerfect Thesaurus . . .**

    A. Suggests words that have the same or similar meanings to the word that you select.

    B. Suggests words that mean the opposite of the word that you select.

    C. Suggests the kinds of words that your sixth-grade English teacher used to use.

    D. Suggests words that will make your document sound impressive and erudite.

    E. Suggests a dinosaur that would be appropriate to mention in your document.

5. **In the classic song "Let's Call the Whole Thing Off," the two people pronounce the following words differently:**

    A. Tomato.

    B. Potato.

    C. Either.

    D. Aunt.

    E. Neither.

6. **The purpose of Grammatik is to . . .**

    A. Make you wish that you had done your English homework during high school.

    B. Fix grammatical errors in your document.

    C. Find incorrect or awkward wording and replace it with better word choices.

    D. Get rid of wording that will make people roll their eyes when they read your document.

    E. Simulate your grandma.

Unit 7 Exercise

The Lexington Toy Company plans to market an old-fashioned circus toy and wants to include a history of circuses.

on the CD

1. Open the document History of Circuses.101.wpd, a history of circuses.

2. Fix any spelling errors (assume names are spelled correctly).

3. Find a better word for *scintillating*.

4. Run Grammatik to check your grammar.

5. Save the improved document with the same name.

Unit 8
• • • • • • • • •

Managing Documents

▶ Job
Application.101.wpd
on the CD

Objectives for This Unit

✓ Understanding how folders organize the files on your hard disk

✓ Creating folders to store your WordPerfect documents

✓ Using multiple folders

✓ Copying, renaming, and deleting files

✓ Finding files and folders by creating Favorites

In the old days before hard disk drives, you organized your computer files by storing them on separate diskettes — for example, one for resume and job notes, another for cover letters, and another for personal correspondence. When you ran out of space, you started a new diskette. Nowadays, people usually use hard disks for routine storage of files, and diskettes for just taking a file somewhere or for keeping a backup. A hard disk can store thousands and thousands of files. So how does anyone ever find anything?

The answer is to use *folders* — which are also called *directories* — to divide the files on your hard disk into groups. Folders help you store documents so that you can find them later.

Think of your hard disk as an infinitely divisible file cabinet — you can decide how many drawers you want it to have, how many categories each drawer should have, and how many file folders each category should have. Each drawer, category, and file folder is a folder (or directory) on your hard disk (or one of your hard disks, if you're lucky enough to have more than one). You may even find that your computer contains your most organized filing system!

All kinds of files, whether they are WordPerfect documents or not, are stored in folders. A folder is not an actual physical part of your hard disk, but a group of files. In addition to files, a folder can contain other folders (called *subfolders*). Putting folders within other folders allows you to create hierarchies, which can make files easier to find (it can also make them more difficult to find, but following the hints that we'll give you about creating folder structure and learning how to search for files should help you avoid that).

a folder is sometimes called a directory

folders contain groups of files and subfolders

subfolder = folder contained in another folder

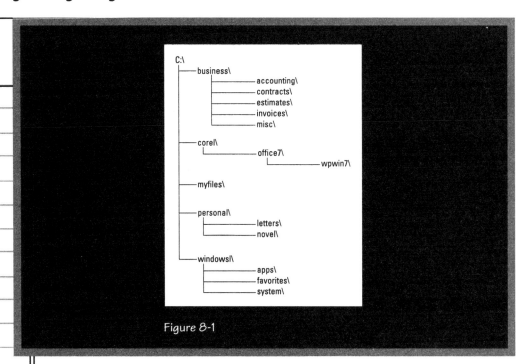

Figure 8-1

root folder = main, top-level folder on a disk

pathname = name that uniquely identifies a file or folder on your computer system

Each hard disk contains a *root folder* — that is, a folder that contains everything else on the hard disk. Each disk drive, whether for diskettes or a hard disk, has a letter. The most common letter for the primary hard drive is C. All the files and folders on the hard disk are in the root folder, or in folders that are in the root folder, or in folders in those folders — you get the idea.

You may want folders for documents pertaining to different activities. For example, if you run a business, you might have folders for invoices, estimates, contracts, and other types of documents pertaining to business. Figure 8-1 shows part of the folder structure of a hard disk. The root folder on the C drive (C:\) contains four folders: Business, Corel, MyFiles, Personal, and Windows. The Business folder contains files (not shown in the diagram) as well as five more folders: Accounting, Contracts, Estimates, Invoices, and Misc. The Personal folder contains some files and two more folders: Letters and Novel. (This is assuming that you're working on the Great American Novel in your spare time.)

The WordPerfect program itself is generally stored in a subfolder of Corel named Office7, in another subfolder named WpWin7. The Windows program is usually stored in the Windows folder and its subfolders.

Suppose that you store a document named Taxes.wpd in the Accounting folder, which is in the Business folder. You may have other files called Taxes.wpd, but not located in the Accounting folder that is in the Business folder. You can use a shorter way to identify this particular file:

```
C:\Business\Accounting\Taxes.wpd
```

This long name uniquely identifies this file (you can think of it as the complete instructions for finding a file) and is called the file's *pathname*. (A pathname can also describe a folder. For example, C:\Personal\Novel is the pathname to the folder in which you store the chapters of the novel that you're working on.)

Here's how you read the pathname above: look on the C hard disk, starting in the root folder (C:\), go to the Business folder, look inside it for the Accounting folder, and look inside that for the Taxes.wpd file. If you're writing a note or an e-mail to someone to tell that person where a file is, you should write the whole pathname. But even the geekiest of us don't often ask (verbally) for a pathname — the exchange goes more like "Where's that file again?" "It's in business accounting on C."

In this unit, you'll learn how to create folders, how to name them, and how to put documents in them. You'll learn how to move a document from one folder to another. While you're at it, you'll find out how to do other things to files, like renaming them and making copies of them. And once you've got lots of files stored in lots of folders, you'll need to know how to find a file that you've lost, because almost everyone loses files!

To work with folders and files in WordPerfect, you need to open one of the dialog boxes that lets you see the files on your disk — the Open, Save As, and Insert File dialog boxes all do this. You can use any of these — we usually use the Open dialog box. When you're done working with folders and files, you can click on one of the Close buttons (or press the Esc key) to avoid opening or saving any documents.

In the process of following the lessons in this unit, you'll create several new folders in which to store your WordPerfect documents. You can use these new folders when you create new documents. And you can move your existing documents into the folders that you create.

pathname takes you to a specific file

Creating Folders for Your Documents   Lesson 8-1

Up to now, you have probably stored all your documents in the WordPerfect default folder, which is probably C:\MyFiles (don't worry if it's something different than that). You can continue to use that folder for all your files. However, if you plan on creating more than a dozen or so documents, storing them all together can get confusing.

You can't have two different files in the same folder with the same name. Once you've created a document called, for example, Letter to Darren.wpd for a letter to your friend Darren, you've got to come up with a different name for the next letter that you write to him (or store a file with the same name in a different folder, which would make finding all your letters to Darren difficult if, one day, you were looking for them).

create separate folders for different types of documents

But if you create a separate folder for letters, you can name the file Darren.wpd, and the next one can be called Darren 2.wpd. By separating your documents into groups using folders, your filenames don't have to be quite as descriptive; because Darren.wpd is in the Letters folder, it is obviously a letter, so its filename doesn't have to convey that information. Despite the fact that Windows 95 lets you use long names, trying not to describe the whole document in the name has some virtue.

If you would like to create several folders to store your documents in, the folder that WordPerfect created for you isn't enough. Rather than use the C:\MyFiles folder that WordPerfect created, you can create your own set of folders or create subfolders in the MyFiles folder to organize your files. Each

*don't use these in file and folder names: * + = [ ] : ; " < > ? / *

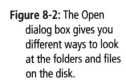

Figure 8-2: The Open dialog box gives you different ways to look at the folders and files on the disk.

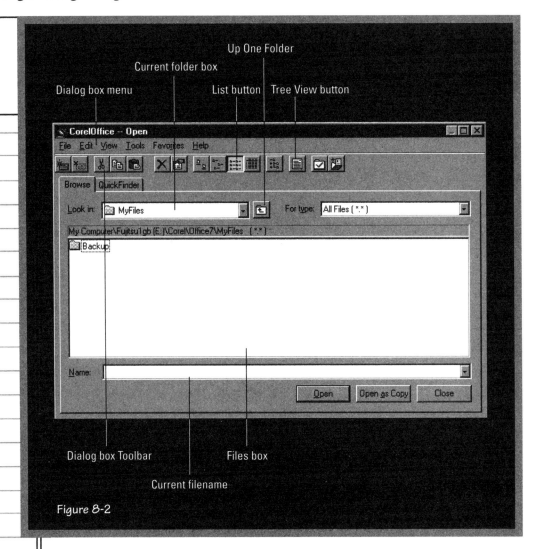

Figure 8-2

folder name can be long, like filenames. But don't use characters such as * + = [ ] : ; " < > ? / \ in folder names or filenames.

Tip: Here are some recommendations for saving documents in folders:

- ◗ Create a set of folders that makes sense to you. Once you get past 20 or so files in a folder, thinking of how to logically "file" your documents in subfolders or new folders is a good idea.

- ◗ Use subfolders but don't overuse them. A project (like this book) might have a main folder named WP101 with subfolders such as Chapters, Figures, and Disk Documents. It shouldn't need a subfolder for each chapter.

- ◗ You may use folders to file documents by date. For example, if you are reluctant to delete old files but find that they get in the way when you're looking for newer ones, you may want to move the older ones to a subfolder called Old or keep files by quarter or half year. For example, you can keep your old estimates from the first quarter of 1996 in a folder named C:\Business\Estimates\1Q96.

◆ Clean out folders and closets regularly. Get rid of what you don't need, or it will just get in the way of your finding what you do need. Consider archiving (copying) files on diskettes or tapes if you're reluctant to delete them altogether.

◆ Make a folder named Temporary to put temporary files in — that is, files that you don't plan to keep for long. From time to time, look through the files in the Temporary folder and delete the ones that you no longer want.

By the way, the MyFiles folder in the root directory is the folder used by all the Office7 applications — so the files in it may not all be WordPerfect documents. They may be spreadsheet files, database files, or graphics files, and nothing stops you from putting program files there (although we strongly discourage it). Keeping different types of files separate, just to make them easier to find, is a good idea, but it isn't mandatory. For example, keeping the spreadsheet files with the documents that analyze and explain them makes sense.

In this lesson, we'll first introduce you to features on the Open dialog box that you haven't learned about yet. Then you'll learn how to create new folders and subfolders and how to change the current folder — the folder that WordPerfect puts your files in.

Note: In Unit 2, you clicked the List button, so that WordPerfect displayed filenames in a neat list on the Open, Save As, and Insert File dialog boxes. If you didn't follow those instructions, you'll need to click on the List button in this unit, so your WordPerfect window will look like the figures in this book. Don't worry! We tell you just when to click on it.

Looking at folders using the Open dialog box

You've seen the Open dialog box (in Figure 2-3 from Unit 2, for instance), but the list of files it contains can appear in many different formats. Figure 8-2 shows you how the Open dialog displays your folders and files in *list format*, which is what you see after you click on the List button. (Incidentally, just about anything you do with folders and files from the Open dialog you can also do from the Save As and Insert File dialog boxes. We're just trying to keep it simple by referring to mainly the Open dialog box.)

You can view your files in four different formats: large icon, small icon, list, and details. And you can view your folder structure in tree view or not at all. Figure 8-2 displays files in List view. The buttons on the Open dialog box Toolbar let you change the way you view your folders and files (the <u>V</u>iew menu on the dialog box gives you the same options). In this unit, we stick with List view. There is no "right way" to view your files — large icon, small icon, and list give you the same thing in different sizes; details also shows you the size and date your file was saved and lets you sort by name, size, and date saved. Table 8-1 lists some things you can do with files in the Open and Save As dialog boxes.

Notes:

Notes:

Table 8-1	Folder and File Management Tricks
When You Want To	**Do This**
View the folders on a drive	Click on the down-arrow button at the right end of the <u>L</u>ook in box, and choose the drive from the menu that appears
See the contents of a folder	Double-click on the folder name
Identify your current folder	Look at the <u>L</u>ook in box
Delete a file or folder	Click on the file or folder once and press Delete (see Lesson 8-3)
Rename a file or folder	Click on the file or folder once, then again, and edit the name (see Lesson 8-3)
Select several consecutive files	Click on the first file to select it and then Shift+click on the last file
Select several nonconsecutive files	Click on the first file and then Ctrl+click on additional files
See a list of recently used files	Click on the down arrow at the right of the <u>N</u>ame box

How about a brief guided tour of the file and folder management features of the Open dialog box? The following exercise will help you learn how to move around the folder structure on your hard disk — and by the time you finish the unit, you'll be a pro.

1 **First open the Open dialog box by clicking on the Open button or pressing Ctrl+O.**

You see the Open dialog box, which may not look exactly like 8-2 yet, but it will in a minute. This dialog box is so fancy that it has its own menu bar and Toolbar.

2 **Move your mouse over the toolbar buttons on the Open dialog box. Notice that, like the regular WordPerfect Toolbar, these buttons have little help screens so that you can figure out what they do.**

Knowing what a button does before you click on it is very useful! And once you learn these buttons, you'll probably see them again — Windows Explorer (which is another way to access files and folders and do many of the things that you'll do here with WordPerfect) uses some of the same buttons.

So that your screen looks like ours, the next two steps make sure that your dialog box shows your files and folders in List view.

3 **If the Tree View button appears to be pushed in, click on it. Otherwise, proceed to Step 4.**

If the button appears depressed, clicking on it makes it pop back out. This unit doesn't describe Tree View, which is another format for looking at files and folders. (If you really want to know how to use all the various ways to list files and folders, see *WordPerfect 7 For Windows 95 For Dummies* by Margaret Levine Young and David C. Kay, published by IDG Books Worldwide, Inc.)

Tree View button

4 **If the List button does *not* look like it's pressed in, click on it.**

Clicking on the un-pressed-in List button presses it in and displays your files in List view. List view shows you your files in a two-column list. The Open dialog box on your screen should now look almost exactly like Figure 8-2 (don't worry if the filenames differ a little).

List button

5 **Click on the down-arrow button at the right of the <u>N</u>ame box at the bottom of the dialog box to see a list of recently opened files.**

It's easy to open a file that you opened recently — just pick it from this list!

6 **Click on the down-arrow button at the right of the <u>N</u>ame box again to make the list of recently opened files go away.**

You're not going to open one right now.

7 **Close the Open dialog box by clicking on the <u>C</u>lose button in the lower-right corner or the <u>C</u>lose button that looks like an X in the upper-right corner.**

When you open the Open dialog box again, it will appear the same — with List view displayed.

You are beginning to learn how to manage your files. You may already have decided how you prefer to view files and folders. For now, work with files in List view. We make sure to point out to you different ways to do things if you prefer a different display.

extra credit

When did I make this file?

By clicking on the Details button on the Open dialog box, you can see details about each file in the current folder. The Details button is the eleventh button on the Open dialog box toolbar. When you click on the Details button, WordPerfect displays the name, size type, and date each file was modified.

You can even sort your files by when they were saved by clicking on the Modified column head above the dates. Just be sure to click on the Name column head again to sort your files back into alphabetical order to avoid confusion the next time you are looking for a file.

Details button

Moving around inside your computer

Well, okay, you won't really move around *inside* the computer, but you'll tell WordPerfect to move from folder to folder on your hard disk so that you can see what's in each one.

WordPerfect (and Windows) calls the folder you are using the *current folder*. You can tell what the current folder is by looking at the <u>L</u>ook in box on the Open dialog box.

current folder = folder that you are using in WordPerfect

1 **Press Ctrl+O or click on the Open button on the Toolbar.**

WordPerfect displays the Open dialog box (shown in Figure 8-2). Chances are that you are looking at the MyFiles folder (C:\MyFiles). The current folder name is shown in the <u>L</u>ook in box. Don't worry if it's not named MyFiles — you are looking at a different folder, that's all! Make a note of the name of the current folder.

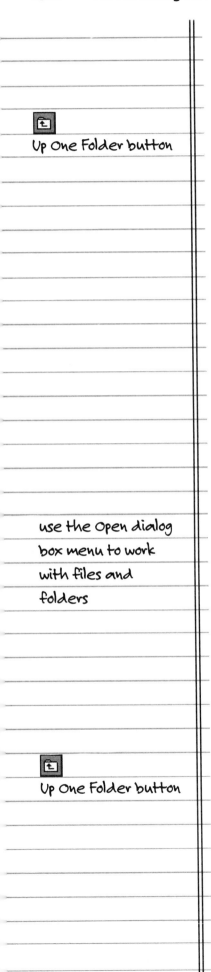

Up One Folder button

use the Open dialog box menu to work with files and folders

Up One Folder button

heads up

2 **Click on the Up One Folder button, the yellow folder button to the right of the Look in box.**

The Up One Folder moves to the folder that contains the folder you've been in. If you think of the structure of folders on your hard disk as a family tree, with folders as parents and subfolders as children, you move to the parent of the current folder. For example, if you were in the C:\MyFiles folder, clicking on the Up One Folder button moves you to the C:\ folder, otherwise known as the root folder.

The Look in box shows the name of the folder that you are looking at now, and the files box shows the folders and files that the current folder contains.

3 **Double-click on the MyFiles folder in the files box.**

(If you didn't start in the MyFiles folder, double-click on the name of the folder that you did start in.) Double-clicking on a folder moves you into that folder. The folder becomes the current folder. The files box shows the files and folders contained in that current folder.

4 **Close the Open dialog box by clicking on either Close button.**

Now you know how to move from folder to folder in the Open dialog box. You can click on the Up One Folder button several times to move upward through the structure of folders toward the root folder of your hard disk. When you reach the root of the hard disk, you see a list of the disk drives on your system. Move down through the tree by double-clicking folder names.

Creating a folder

Unlike many inferior word-processing programs, WordPerfect can create a new folder for you. Other word processors require that you use another program — like My Computer or Windows Explorer — to create folders. But why bother to learn a new program when WordPerfect can do it perfectly well?

In this lesson, you create a new folder on your hard disk for all your WordPerfect documents and name the folder Personal.

Note: Your hard disk may already have a folder named Personal, if you or someone else created it. Don't worry — we tell you how to see if a folder already exists and what to do if this is the case.

1 **Press Ctrl+O or click on the Open button on the Toolbar.**

WordPerfect displays the Open dialog box (shown in Figure 8-2).

2 **Click on the Up One Folder button until you see a list of the disk drives on your computer.**

If your computer is on a network, you may see *network drives*, which are disk drives on other computers that you can access from your computer. You also see things on your Windows 95 desktop, which may include things like Control Panel, Dial Up Networking, and Printers.

3 **Double-click on the C disk drive, or whatever disk drive you usually store your files on.**

You see tons of folders and files in the files box — these are the folders and files in the root folder of C (C:\), or of whatever disk drive you double-clicked.

Make sure that you've clicked the right drive before you create a new folder — you don't get a chance to approve of where WordPerfect puts the new folder. If you want to create a folder within another folder, move to the folder in which you want to create the new folder. For example, if you want to create a folder in the MyFiles folder, you move to that folder and select it before creating the new folder.

4 **Check whether the disk drive already contains a folder named Personal by looking at the names of the folders listed in the files.**

You may need to use the scroll bars on the bottom side of the box to see all the folders stored in the C drive (or whatever disk drive you chose). WordPerfect displays the folders in the box in alphabetical order. Many of the folders contain program files.

If a folder called *Personal* already exists, use another name for this folder, like *101 Personal*. If you share your computer, you may want to give the new folder your name.

5 **Choose File⇨New⇨Folder from the Open dialog box menu.**

WordPerfect creates a new folder for you and calls it *New Folder*. This is a little annoying, because you were planning to call the folder Personal. But you'll take care of that. The new folder appears with a box around it — that means it's ready for you to name it.

6 **Type the name of the new folder — in this case,** Personal**.**

When New Folder is highlighted and a box is around it, it's ready to be edited. Type a new name to change the name from New Folder to something more descriptive. You can use the left- and right-arrow keys to move around the filename, and the Delete and Backspace keys to delete characters you don't want.

7 **Press Enter.**

WordPerfect creates the new folder, C:\Personal. This may be a little slow — WordPerfect has to figure out where the new folder goes in the list. The Open dialog box is still on the screen.

Create a new folder by choosing File⇨New⇨Folder from the menu on the Open or Save As dialog box. Then give the folder a new name by typing it and pressing Enter. The new folder will be stored in the folder that is the current folder when you give the menu command.

You can edit the name of the already existing folder (or a file) by clicking on it twice and typing the new name. Be sure to leave a pause between two clicks — double-clicking has a totally different effect!

You can rename any file or folder by clicking it twice (this works in Windows Explorer, too).

heads up

Warning: Don't rename program files or the folders that contain them. If you change the name of a program file or the folder it is stored in, Windows 95 won't be able to find the program file when you want to run the program.

Creating a subfolder

In the C:\Personal folder, create a subfolder named Letters for letters to friends that you create with WordPerfect. Then, as an extra credit project, create another folder for another type of document. Just follow these steps:

1 **In the files box on the Open dialog box, double-click on the Personal folder to make it the current folder.**

WordPerfect updates the Look in box to say *Personal*. The files box is blank because this new folder doesn't contain any files or folders.

2 **Choose File⇨New⇨Folder from the Open dialog box menu.**

WordPerfect creates a new folder: C:/Personal/New Folder, and highlights it with a box around it so that you can rename it.

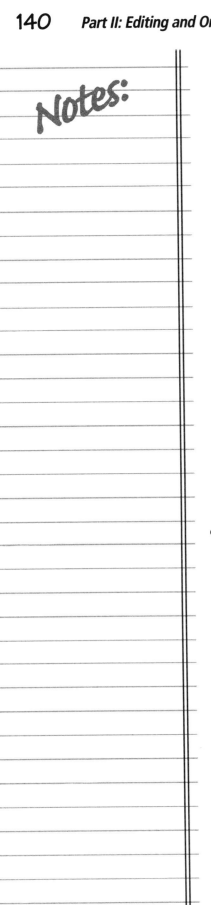

Notes:

3 **Type the new name,** Letters.

WordPerfect creates a folder named C:\Personal\Letters. Letters appears as a subfolder of Personal in the files box.

4 **Just to make sure that you have this skill down, create another folder in the C:\Personal folder to contain another type of document by repeating Steps 1 through 3.**

This time, choose the folder name to reflect the type of documents that you're likely to store there. Here are some suggestions: Memos, Reports, Budget, Class, Poems, Novel, or Recipes.

5 **Click on one of the Close buttons on the Open dialog box to close the dialog box.**

Don't worry — clicking on this button doesn't cancel the folders that you just created! It just tells WordPerfect that you don't want to open a file after all.

The File⇨New⇨Folder choice on the Open dialog box menu allows you to create a new folder. Now you're ready to organize your WordPerfect documents into folders.

Congratulations! Many computer users never understand folders well enough to create or use them. You've achieved an important feat: creating your own folders and subfolders in which to store your files.

heads up

If you create a folder that you later decide you don't need, you can delete it by clicking on it and pressing delete. Be warned, though, that when you delete a folder, you also delete all the files it contains.

extra credit

Changing the default folder

When WordPerfect is installed, it creates a folder for your documents, usually named C:\MyFiles. This is the *default folder* for documents — that is, each time you start WordPerfect, it assumes that the files that you're working with are in that folder. The list of files that you see in the Open dialog box is in the default folder. And when you save a file without changing the folder, WordPerfect saves it in the default folder. If you usually use a different folder, changing the WordPerfect default folder saves you some extra clicking each time you save or open a file.

Follow these steps to change the default folder:

1. Choose Edit⇨Preferences from the menu bar.

You see the Preferences dialog box, with lots of cute icons (see Figure 8-3).

2. Double-click on the Files icon.

The Files Preferences dialog box appears, as shown in Figure 8-4. If your Files Preferences dialog box doesn't look like Figure 8-4, click on the Document tab in the upper-left corner of the dialog box so that you see the document-related settings.

(continued)

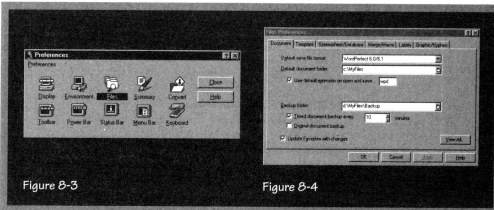

Figure 8-3

Figure 8-4

Figure 8-3: The Preferences dialog box.

Figure 8-4: The Files Preferences dialog box.

(continued)

The Default document folder setting is the second setting on the dialog box. It is usually set to C:\MyFiles. Now you can change it to the folder in which you store most of your documents, or plan to.

3. **To change your default folder, click on the small file folder button to the right of the Default document folder box.**

WordPerfect displays the Select Default Document dialog box, which looks a lot like the Open dialog box, where you can view your folder structure and choose a folder. If you prefer to type the path of the new default folder into the Default document folder box, you may do that instead.

4. **Move to the folder that you want as the default folder.**

Click on the Up One Folder button to move to the parent of the current folder and double-click on a folder name to move down into it. When you find the folder you want to use as your default folder, click on the folder name so that it appears in the Look in box.

5. **Click on the Select button when your desired folder is selected as the current folder.**

You see the File Preferences dialog box again. The Default document folder box now has the name of the folder that you selected.

6. **Click on OK.**

The File Preferences dialog box closes, and you see the Preferences dialog box.

7. **Click on Close.**

Now when you run WordPerfect, it assumes that you want to work on files in the new default folder rather than the C:\MyFiles folder. Be aware, though, that unless you specified a different folder when you installed the files that came with this book, they are stored in C:\MyFiles. If you are continuing with the exercises in this book, you will need to either change the default folder back to what it was or change the current folder to C:\MyFiles (you'll learn how in Lesson 8-2) each time you need one of the files that came with this book.

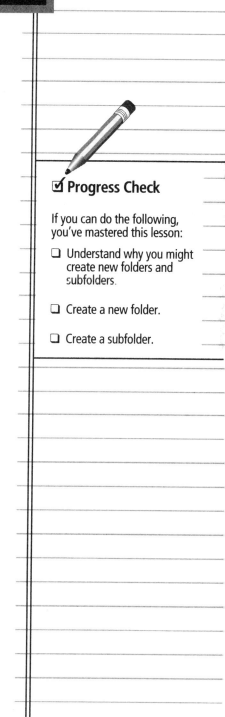

☑ **Progress Check**

If you can do the following, you've mastered this lesson:

❑ Understand why you might create new folders and subfolders.

❑ Create a new folder.

❑ Create a subfolder.

Opening and Saving Files in Other Folders

default folder is where WordPerfect usually opens and saves files

current folder is the last folder you used in WordPerfect

Even though WordPerfect has one default folder (the folder that WordPerfect opens and saves folders in unless you've specified another folder), you can save files to and open files from other folders. For example, if the default folder is C:\MyFiles, you can still use files in C:\Personal\Letters or (if you have one) C:\Personal\Poems. You'll learn how to change the *current* folder (which is where WordPerfect is currently saving files to and opening files from) so that you can open or save files in another folder.

Saving a document to another folder

First, you'll save a document to a folder other than the folder from which you opened it, using the File⇨Save As command. This command makes a copy of the file with any changes you make while it's open — the file still exists in the folder in which you opened the document, and the new file is saved in the folder to which you saved it.

on the CD

You can use the Save As dialog box to make a copy of the Job Application.101.wpd document that you used in Unit 7. It is currently stored in C:\MyFiles. Follow these steps to save a copy to the C:\Personal\Letters folder:

1 Open the Open dialog box.

Notice a few new things this time. First, notice that the name of the current folder is listed in the Look in box. All files and folders listed in the Open dialog box are stored in the current folder.

2 Open the Job Application.101.wpd document.

The file should be in the default folder, C:\MyFiles (unless you specified a different location when you installed the files). Once you see this familiar letter on the screen, go on to the next step.

3 To save the document to the new C:\Personal\Letters folder, choose File⇨Save As from the menu bar (or press F3).

WordPerfect displays the Save As dialog box (see Figure 8-5). Notice that the Name box at the bottom of the dialog box lists the name of the file. Sometimes this box lists a full pathname, which is where the file will save to when you click on Save. Make sure that this setting is correct before you save a file to a new folder.

Before you can save the document to the C:\Personal\Letters folder, you must change the current folder to C:\Personal\Letters — the next three steps tell you exactly what to do. You may not be able to see that folder at first because WordPerfect may be displaying only one branch of the folder tree in dialog boxes — in this case, you see just the C:\MyFiles branch.

4 Click on the Up One Folder button (the one with the little yellow folder, just to the right of the Save in box) once.

You move to C:\ (the root folder of C:). You see all the folders and files in the root folder, including the Personal folder.

Up One Folder button

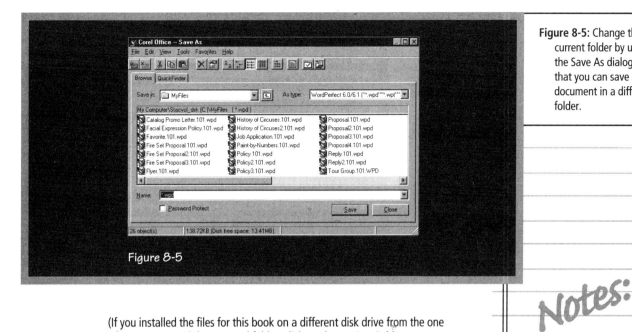

Figure 8-5

Figure 8-5: Change the current folder by using the Save As dialog box so that you can save a document in a different folder.

(If you installed the files for this book on a different disk drive from the one where you created the Personal folder, click on the Up One Folder one more time and then double-click on the disk drive that contains the Personal folder.)

5 Double-click on the Personal folder.

Now C:\Personal is the current folder, and WordPerfect shows you the files and subfolders that it contains, including the Letters folder.

6 To make the Letters folder the current folder, double-click on the Letters folder.

Now C:\Personal\Letters is the current folder. You can check that by looking at the folder listed in the Save in box. The Name box contains the same name that the document had when you opened it, Job Application.101.wpd.

7 Check that the name is correct in the Name box.

8 Save the file by clicking on Save.

The file is saved to the current directory (which appears in the Save in box) with the name in the Name box. WordPerfect saves the document in the C:\Personal\Letters folder with the filename: Job Application.101.wpd. Notice that you can have two files with the same name saved in different folders.

9 Close the Job Application.101.wpd document, using the File⇨Close command.

You've just learned how to save to an alternate folder, using the File⇨Save As command and the Save As dialog box.

To change to another folder to open a document, use exactly the same techniques to move around your folder and drives. The Open and Save As dialog boxes work in the same way, so the way you learned to move to a folder on the Save As dialog box works when you need to move among folders on the Open dialog box.

The Open and Save As dialog boxes display part of the folder structure on your hard disk. To change the active folder and see other folder branches, click on the Up One Folder button to move upward through the tree, or double-click on folder names to move down into the folders.

Notes:

☑ **Progress Check**

If you can do the following, you've mastered this lesson:

❏ Save a document in a folder other than the active (default) folder.

❏ Change the current folder.

❏ See a list of the subfolders of the current folder.

The same technique works when you want to save to a different drive (or to a diskette): Simply click on the Up One Folder button until you see the list of disk drives, select the drive you want, and then change the folder as needed.

When you next use the Open or Save As dialog boxes, they will show you details of the default folder. If you want them to show you details of the last folder you worked with (the last current folder), choose Edit⇨Change Default Folder from the dialog box menu on the Open or Save As dialog boxes so that there is a check next to it.

Recess

If you want to take a break, leave WordPerfect by choosing File⇨Exit from the menu bar. When you come back, you'll be ready to learn some other file and folder maneuvers!

Lesson 8-3

Copying, Moving, Renaming, and Deleting Documents

WordPerfect provides you with easy ways to copy, rename, and delete documents. Each document is stored in a file, with a filename. You can use the Windows Explorer or My Computer programs for these tasks, but if you're comfortable using WordPerfect, why not use it for your file management as well as word processing?

Here are some reasons why you might want to rename, copy, move, or delete documents:

▸ **Rename a document** if you chose a bad name for it when you saved it for the first time. If the name turns out not to describe the contents of the document, it's a good idea to change its filename.

▸ **Copy a document** if you want to create a new document based on the file or if you want to save a copy of the file to a new folder or disk. You've already created a copy of a document by using the File⇨Save As command to save a copy. You also created a copy of a document back in Lesson 2-3, when you used the Open as Copy button in the Open File dialog box. In this lesson, you learn how to make a copy of a document without opening the document.

▸ **Move a document** from one folder to another if you decide that the document is stored in the wrong folder. For example, now that you know how to create folders, you can move documents from the default folder to new folders that you create. Moving documents is the way to get your documents organized into folders.

▸ **Delete a document** if you're sure that you will never need it again.

heads up

If you get an error message while trying to perform any of these tricks with files, the file is probably open — you can't move, rename, or delete an open file.

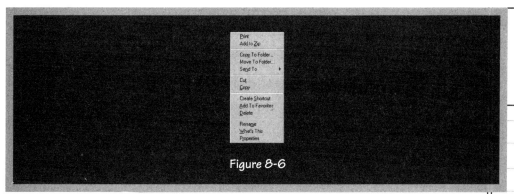

Figure 8-6

Figure 8-6 : Display this QuickMenu by right-clicking on a file on the Save As or Open dialog boxes.

Notes:

Making a copy or moving a document

on the CD

To copy or move a document, you tell WordPerfect which file you want to copy or move by selecting the file.

You don't have to open the document you want to copy. Instead, you can use the Files QuickMenu to copy the file from its current location (with its current name) and paste a copy back into the same folder or a different folder. If you paste a copy of a file into the same folder as the original file, WordPerfect adds *Copy of* to the beginning of the filename so that the two files don't have the same name.

To copy a file, right-click on the file and choose Copy To Folder. Then choose the folder that you want to copy it to. To move a file, use the Files QuickMenu, but choose Move To Folder instead.

How about copying Toy Letter or Toy Letter2 to your new \Personal\Letters folder? Follow the steps below.

1 Choose File⇨Save As from the menu bar or press F3.

You see the Save As dialog box (refer to Figure 8-5). (You could have opened the Open dialog box instead — it doesn't matter which dialog box you use.) If the current folder isn't C:\MyFiles, change the current folder to that folder.

2 In the files box, which contains a list of files and folders in the current folder, right-click on the file that you want to copy: Toy Letter.wpd or Toy Letter2.101.wpd.

WordPerfect displays the Files QuickMenu of things you might want to do to a file, as in Figure 8-6.

3 Choose Copy To Folder.

WordPerfect displays the Select Destination Folder For Copy dialog box, which looks very similar to the Open and Save As dialog boxes and works in much the same way.

If you want to move the file instead of copying it, choose Move To Folder from the QuickMenu. WordPerfect then displays the Select Destination Folder For Move dialog box.

4 Now use the by now familiar method of clicking on the Up One Level button and double-clicking on folder names to move to C:\Personal\Letters.

When you're there, Letters will appear in the Look in box.

5 Click on the Copy button.

WordPerfect copies the file to \Personal\Letters.

If you're moving the file, the button you need to click is the Move button.

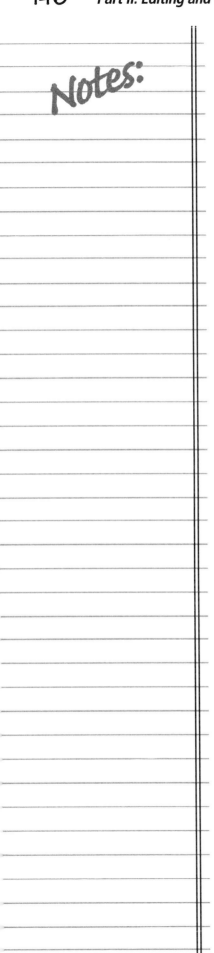

on the test

6 **Close the dialog box by clicking on the Close button.**

Use the Copy To Folder and Move To Folder options on the Files QuickMenu to copy or move a file to another directory. If you're copying to a floppy disk, use the Send To option and pick the disk drive — it's quicker than going through the copying steps, but gives you the same result.

You can also copy a file to the Windows Clipboard by choosing Edit⇨Copy from the dialog box menu or pressing Ctrl+C. You use the same commands to copy text in Unit 5! To paste the file from the Clipboard back into a file, choose Edit⇨Paste from the dialog box menu or press Ctrl+V.

Changing the name of a document

Renaming a document is extraordinarily easy in WordPerfect 7. Try it:

1 **Press Ctrl+O or click on the Open button on the Toolbar.**

You see the Open dialog box (refer to Figure 8-2). (As usual, you could use the Save As dialog box for this exercise, too.)

2 **Navigate your way to the \Personal\Letters folder.**

Use the Up One Level button to move to the root folder, double-click on the Personal folder, and then double-click on the Letters folder. Letters should appear in the Look in box.

3 **In the files box, click on the file that you want to change the name of: Job Application.101.wpd.**

4 **Now click on the filename again after it's selected. Note that this is different than double-clicking on it, which would open it.**

A little box appears around the filename, indicating that it is ready to be edited. Probably the whole name is selected, which means that if you start typing, what you type will replace what is already there. But you can also click somewhere in the name to get the cursor to appear there and then delete and type characters.

5 **Type the new name,** Application Letter.wpd.

If the name was selected when you started to type, the new name replaces the old. If not, you may need to delete some of the characters of the old name.

6 **Press Enter after you've finished editing the name.**

That's all there is to it!

7 **Click on the Close button in the Open dialog box to close the dialog box.**

You can rename a file by clicking on it after it has been selected and then editing the name.

Deleting a document that you never want to see again

heads up

You can delete the Letter to Gardner.wpd document that you created in Unit 2. If the Look in box on the Open dialog box doesn't display the name of your default directory (which is where Letter to Gardner.wpd should be), you need to go there by using the methods you've already learned —

double-clicking on the folders and clicking on the Up One Folder button. (If you've gotten really fond of it, make a copy of the document with another name before following the steps in this lesson to delete it.)

1 Click on the Open button or choose File⇨Open to display the Open dialog box.

First, you need to move to the folder that contains the file to delete.

2 Select the file that you want to delete by clicking on it once.

Select the document Letter to Gardner.wpd. Just click once — if you double-click on it, you'll open the document.

3 Press the Delete key.

WordPerfect displays the Confirm File Delete dialog box, asking if you're sure that you want to move this file to the Recycle Bin.

4 If the name of the file in the box is correct, click on Yes.

Poof! It's gone. Easy (as long as it was the right file)!

5 Click on Close to close the Open dialog box.

Delete a file by choosing it in either the Open or Save As dialog box and pressing the Delete key.

If you change your mind, you can retrieve most files by double-clicking on the Recycle Bin icon on your Windows 95 desktop, selecting the file that you've decided you shouldn't have deleted, right-clicking, and choosing Restore. You should visit the Recycle Bin once in a while to empty the trash — it frees up space on your hard disk.

extra credit

Finding lost documents

Now that you know how to change the current folder, save documents in different folders, notice what folder a document is saved to, and create a sensible folder structure for documents on your hard disk, you should never lose a document. And pigs can fly, too, right? Wrong — people lose files all the time. "Where did I store that December Estimate.wpd file, anyway? In C:\Estimate? In C:\Dec96? In C:\Personal? Drat!"

Fortunately, WordPerfect has a terrific feature to help you find lost documents: It's called QuickFinder. QuickFinder lets you look in one folder or more for specific filenames, or for filenames that have particular characters in them, or documents with particular words or phrases. To use QuickFinder, display the Open or Save As dialog box and click on the QuickFinder tab, right below the dialog box Toolbar. WordPerfect displays the QuickFinder settings, in which you tell WordPerfect what you're looking for. (See Figure 8-7.)

For example, here's how you can search for files that have the word *toy* in them:

1. Click on the Open button on the Toolbar or choose File⇨Open from the menu bar.

You see the Open dialog box.

2. Click on the QuickFinder tab.

The QuickFinder settings appear.

3. In the Content box, type toy.

(continued)

Up One Folder button

☑ **Progress Check**

If you can do the following, you've mastered this lesson:

❏ Move a file to a different folder.

❏ Copy a file.

❏ Rename a file.

❏ Delete a file for good.

Figure 8-7: The QuickFinder dialog box helps you find lost files — too bad it doesn't find keys!

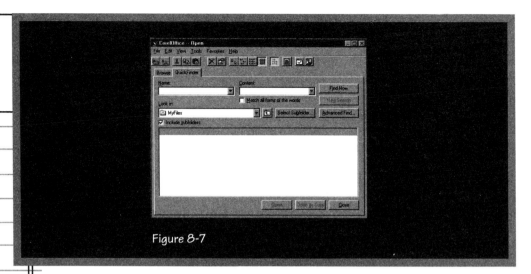

Figure 8-7

Notes:

(*continued*)

The Content box is where to put the words or phrases that you're looking for. WordPerfect assumes that two words are a phrase unless you specify And, Or, Not, and so on. For instance, typing "toy not fire" in the content box (without the quotes) will find documents that have the word "toy" in them, but not the word "fire."

4. **Tell WordPerfect where to look using the Look in box. Select a particular folder by using the Select Subfolder button. Tell WordPerfect to look in all subfolders of whatever you've selected by clicking on the Include subfolders setting so that a check mark appears in the box.**

   You can search all disks by choosing My Computer in the Look in box, or you can be more specific (which speeds up the search).

5. **Click on Find Now to tell WordPerfect to search.**

   QuickFinder searches for files containing the word *toy.* While it's searching, you can click on the Stop Find button if (a) you think it has already found what you need or (b) it's taking too long.

   When the search is finished, WordPerfect displays the files it's found. All the files with the word *toy* in the text are displayed in a list, showing the filename and the folder that each file is stored in.

   If you want to open a file that the search found, click on the document once and then click on Open. WordPerfect closes the dialog box and opens the document.

6. **When you're done looking at the documents that QuickFinder found, click on Close.**

The QuickFinder is a good way to find a lost document — you can use it whenever you have the Open or Save As dialog box open.

Using the Favorites Folder to Find Files Quickly

Lesson 8-4

Once you set up folders to store your WordPerfect documents in, you have to change the current folder to the folder that you want to use each time you open or save a file. If clicking through lots of folder names annoys you, learn to use Windows 95's *Favorites* feature. This feature lets you see a list of the names of the folders and files that you use most often.

Windows 95 creates a folder named Favorites, usually on your C disk drive. You can tell WordPerfect to make the files and folders that you use often *Favorites,* which means that you won't have to do as much navigation to find them. When you tell WordPerfect to make a certain file or folder a Favorite, WordPerfect (and Windows 95) creates a shortcut, stored in the Favorites folder, to the file or folder that you want easy access to. Because the Favorites folder is used by all Windows 95 programs, it can contain shortcuts to many different types of files, not just WordPerfect documents.

Both the Open and Save As dialog boxes contain a button on their Toolbars that take you straight to the Favorites folder — the Go To/From Favorites button. They also contain an Add to Favorites button that adds the file or folder you select to the Favorites folder.

Adding a folder to Favorites

Stick your favorite folders or files in the Favorites folder, and you'll be able to open them much more quickly. When you add a folder to your Favorites folder, WordPerfect doesn't actually move or copy the original folder. Instead, it adds a *shortcut* to the folder. A shortcut looks like a folder, and when you double-click on a shortcut, you open the folder. Shortcuts are a way for files and subfolders to appear in two folders at the same time.

shortcuts let files and folders be in two places at the same time

Here's how to add the C:\Personal\Letters folder to your Favorites folder:

1 **Display the Open dialog box by clicking on the Open button on the Toolbar.**

WordPerfect displays the Open dialog box.

2 **Move to the C:\Personal\Letters folder.**

By now, moving to another folder is old hat, right?

3 **Click on the Add to Favorites button, the rightmost button on the toolbar in the Open dialog box.**

A little menu appears, giving you the choice between adding Add Favorite Folder and Add Favorite Item.

Add to Favorites button

Figure 8-8: Your Favorites folder can contain folders, WordPerfect documents, and other types of files.

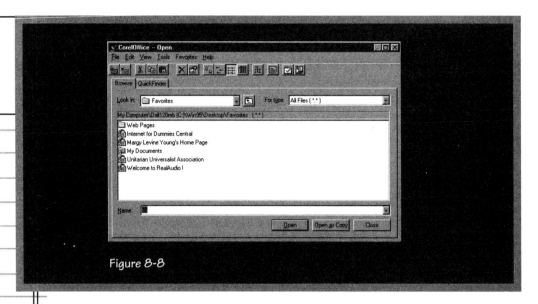

Figure 8-8

4 Select Add Favorite Folder from the menu that appears.

Nothing appears to happen, but WordPerfect just added the folder to your Favorites folder. You can add a file in the same way — just select the file before you click on the Add to Favorites button and then choose Add Favorite Item from the menu that appears.

5 Close the Open dialog box.

To add a file or folder to your Favorites folder, select the file or folder and click on the Add to Favorites button.

Using Favorite folders and files

Folders and files in your Favorites folder don't do you any good unless finding those folders and files is easy. And it is! To use a favorite file or folder, click on the Go To/From Favorites button on the Open or Save As dialog box. You jump directly to the Favorites folder.

1 Open the Open dialog box.

It's time to jump to your Favorites folder.

2 Click on the Go To/From Favorites button, the second-to-last button on the toolbar on the dialog box.

Poof! You move to C:\Windows\Favorites. Our Favorites folder is shown in Figure 8-8. The MyFiles entry is a shortcut to the C:\MyFiles folder.

To use files in a folder in your Favorites folder, double-click on the folder.

3 Double-click on the Letters folder.

You jump to C:\Personal\Letters, the same folder you've been using throughout this unit.

Go To/From Favorites button

☑ Progress Check

If you can do the following, you've mastered this lesson:

❏ Add a folder to the Favorites folder.

❏ Jump to your Favorites folder.

❏ Use the files and folders in your Favorites folder.

Unit 8 Quiz

For each of the following questions, circle the letter of the correct answer or answers. Remember, there may be more than one right answer for each question!

1. **A folder is . . .**

    A. Where you look to find phone numbers.

    B. An object created using origami, the Japanese art of paper-folding.

    C. Something that contains files and other folders.

    D. The contortionist at the circus.

    E. A place on your hard disk to store files.

2. **A subfolder is . . .**

    A. A small folder that isn't very important.

    B. A military rank.

    C. A folder that is stored in another folder.

    D. A new contraption that keeps your sub sandwich (or hoagie, for you folks from Philadelphia) fillings from messing up your clothes.

    E. An entry in a folder that consists of another folder, where you can store files and folders.

3. **A folder can contain . . .**

    A. Files.

    B. Folders.

    C. Subfolders.

    D. Submarines.

    E. Hard disks.

4. **You may want to create a folder to contain . . .**

    A. Love letters.

    B. Memos to coworkers.

    C. The chapters of the book that you're writing.

    D. Press releases for your organization.

    E. Papers that you've written for a course.

5. **The Favorites folder helps you . . .**

    A. Choose your best friend faster.

    B. Change the current folder faster.

    C. Open a frequently used file faster.

    D. See the files in a folder faster.

    E. Choose the folder that you want to use faster.

Notes:

Unit 8 Exercise

1. Create a folder on your hard disk for one type of document. For example, create a folder named Memos to contain memos that you write. Create it in the C (root) folder or in another folder (for example, in the C:\Personal folder that you created in Lesson 8-2, making the new folder C:\Personal\Memos).

2. Move a file into the new folder that you just created. For example, if you've written a memo and stored it in the C:\MyFiles folder, move it to the folder that you just created.

3. Rename a document. Choose one that has a name that isn't particularly descriptive and change it to a name that better describes the document's contents.

4. Add the folder that you created in Step 1 to your Favorites folder.

Part II Review

Unit 5 Summary

- **Selecting text:** Select text by painting it with the mouse (clicking and dragging), by using the Shift key with the cursor movement keys, or by using the mouse button to click on the text or in the margin.

- **Deleting text:** Delete a bunch of text by selecting it and pressing Delete.

- **Using the Undo Command:** Undo what you just did by pressing Ctrl+Z or choosing Edit⇨Undo from the menu.

- **Copying text:** Copy text to the Clipboard by selecting it and pressing Ctrl+C or clicking on the Copy button on the Toolbar. Copy text from the Clipboard to the point where the cursor is by pressing Ctrl+V or clicking on the Paste button on the Toolbar. Alternatively, select the text and then hold down the Ctrl key while clicking on it and dragging it to its new position.

- **Moving text:** Move text by selecting it, cutting it to the Clipboard by pressing Ctrl+X, or clicking on the Cut button on the Toolbar. Insert text in its new position by moving the cursor to that position and pressing Ctrl+V or clicking on the Paste button on the Toolbar. Alternatively, select the text, then click on it and drag it to its new position.

Unit 6 Summary

- **Searching for words or phrases:** Press F2 to search for a word or phrase (by using the Find and Replace Text dialog box).

- **Continue searching:** Click on Find Next to continue the search.

- **Searching for whole words:** Use the Match⇨Whole Word option from the dialog box menu when you are looking only for a whole word, and not for a portion of a word.

- **Replacing words or phrases:** Use the Replace All button when you want to replace all instances of the word or phrase in the Find box with the word or phrase in the Replace With box. Always save your document before doing a global search and replace.

- **Using the Go To command:** Use Ctrl+G to Go To a particular page.

Part II Review

Unit 7 Summary

▶ **Correcting spelling:** Right-click on a word with a squiggly red line under it to correct its spelling using Spell-As-You-Go.

▶ **Using Spell Check:** Click on the Spell Check button on the Toolbar or choose Tools➪Spell Check to check the spelling of a document using Spell Check.

▶ **Adding words to the dictionary:** Use the Add button on the Spell Checker or the Add option on the Spell-As-You-Go menu to add words you frequently use to WordPerfect's dictionary.

▶ **QuickCorrect:** Add commonly misspelled words and abbreviations for commonly used words or phrases to QuickCorrect. Display the QuickCorrect dialog box by choosing Tools➪QuickCorrect from the menu.

▶ **Thesaurus:** Use the Thesaurus to find a better word: Select a word and choose Tools➪Thesaurus to let the WordPerfect Thesaurus suggest alternative words.

▶ **Grammatik:** Use Grammatik to check your grammar when you don't have an editor in the family: Click on the Grammatik button on the Toolbar or choose Tools➪Grammatik from the menu bar.

Unit 8 Summary

▶ **Folders:** Use folders to organize files on your hard disk.

▶ **Navigating folders:** Find your way around folders in the Open or Save As dialog boxes by double-clicking on a directory name to see the files and subfolders in it and clicking on the Up One Level button to see the previous folder in the folder structure.

▶ **Current folder:** Double-clicking on a folder makes it the *current* folder, which is the folder currently in use for opening and saving files.

▶ **Default folder:** The default folder is C:\MyFiles.This is the folder that files are saved to and loaded from unless you make another folder the current folder.

▶ **Creating new folders:** Create a new folder for your documents by choosing File➪New➪Folder from the Open or Save As dialog box menu. Give it a name of your choice by typing the new name while the new folder is selected and then pressing Enter.

▶ **Copying and moving files:** Right-click on filenames in the Open and Save As dialog boxes to display a menu with Copy To Folder, Move To Folder, and Send to options to move and copy files to different drives and folders.

▶ **File Options:** Right-click on filenames in the Open and Save As dialog boxes to display a menu with Cut, Copy, Delete, Rename, and Send to options.

▶ **Favorites:** Use the Go to Favorites and Add to Favorites buttons on the Open and Save As dialog boxes to make files and folders easy to find. Use the Go to Favorites button to display favorite files and folders and use the Add to Favorites button to add a file or folder to Favorites.

Part II Test

The questions on this test cover all of the material presented in Part I and II, Units 1-8.

True False

T F 1. It's a good idea to keep all your documents in one folder, preferably the same folder that contains the WordPerfect program files.

T F 2. There is only one way to select text.

T F 3. WordPerfect's Grammatik feature helps make your writing more like Stephen King's.

T F 4. The Edit⇨Find and Replace command can be used to remove all the spaces from your document.

T F 5. Mister Rogers is a Presbyterian minister.

T F 6. Spell-checking your doumnets is a good idea.

T F 7. You can move text by selecting it and using the mouse to drag it to its new position.

T F 8. The Clipboard is where Windows stores your grocery list.

T F 9. You can use WordPerfect's search feature to find your car keys.

T F 10. If WordPerfect doesn't know how to spell a word, you can add it to the dictionary.

Multiple Choice

For each of the following questions, circle the correct answer or answers. Remember, there may be more than one right answer for each question!

11. **What's the default document folder?**

   A. The folder where WordPerfect stores documents, unless you change to a different folder.

   B. C:\MyFiles.

   C. Where the bank looks when WordPerfect defaults on a loan.

   D. Whatever you want it to be.

   E. WordPerfect\Default\Folder.

12. **How do you copy some text from one part of your document to another?**

   A. Select the text, hold down the Ctrl key, and drag the text to the new location.

   B. Select the text, press Ctrl+C, move the cursor to the new location, and press Ctrl+V.

   C. Print the document and photocopy the section that needs to be copied and cut and paste the document to look like you want it to.

   D. Select the text, click on the Copy button on the Toolbar, move the cursor to the new location, and click on the Paste button on the Toolbar.

   E. Click your heels three times and wish for a tornado to move the text to the new location.

13. **What does K.I.S.S. stand for?**

   A. Kill Innocent Single Snakes.

   B. Keep It Simple, Stupid.

   C. What do you mean, "stand for"? Isn't "kiss" a word?

   D. Keep It Simple, Smarty.

   E. Korea, Indonesia, Samoa, and Singapore.

14. **What does Ctrl+X do?**

   A. The same thing as the Cut button on the Toolbar.

   B. Erases the selected text and stores it on the Windows Clipboard for later use.

   C. Capitalizes the text.

   D. Replaces all the characters in the document with Xs.

   E. Displays an episode of *The X-Files*.

Part II Test

15. What are Favorites for?

    A. Speeds up creation of your grocery list by automatically listing your kids' favorite foods such as chocolate syrup, hamburger, tortilla chips, and salsa.

    B. Helps you move to the folder you want.

    C. Lists the folders that you actually use.

    D. To please WordPerfect's engineers who got to add two cute buttons to the Open and Save As dialog boxes.

    E. Lists favorite singles in your neighborhood (of the requisite gender, of course).

16. When the WordPerfect Spell Checker finds a word it doesn't know, what can you do?

    A. Add it to the dictionary.

    B. Replace it with a correctly spelled word.

    C. Skip it just this once.

    D. Skip it whenever it occurs, but just in this document.

    E. Burst into tears.

17. Which of the following things can the WordPerfect Edit⇨Find and Replace command do?

    A. Replace your kids with kids who clean up the house and set the table without being asked.

    B. Replace one whole word with another whole word.

    C. Replace all the incorrectly spelled words with correctly spelled words.

    D. Replace a word or phrase with another word or phrase.

    E. Replace all the spaces in your document with question marks. (But save the document first!)

18. Which aren't actually as bad as they sound?

    A. English muffins with strawberry jam and cheddar cheese (melt the cheese).

    B. Lentils.

    C. Black beans, especially in feijoada, the Brazilian national dish.

    D. Cottage cheese and ketchup. (President Nixon is reported to have loved it.)

    E. Creating and using folders.

Part II Test

Matching

19. Match up the following Toolbar buttons with the corresponding commands:

    A. ☐ 1. Edit⇨Copy.

    B. ☐ 2. Edit⇨Paste.

    C. ☐ 3. Edit⇨Undo.

    D. ☐ 4. Edit⇨Cut.

    E. ☐ 5. Tools⇨Spell Check.

20. Match up the descriptions with the buttons on the Toolbar:

    A. Displays the Print dialog box. 1. ☐

    B. Inserts the information from the Clipboard at the cursor. 2. ☐

    C. Displays the Open dialog box. 3. ☐

    D. Copies the selected text to the Clipboard. 4. ☐

    E. Checks the spelling in the document. 5. ☐

21. Match up the following keyboard shortcuts with the corresponding feature.

    A. Ctrl+X.   1. Save.

    B. Ctrl+S.   2. Cut.

    C. Ctrl+V.   3. Undo.

    D. Ctrl+C.   4. Paste.

    E. Ctrl+Z.   5. Copy.

22. Match the following characters with their TV shows:

    A. Mulder.   1. *The Simpsons.*

    B. Maggie.   2. *The X-Files.*

    C. Data.   3. *Sesame Street.*

    D. Bart.   4. *Star Trek: The Next Generation.*

    E. Oscar.   5. *Northern Exposure.*

Part II Lab Assignment

In this assignment, you will write instructions for the design criteria for stuffed animals to be manufactured by Lexington Toys.

Step 1: Write the first draft

Starting with a blank document, write instructions for how to design teddy bears. Mention size, color, accessories, and facial expression.

Save the document as Teddy Bears.wpd.

```
Lexington Toy Company
Design Criteria for Teddy Bears

1. Teddy bears should be no more than three feet (36 inches)
high, so they won't be too scary for small children.

2. Teddy bear colors are limited to white, brown, and
pastels, so they look cheery.

3. Teddy bears may come with accessories, such as clothing,
hats, bags, flags, etc. Attached accessories must be
washable. Detachable accessories do not have to be washable.
All accessories that come with Teddy bears should be safe
for children aged three and under (nothing that can be
swallowed, such as buttons).

4. Teddy bear facial expressions must be pleasant or blank.
No ferocious Teddy bears, please!

5. Teddy bears should look well-fed without appearing obese.
We are going for the "pleasantly plump" look.
```

Step 2: Change the subject of the document

Oops! You were *supposed* to write about design criteria for toy dinosaurs! Now they tell you! No problem — use the WordPerfect search-and-replace feature to change all the references to teddy bears to references to dinosaurs. Proofread the document after making the replacements to make sure that it still makes sense. Some adjustments may be needed.

Step 3: Switch the order of the topics

Move point 5 up to come after point 2, and renumber the points.

Step 4: Check your spelling

Spell check the document and save it again.

Adding Pizzazz

Part III

In this part . . .

We know you've been waiting anxiously to learn about the features in WordPerfect 7 that will make you look like a real word-processing pro. This part teaches you how to format your characters, paragraphs, and pages, and even shows you how to untangle formatting mishaps.

Using a powerful word processor such as WordPerfect 7 to produce documents that look like they could have been produced on a typewriter would be a shame. After all, WordPerfect makes controlling the fonts, spacing, centering, and justification of the text in your document easy.

When you follow the lessons in this part of the book, you learn how to use boldface, italics, and different fonts to jazz up your characters, how to center and indent to jazz up your paragraphs, and how to use headers and page formatting to jazz up your pages — not to mention other WordPerfect 7 features that will dress your text for success!

Formatting Fancy Characters

Prerequisites
♦ Opening an existing document (Lesson 2-2)
♦ Selecting text (Lesson 5-1)

♦ Proposal.101.wpd
♦ Proposal2.101.wpd
♦ Proposal3.101.wpd
on the CD

Objectives for This Unit

✓ Adding bold, italics, and underline to text that you've already typed

✓ Making text that you're about to type bold, italic, and underlined

✓ Changing the font and font size of text

✓ Capitalizing and decapitalizing (not to be confused with *decapitating*) chunks of text

✓ Copying nice-looking character formatting to less attractive text

You know how other people with word processors can do neat stuff with their characters? (We're not talking about character development, like having a better sense of humor or becoming more outgoing.) Some folks can spruce up their writing by making characters italic or bold, using different fonts and characters of different sizes — in short, their documents look pretty snazzy.

This part of the book shows you how to add some pizzazz to your documents. What's the point in using a powerful word processor like WordPerfect if your documents end up looking as if you typed them on a manual typewriter? You learn about using lots of different sizes and shapes for the characters in the document, as well as how to center text, make hanging indents, fool around with margins, and stick things in the margins (like page numbers, headers, and footers).

We want to warn you, though, about using these new skills to excess — formatting should enhance the meaning of the text, not overwhelm it. *No one* <u>likes</u> to read **text** that has been ***<u>overly formatted!</u>***

In this unit, you work on making the proposal for the Firehouse Set look more appealing. We give you the text, and you do the formatting. If you want to work on something of your own, feel free to format your own text.

Lesson 9-1 — Basic Formatting: Bold, Italics, and Underline

Bold button

Italics button

Underline button

Now is the time to use what WordPerfect calls *text styles,* otherwise known as making text bold, italic, or underlined. Good news — these are the easiest of formatting tricks. Why? Because WordPerfect gives you easy-to-use buttons on the Toolbar for these three formatting functions. All you need to do is select the text and click on the relevant button. Or if you have a phobia of buttons, you can use Ctrl+B, Ctrl+I, or Ctrl+U (nice mnemonic keystrokes for a change) to make text bold, italic, or underlined. (If you're not confident about selecting text, have a look at Unit 5.)

on the test

WordPerfect has two ways to make text bold, italic, or underlined, using either the Toolbar buttons or the keyboard:

- ▶ If you haven't typed the text yet that you want to format, click on the Toolbar button or press the keys to turn on bold, italics, or underlining. Then type the text. Click on the Toolbar button or press the keys to turn the formatting off again.

- ▶ If you've already typed the text that you want to format, select the text and then click on the Toolbar button or press the keys to format it. After the text is selected, you can go on formatting it by clicking on yet another button or using the keystroke command. And if you decide that having your text bold, italic, **_and_** underlined obscures what you're trying to say, just click on one of the three buttons again or give the keystroke command again to undo the formatting (with the text selected).

Formatting text you've already typed

on the CD

The document Proposal.101.wpd contains the proposal for Matt's Firehouse Set. You can make it look more interesting, first by using bold to make the important stuff stick out and then by experimenting with italics and underlining. In the process, you learn to undo text-style formatting.

1 Open the document Proposal.101.wpd (if you trashed it somehow, we've provided an identical document — Proposal2.101.wpd).

The memo reads okay, but it looks pretty boring. No one is going to get excited by the appearance of this letter. Where's the playful atmosphere? (Find it in Figure 9-1.)

2 Select the first heading within the text of the letter, Overview.

You can select it by using the mouse or the keyboard — see Unit 5 for ways to select text.

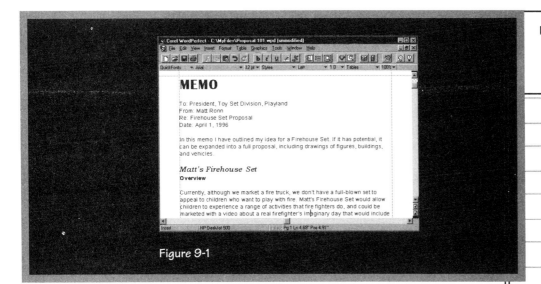

Figure 9-1

Figure 9-1: The Proposal.101.wpd memo the way it will look in a few exercises!

3 **Click on the Bold button on the Toolbar.**

Take a look at the Bold button on the Toolbar: the button appears depressed when the cursor is in the bold text. The line is now . . . boldified? Boldfacized? The characters look darker. (To see what the bold text looks like when it's not selected, click once somewhere else in the document.)

4 **Now select the first paragraph of the letter, starting** In this memo.

A good way to select a paragraph is to double-click in the margin.

5 **Click on the Italics button on the Toolbar.**

The first paragraph of the letter is italicized.

6 **With the first line of the letter still selected, click on the Underline button on the Toolbar.**

Hmm . . . It doesn't look very good that way. Time to undo it.

7 **While the text is still selected, undo the underlining by clicking on the Underline button again.**

Voilà! Back to just italic text — the underline goes away.

8 **Make the italics go away by clicking on the Italics button again while the text is still selected.**

Back to regular old text. Sometimes, simple is better!

Using these three types of formatting is as simple as selecting and clicking on a button.

Formatting as you type

You can also tell WordPerfect how you want text to look *before* you type it. Just click on the appropriate button — or use Ctrl+B for bold, Ctrl+I for italics, or Ctrl+U for underline — before you start typing. After you're finished typing, turn the text style off in the same way. Try it:

Notes:

Ctrl+B turns boldface on/off

Ctrl+I turns italics on/off

Ctrl+U turns underline on/off

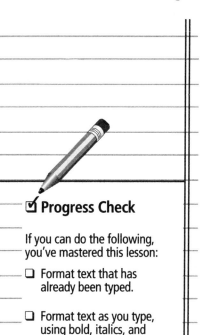

1 **Put your cursor at the beginning of the blank line before the** `Overview` **heading.**

You're going to add a title.

2 **Press Ctrl+I or click on the Italics button on the Toolbar.**

Now any text that you type is italic. The Italics button on the Toolbar appears depressed (looks downhearted to us, anyway).

3 **Type** matt's firehouse set.

The text appears in italics (and you'll change the capitalization later).

4 **Press Ctrl+I or click on the Italics button again to turn italics off.**

The Italics button on the Toolbar pops back out — that is, it doesn't look like it's pushed in. Now if you type something else, what you type is not italicized.

5 **Press Ctrl+S to save your document, just in case the cat knocks your coffee into your computer keyboard and shorts out your PC.**

If you prefer to format as you type, you can turn formatting on before you type text, by using Ctrl+B, Ctrl+I, or Ctrl+U or by clicking on buttons on the Toolbar.

Note: You don't need to turn formatting off if you aren't going to type anything else where the cursor is. For example, if you turn on underlining, type some underlined text, move the cursor to another location in the document, and start typing again, underlining probably isn't turned on at your new location. You can always tell whether bold, italics, or underline is turned on by looking at the buttons on the Toolbar: If they appear to be pushed in, the formatting is on.

Lesson 9-2   Choosing Fonts and Font Sizes

So what is a font, anyway? A *font* is a set of shapes for letters, numbers, and punctuation. In the old days, just a few fonts existed, with names like Times Roman, Courier, Prestige, and Elite. Nowadays, if our computers are anything to go by, fonts are on a mission to take over the world. Just imagine — some people get paid to think up new ones!

A font is a set of character shapes

Fonts are often broken down into two major categories: ones that have little thingies called *serifs* off the main strokes of the letters, and plainer ones (called *sans serif*) without the thingies (you may need to brush up on your French to remember these names). We can explain it better by example: The type that you're reading right now is a serif font, and the extra credit text (in the sidebars) is a sans serif font. Usually WordPerfect will automatically use a serif font called Times Roman (or some variation on that name, such as Times New Roman or Tms Roman) unless you tell it to use another font. Common sans serif fonts are Helvetica, Swiss, and Arial. Sans serif fonts are a good choice for headings in a document that uses Times Roman for text, because they're easily distinguishable but still readable, and they don't clash with the serif font. Figure 9-2 shows some commonly used fonts.

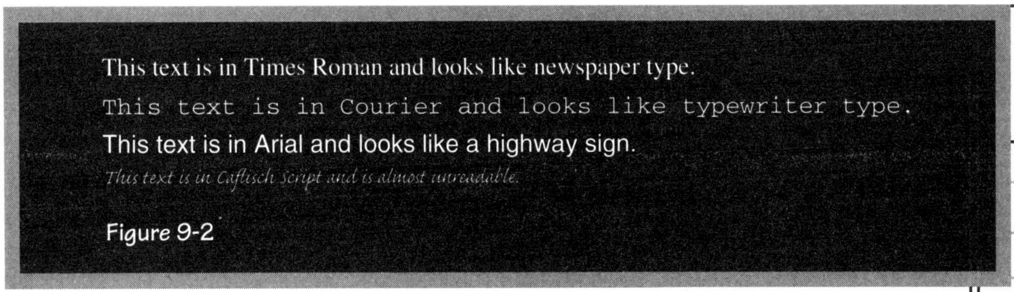

This text is in Times Roman and looks like newspaper type.

This text is in Courier and looks like typewriter type.

This text is in Arial and looks like a highway sign.

This text is in Caflisch Script and is almost unreadable.

Figure 9-2

Figure 9-2: Examples of some commonly used fonts.

Windows comes with a bunch of fonts, and so do WordPerfect and your printer. You can also buy more or get some with other software that you buy. In this lesson, you see how to display a list of the fonts that you can use in your WordPerfect documents.

Most fonts are *proportionally spaced,* which means that different characters take up different amounts of space. A capital *W* is usually the widest letter, and a small *i* is usually the narrowest: Look at the difference in the width of those two letters on this page. *Fixed-space* or *fixed-pitch fonts* are like those on a typewriter — each character takes up the same amount of space. A common fixed-pitch font is Courier.

on the test

Fonts also come in sizes, which are measured in points or pitch. A *point* is $1/72$ of an inch, and normal readable type is usually 10 or 11 points high. Headlines can be 14, 24, or even 36 points high. The larger the point size, the larger the font looks.

You can make a so-so document look terrific (and waste a lot of time trying) by changing the font and by putting headings in a font that's different from the one you used for the text. This lesson describes different ways to fool around with fonts. The easiest way to change fonts and type sizes is by using the first three buttons on the Power Bar: the QuickFont, Font, and Font Size buttons.

Seeing what fonts you have

The easiest way to work with fonts is by using a button on the Power Bar. The Power Bar is the gray row of buttons directly below the Toolbar. Each button has a downward-pointing triangle at its right end, indicating that if you click on it, a list of options will drop down from the button.

Tip: If no row of rectangular buttons appears below the Toolbar, choose View⇨Toolbars/Ruler from the menu bar and see if an x appears next to the Power Bar command — if not, click on the Power Bar box, and then OK, and the Power Bar appears.

The second box (button) on the Power Bar is the Font button. The button displays the name of the font currently in use (where the cursor is).

Notes:

Power Bar: gray buttons below Toolbar

Times New Roman ▼

Font button on Power Bar

clicking on Font button displays list of fonts

Notes:

To see a list of fonts on your system:

1 Click on the Font button once.

A list of fonts appears below the Font button. It's probably quite a long list.

2 You can scroll through the list of fonts, using the scroll bar along the right edge of the list.

3 To make the list disappear again, click in the typing area of the WordPerfect window.

So far, you haven't changed anything in your document. You just took a peek at the names of fonts that you can use. To see what they actually look like, you have to format some text with them.

Changing the font and size of selected text

on the CD

Start playing with fonts by changing the font of one line of text. (If Proposal.101.wpd isn't open, open it now.)

Note: If you don't have the fonts we suggest, use fonts that you do have. The point isn't to use particular fonts, but to practice changing the font of selected text.

1 Select the first line of the document, MEMO.

2 Click on the Font button.

The Font button appears pressed in, and a list of available fonts appears. If the list is long, it has a scroll bar.

3 Pick a new font for the line — try Britannic Bold if you have it, or Century Gothic, or Braggadocio.

We like something big and bold at the top of the memo, but you can decide whether you prefer fancy or plain. After all, choosing fonts is one of the funnest parts of having WordPerfect, and we have no intention of spoiling your fun.

After you click on the font, the list disappears, and the font of the selected text changes. The text stays selected, though, so that you can try out a different font by clicking on the Font button again and picking another font from the list.

The text looks different now, but try making it bigger to see what it really looks like.

4 (If the first line is no longer selected, select it again.) Now make the selected text larger by clicking on the Font Size button.

It's next to the Font button on the Power Bar.

The button looks depressed (any shrinks out there?), and a list of font sizes appears, shown in points ($1/72$ of an inch).

5 Choose a larger size — say, 30.

After you click on the size, the list disappears, and the size of the selected text changes.

`12 pt ▾`

Font Size button on Power Bar

6 **Try another line. Select the** `matt's firehouse set` **line.**

It's the first heading in the body of the letter. Wouldn't the headings look nicer if they stood out a little? In the next couple of steps, you'll format this heading to make it a different font and slightly bigger than it is now — say, 14-point or 16-point.

7 **Click on the Font button and choose Bookman Old Style or another font.**

Hmm . . . Looks kind of small. Make it bigger.

8 **Click on the Font Size button and choose 16.**

The line still needs to be selected. If you don't like the look of it, select some other size and/or font.

9 **As you move your cursor around the document, take a look at the Font and Font Size buttons on the Power Bar.**

They show which font and size are in use wherever your cursor is. When your cursor is on the first line of the document, the Font button displays *Britannic Bold,* or *Century Gothic,* or *Braggadocio,* or whatever font you chose, and the Font Size button shows *30 pt.*

> Font and Font Size buttons show font and size in use at cursor position

That's it. All you have to do to pretty up the font of selected text is to select it and choose the font and font size by using the buttons on the Power Bar.

heads up

Incidentally, you change the font or font size for the rest of the document if you don't select text before selecting a font or font size. We don't recommend that approach, though — see our suggestions below for safe formatting.

Choosing a font for the whole document

on the test

The *initial font* for the document is the font that all text will use (including headers, footers, and page numbers) unless you specify otherwise. Following is how to set the initial font for a document:

1 **Unlike most commands that change a font, the location of your cursor is unimportant when you give this command.**

This command affects the whole document, not the text where the cursor is. Do make sure, however, that no text is selected.

2 **Choose Format⇨Document⇨Initial Font from the menu bar.**

WordPerfect displays the Document Initial Font dialog box, which you see in Figure 9-3.

> Format→Document→ Initial Font to set initial font for document

3 **Select the Font face, Font size, and Font style that you want as the defaults for the document. For the Proposal.101.wpd memo, choose Arial, 12-point type (or any other font whose look you like).**

The Font style enables you to set the initial font to be italic, bold, or even bold italic. We have trouble thinking of a reason for going that far, though. Whatever changes you make, the text in the preview box displays how your text will appear.

You can change the initial font of all documents by using the Set as printer initial font check box at the bottom of the Document Initial Font dialog box. Set the initial font for the document you're working on to a font that you would like to be the initial font for all documents.

Figure 9-3: What font do you want your document to use?

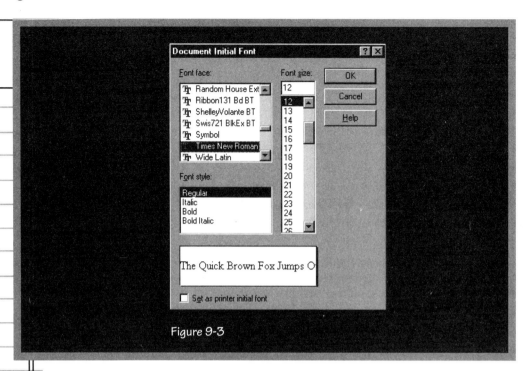

Figure 9-3

 Click on OK to make the change.

Any text that doesn't have a specified font changes to the initial font you just defined.

 Press Ctrl+S to save your document, just in case lightning strikes your building before you finish this unit.

In the Proposal.101.wpd memo, you formatted the first line (*Memo*) using Britannic Bold, or whichever font you chose, and it doesn't change. The memo heading hasn't been formatted, so it changes to the new initial font — as does the rest of the document except the two headings, which you formatted with different fonts.

The Document Initial Font dialog box allows you to set the initial font for the whole document. You can then change fonts for selected text or for the rest of the document starting from where the cursor is by using the Font button on the Power Bar.

Tip: In case you haven't guessed, you can easily get carried away with fonts (because they're so much fun) and overformat a document. Normally, we (Alison and Margy) try to use a maximum of three fonts in a document — usually a serif and sans serif font that complement each other (like Times Roman and Arial) — one for headings and one for regular text, with perhaps a third font thrown in for spice. But fonts are fun, so enjoy yourself and trust your judgment.

heads up

You've now learned a lot of ways to change the font of text in your document, so we want to give you some safe formatting guidelines. Ready?

- Set the initial document font to a font that will be used for most of the text in the document.

♦ Format selected text, like headings, by selecting the text and changing the font. Changing fonts in this way insures that the text after the heading reverts to the document initial font.

♦ In general, we don't recommend changing the font for the rest of the document (which you can do by selecting a font or font size from the Power Bar lists without selecting text first) — too easily, you can end up with a badly formatted document (with the font and font size changing here and there).

extra credit

The master panel for text appearance

If you are doing serious formatting and find yourself wishing for a place where you could specify exactly how you want your text to look, look no further than the Font dialog box, which appears in Figure 9-4. To view it, press F9 (or choose Format⇨Font from the menu bar). It works like other commands that change the appearance of your text — if text is selected, that text is formatted, and if no text is selected, WordPerfect changes the appearance of text from the point where the cursor is to the end of the document (or until it reaches a point where you've given another formatting command).

In addition to changing the formatting of your text in ways you've already seen, you can also use some new formatting options. The Appearance part of the Font dialog box (in the center top of the dialog box) contains not only Bold, Italic, and Underline, but also Double Underline, Outline Shadow, Small cap, Redline, and Strikeout (and Hidden, which is for comments that you don't want printed).

You can create superscripts and subscripts by changing the Position setting. If you want your superscript or subscript in a smaller font, use the Relative size setting.

Some more-obscure text formatting options are as follows:

Text Formatting	When to Use It	What It Looks Like
Outline	To make text look funky	Outlined text
Shadow	To give letters a shadow	Shadowed text
Small Cap	To make all-caps text ultra-readable	SMALL CAPS
Redline	To make some text, such as editorial comments, stand out in red letters	Redlined text
Strikeout	To put a line through the text	Struckout text
Superscript	To put some smaller-sized text above the normal text position, as with mathematical expressions	$4^2 = 16$
Subscript	To put some smaller-sized text below the normal text position, as with chemical formulas	H_2O

Format to your heart's delight, and if you suddenly become frightened that you've done too much, just press Esc or click on Cancel to forget the whole thing. Click on OK to keep the changes that you've made.

☑ **Progress Check**

If you can do the following, you've mastered this lesson:

❑ Change the font and font size for selected text.

❑ Change the font and font size for the rest of the document.

❑ Set the default font and font size for the document.

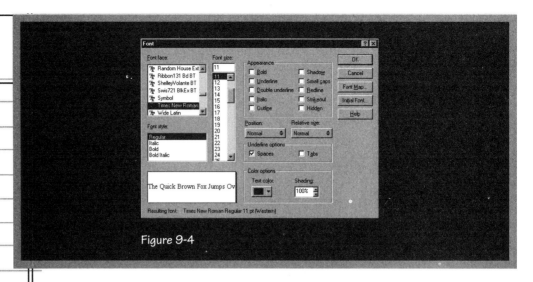

Figure 9-4: The Font dialog box is like Mission Control for formatting.

Figure 9-4

Lesson 9-3   Changing Capitalization

Ctrl+K switches capitalization

☑ Progress Check

If you can do the following, you've mastered this lesson:

❑ Change the capitalization of selected text.

❑ Impress your coworkers by showing them that they don't have to retype their text if they press the Caps Lock key by mistake.

dON'T YOU HATE IT WHEN YOU PRESS THE cAPS lOCK KEY BY MISTAKE? Having the option of changing the capitalization of your text saves you from having to retype. Or maybe you're trying to figure out if a title looks better in all caps or just with the initial letter of each word capitalized. WordPerfect gives you an easy way to try out these options.

Making a title all caps

In the proposal, make the word *Memo* all capital letters. If you don't already have the Proposal.101.wpd document loaded, open it now. Then follow these steps:

1 **Select the word *Memo* at the beginning of the document.**

2 **Choose Edit➪Convert Case from the menu.**

WordPerfect gives you three choices: Lowercase, Uppercase, and Initial Capitals, which pretty much cover the options.

3 **Choose Uppercase.**

WordPerfect changes the capitalization of your text. Some fonts are almost unreadable in all caps — if you don't like the looks of your title, while it's still selected, you can change the font (by clicking on the Font button).

Tip: You can also press Ctrl+K to change selected text from uppercase to lowercase and back again.

When you need to change the capitalization of your text, the Edit➪Convert Case command saves you from the boredom of retyping it (although you may still need to edit a few letters to get them right).

Changing capitalization to initial caps

Try a different option:

1 Select the text matt's firehouse set. **You added this title earlier.**

2 Choose Edit⇨Convert Case from the menu.

3 Choose Initial Capitals.

WordPerfect changes initial letters to capitals, but it's smart about it — small words like *a, an, the,* and *and* will stay uncapitalized, which is how they should be.

Copying Character Formatting

Lesson 9-4

on the test

WordPerfect provides an easy way to format several different selections of text the same way — QuickFormat. QuickFormat is useful when you have more than one heading in a document: After you've formatted one of the headings to look good, you can format the other headings without going through all the steps again.

Following are three ways to use QuickFormat:

▶ Click on the QuickFormat button.

▶ Click on the right mouse button anywhere in the typing area to display the text QuickMenu and then choose QuickFormat.

▶ Choose Format⇨QuickFormat from the menu bar.

QuickFormat button

Using QuickFormat

on the CD

You can use the QuickFormat option on the Proposal.101.wpd letter to copy formatting from one heading to other headings. (If Proposal.101.wpd isn't open, open it now. If you haven't followed the first three lessons in this unit, open Proposal3.101.wpd instead so that your document has the same fancy formatting that it would have if you had followed the steps.) Follow these steps:

1 Select the Overview **heading that you formatted earlier.**

It's bold. In a minute you'll add even more formatting to it.

2 While the heading is still selected, turn QuickFormat on by clicking on the QuickFormat button on the Toolbar.

Alternatively, you can choose Format⇨QuickFormat from the menu bar or click on the right mouse button anywhere in the typing area and then choose QuickFormat from the QuickMenu that appears. Whichever method you use to start QuickFormatting, WordPerfect displays the QuickFormat dialog box (see Figure 9-5).

Figure 9-5: You can copy formatting from one chunk of text to another by using the QuickFormat dialog box.

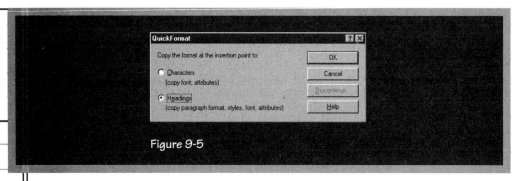

Figure 9-5

Turning QuickFormat on means that you want WordPerfect to remember the format of the text that the cursor is in, because you want to format other text to look the same.

You have the option of copying character format only (Characters) or including paragraph formatting (Headings). Because you're formatting a heading, use the Headings choice. If you were copying the format of a piece of text that wasn't a whole paragraph (meaning it doesn't have carriage returns before and after it), you could use the Characters option.

3 **Choose Headings and click on OK.**

The dialog box goes away, and the mouse pointer turns into a tall *I* with a paintbrush next to it, indicating that you can paint new text to look like your already prettified text.

4 **Select the next heading,** Matt's Firehouse Set Components, **to format.**

When you're copying a headings format, you need only to click somewhere in the paragraph (or line, in this case) to indicate that the format should be copied to the whole paragraph.

As soon as you select the text, WordPerfect immediately formats it the same way that the first heading is formatted. Very Quick! The mouse pointer still looks funny, though, with its tiny paintbrush. As long as the mouse pointer includes a paintbrush, WordPerfect is still ready to QuickFormat.

5 **Select the rest of the headings to make them all look the same.**

The other headings are Competing Toys and Market. The other headings are really subheadings of the Components heading. If you format any other text by accident, don't worry: In Unit 10, you learn how to get rid of formatting that you don't want. (You could also press Ctrl+Z to undo any formatting you do accidentally.)

You can also format text when QuickFormat is off — select the text to be formatted (with a headings format, you actually only need to have the cursor in the paragraph to be formatted) and choose QuickFormat1 from the Select styles button on the Power Bar.

6 **Turn QuickFormat off by clicking on the QuickFormat button on the Toolbar, choosing Format⇨QuickFormat from the menu bar, or using the QuickMenu by right-clicking and choosing QuickFormat to turn off the feature. In other words, turn it off the same way you turned it on.**

Another way to turn off QuickFormat is just to start typing. You can tell when WordPerfect is finished QuickFormatting: The mouse pointer returns to its usual pointy shape.

Your headings now all match. QuickFormat is a good way to give your document consistent formatting. Fancying up your document is fine — making each heading look different will just confuse your readers!

extra credit

Stylish concepts

Styles are one of the most powerful features of WordPerfect . A style is a set of formatting that you give a name. Styles enable you to create beautifully formatted documents with consistent formatting for all your headings, captions, quotations, and other specially formatted text. And styles make formatting faster and easier.

Why bother to use a style? Imagine the following scenario: You've just turned in a 300-page proposal to your boss. She has only a few minor content-related criticisms, but she really hates the way the headings look. To change the headings (all three levels), you have to go through the whole document and change the font and size of each heading manually. Yeech!

How does this scenario differ if you use styles? If you do, each heading level has a style (perhaps *Heading 1, Heading 2,* and *Heading 3,* which are predefined styles — ready and waiting for you to use to format text). All you have to do is change the formatting of the *styles* for the three headings to change the format of all the headings in the document. All the headings in the whole document are then reformatted automagically. Sound easier?

WordPerfect has three different kinds of styles:

- **Character**: Font formatting for selected text

- **Paragraph**: Paragraph spacing, font for the whole paragraph, line spacing for the paragraph, and other formatting that affects the entire paragraph

- **Document**: Formatting for the whole document, such as the default font

The process of using styles in a document may go something like the following:

- You realize that you'll be doing a lot of formatting in a document. You think that using styles will help you keep formatting consistent and let you make global formatting changes if you don't like the way you do it the first time.

- You create styles as you go along, using QuickStyling.

- After you've created a style the first time, you apply it to other text that should look the same.

- After you've finished the document, you look at the overall format. If necessary, you edit the styles, using the Styles Editor.

Changing the format of QuickFormatted text

After you've used QuickFormat to format headings, you can change the format of one heading, and the format of the rest will change to match.

1 **Select one of the headings you just formatted.**

You have a bunch to choose from — any will work.

Notes:

Notes:

Progress Check

☑ **Progress Check**

If you can do the following, you've mastered this lesson:

❑ Find different parts of your text that should have the same formatting.

❑ Use QuickFormat to copy formatting.

❑ Paint with the mouse pointer.

2 **Change the font by using either the Font button or the QuickFont button (QuickFont lists fonts that you've used recently — and as an added bonus, it lists them the way they look).**

You can choose a font that you've used before or a new one (we used Caslon Opnface BT 16pt, just for fun).

Have a quick look through your document. Notice that not only the format of the heading you selected changed — but the format of the other headings you formatted with QuickFormat changed also.

3 **Close the Proposal.101.wpd document. Be sure to save your changes, now that all the headings are formatted in a nice, consistent way.**

QuickFormat is an easy way to format a number of items in your document the same way. Another way is by using styles, which are described in two extra credit sidebars in this unit.

Recess

You've come to a great place to take a break — save Proposal.101.wpd and exit WordPerfect. But come back soon to take the quiz.

extra credit

Making a character style by QuickStyling

The WordPerfect QuickStyle feature is an easy way to make a style. All you do is follow these steps:

1 **Format some text.**

2 **With your cursor in the formatted text, click on the Select Style button on the Power Bar, and choose QuickStyle.**

After you choose the QuickStyle option, the QuickStyle dialog box appears (see Figure 9-6).

3 **In the Style name box, type the name you want to use for the style, for example,** Jargon.

All styles need names, which must be 12 or fewer characters. Names have to be unique, so you can't give a new style the name of a style that already exists. You can also give the style a description — for example, *Used for titles and other large headings*. This description is optional — you can skip it this time.

4 **Click on Character to tell WordPerfect that this is a character style.**

A character style can format characters and can contain formatting that applies to characters. It can't contain formatting that applies to paragraphs (like line and paragraph spacing) or pages or documents (like margins). You use character styles to format words and phrases within paragraphs rather than entire paragraphs.

5 **Click on OK to return to the document.**

WordPerfect creates the Jargon style in this document. To use this style to format other words and phrases, select the text to be formatted, click on the Select Style button on the Power Bar, and choose the name of the style.

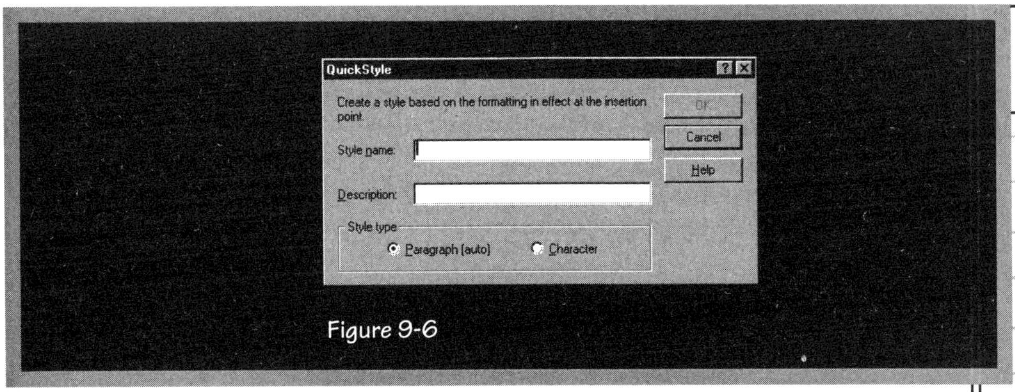

Figure 9-6

Figure 9-6: The QuickStyle dialog box.

For each of the following questions, circle the letter of the correct answer or answers. Remember, we may have included more than one right answer for each question!

1. **What does this button do?**

   A. Types a *B*.

   B. Makes characters look darker than usual.

   C. Tells WordPerfect that it's time for breakfast.

   D. Applies bold formatting to characters.

   E. Causes the spoken word "Bingo!" to come out of the computer's speaker.

2. **What is a font?**

   A. An old-fashioned fountain.

   B. A source; for example, this book is a *font* of information.

   C. A set of shapes for letters, numbers, and punctuation.

   D. A choice on the Font button menu.

   E. The name of a WordPerfect dialog box.

3. **If you click on the Font button and choose a different font when your cursor is in the middle of a document . . .**

   A. The default font for the document changes.

   B. The font changes from that point until another font code is encountered.

   C. The font changes for the line of text where the cursor is.

   D. You create a new font — a combination of the document default font and the new font chosen.

   E. You'll get nothing for dinner.

4. **In WordPerfect, font size is measured in . . .**

A. Feet.

B. 72nds of an inch.

C. Points.

D. Miles.

E. Furlongs per fortnight.

 5. **Which button is this?**

A. Paint Me a Picture.

B. QuickFormat.

C. Apply Wallpaper.

D. Warning! Exploding Letters!

E. Spell Checker.

6. **What does QuickFormat do?**

A. Guesses how you want to format your text and does it quickly.

B. Quickly copies character and paragraph formatting.

C. Remembers the formatting of the selected text and applies it to other text that you select.

D. Formats your text like a duck.

E. No one knows.

Unit 9 Exercise

You've decided to hold a yard sale. Make a flyer with the appropriate formatting.

1. Create a new document in WordPerfect by closing any document that is open.

2. Type your name and address and information about a yard sale that you're thinking of holding. Alternatively, type your company's name and address and information about an upcoming marketing seminar.

3. Choose a default font for the document.

4. Format your name (or your company's name) in a nice-looking font, and make it big.

5. Format the other lines of the document so that they stand out but are still readable.

6. Save your document.

7. Print your document.

8. Pass the printout around to impress people with your formatting skills.

Secrets of Formatting: Using WordPerfect Codes

Objectives for This Unit

- ✓ Knowing what codes are
- ✓ Using the Reveal Codes window
- ✓ Deleting codes
- ✓ Fixing formatting problems
- ✓ Editing codes

Prerequisites
- ◗ Opening an existing document (Lesson 2-2)
- ◗ Using dialog boxes (Lesson 2-3)
- ◗ Making your text bold, italicized, and underlined (Lesson 9-1)
- ◗ Using different fonts and sizes (Lesson 9-2)

on the CD
- ◗ Toy Letter2. 101.wpd
- ◗ Proposal.wpd
- ◗ Proposal4.101.wpd
- ◗ Catalog Promo Letter.101.wpd
- ◗ Flyer.101.wpd

We hear that the folks at WordPerfect were tempted to require membership in a secret club before allowing you to use any formatting commands, keystrokes, or buttons, but instead they settled for putting secret codes in your documents. Just like a secret club, codes have their hassles and benefits. The hassles include dealing with cryptic codes (quick, guess what *HRt* means!) and having to be careful where your cursor is when you give formatting commands (because you can't see where the formatting codes are unless you open up a special window to see them). The benefits of WordPerfect codes include being able to clearly see how WordPerfect is formatting your document and being able to fix your documents when the formatting gets screwy (which is truly WordPerfect's advantage over its major competitor).

So what are these codes, anyway? Codes are what WordPerfect uses to turn special features on and off. WordPerfect has three kinds of codes:

- ◗ **Character codes:** Represent a special character such as Tab or a soft hyphen.
- ◗ **Single codes:** Turn a feature on or change formatting starting at the point in the document where the code is (for example, changing the font). WordPerfect usually inserts the code wherever the cursor is when you give the command, click on the button, or press the keys that create the code. In some cases, WordPerfect sticks the code at the beginning of the line, paragraph, page, or document where the cursor is.

Left Tab

this is a character code

Font: Arial

this is a single code

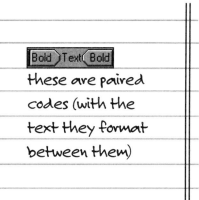

these are paired codes (with the text they format between them)

▶ **Paired codes:** (WordPerfect calls these revertible codes — we won't.) One to turn a feature on and one to turn it off again. When you make text bold, for example, by using either the Bold button on the Toolbar or pressing Ctrl+B, WordPerfect sticks two codes into your document: One code turns bold on, and another turns it off. If text is selected, WordPerfect puts the codes at the beginning and the end of the selected text. If no text is selected, WordPerfect puts the codes on either side of the cursor so that whatever you type next comes between the two codes. Some formatting codes can be paired or single, depending on how you format the text.

Don't get nervous — this detail all sounds kind of technical, but the fact is that you rarely have to deal with codes. Knowing how codes work makes understanding how formatting commands work easier and gives you the power to untangle your document when the formatting goes awry.

Lesson 10-1   Seeing the Codes in Your Document

View→Reveal Codes to see formatting codes

WordPerfect provides you with a special little window at the bottom of the WordPerfect window in which to view all these special codes. You may be staring in confusion at your WordPerfect screen, wondering where this window is — the answer is, it's not there yet. And the way to view it is a secret — just kidding! To see the Reveal Codes window, you choose View⇨Reveal Codes from the menu bar, making your screen look something like Figure 10-1. When you open the Toy Letter.wpd document, you see the regular view of the document in the typing area, and the codes in the Reveal Codes window.

In the Reveal Codes window, WordPerfect displays the text of your document, with the formatting codes and special characters visible. Each of the rectangles in the Reveal Codes window represents a code. For example, the first code in Figure 10-1 is an Open Style code, a code that determines how the overall document is formatted. The next code in Figure 10-1 is a Left Tab code — you guessed it! It's a tab. You also see regular old characters, like letters and punctuation. Spaces appear as little diamonds, and carriage returns (line endings) appear as HRt (which stands for *hard return*) codes. Carriage returns that WordPerfect puts in to end lines appear as SRt (which stands for *soft return*). WordPerfect puts in soft codes such as returns and hyphens (if you use hyphenation) and moves them around as needed. The cursor appears as a red block in the Reveal Codes window. It corresponds with the cursor in the regular typing window — they move together.

In Unit 9, you learned how to create lots of different codes to format your documents — codes to turn bold, italics, and underline on and off and codes to change the font. Most of the time, you don't need to look at them in the Reveal Codes window, but the codes are hiding there, waiting for you to take a peek!

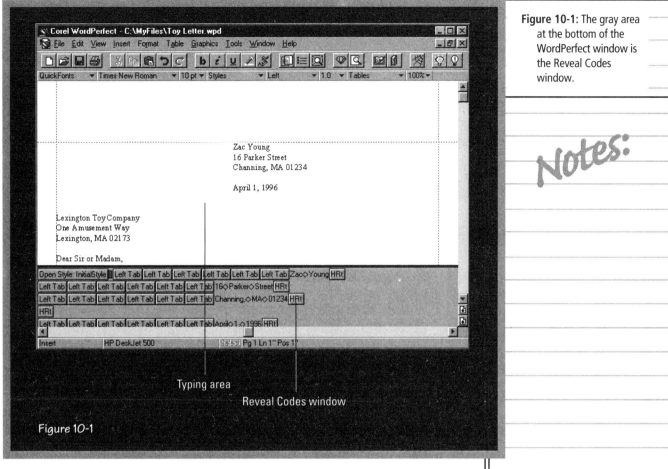

Typing area

Reveal Codes window

Figure 10-1

Reveal your codes in one of the following ways (and see the extra credit sidebar if neither of these methods appeals to you):

- Press Alt+F3.
- Choose View⇨Reveal Codes.

Make the Reveal Codes window disappear by giving the same command again.

Alt+F3 also shows formatting codes

Alt+F3 again to make codes disappear

Notes:

More ways to reveal codes

As usual, WordPerfect gives you lots of ways to give commands. Any of these methods displays the Reveal Codes window:

- Choose View➪Reveal Codes from the menu bar.

- Press Alt+F3.

- Click the *right* mouse button anywhere in the Typing area and choose Reveal Codes from the QuickMenu that appears.

- Put your mouse pointer in the black space at the top or bottom of the scroll bar. The mouse pointer turns into a double-headed arrow. Click and drag the pointer to somewhere in the middle of the Typing area. (The exact position determines how big your Reveal Codes window is.)

Following are lots of ways to make the Reveal Codes window go away:

- Choose View➪Reveal Codes.

- Press Alt+F3.

- Click and drag the dividing line between the typing area and the Reveal Codes window to the top or bottom of the typing area.

- Click anywhere in the Reveal Codes window with the *right* mouse button and choose Hide Reveal Codes (which seems a little contradictory).

- Click in the regular part of the screen with the *right* mouse button and choose Reveal Codes (to make the check mark beside it disappear).

Choose your favorite method and stick with it!

Now we dive into the World of WordPerfect Codes!

Revealing codes

To see some codes, start by opening a document that doesn't have much formatting in it and looking at what appears in the Reveal Codes window.

on the CD

1 **Open Toy Letter.wpd, the letter to the toy company that you wrote in Lesson 1-3.**

If you didn't follow the steps in Lesson 1-3 and don't have a document named Toy Letter.wpd, open Toy Letter2.101.wpd, which we provide, instead.

2 **Reveal your secret codes by choosing View➪Reveal Codes from the menu bar or by pressing Alt+F3.**

At the bottom of your WordPerfect window appears a gray area with some text and a lot of little boxes with letters in them. This area is the Reveal Codes window (you see it in Figure 10-1).

3 **Yell, "Aaarghhh!"**

Codes can seem difficult in this day and age when computers are supposed to work for us! But then look carefully at the Reveal Codes window and you'll see that it's not so complicated — it's just another view of your document. Your text is there, but also you see lots of boxes, which are codes. The red block is your cursor.

4 **Move down in the document until your cursor is at the beginning of the second paragraph in the body of the letter.**

Use your favorite method for moving around in a document. Be sure to move the cursor, not just the mouse pointer.

One piece of advice: as you move, don't watch the Reveal Codes window — watch the regular typing area instead (as a dancing teacher once said to the men in a class, "Don't watch the women; they'll just confuse you!"). The exception is when you're trying to move to a specific code, but if you're moving to specific text, watch the window with just text.

5 **Now notice the codes in this part of the letter.**

First, find your cursor in the Reveal Codes area. Notice that at the end of each line is a SRt code (*Soft Return,* which is what WordPerfect puts in when you type past the end of a line). Also notice how hyphens appear — as -Hyphen codes (which seem a bit redundant).

6 **After you've seen enough, get rid of the Reveal Codes window by choosing View➪Reveal Codes again or pressing Alt+F3.**

The Reveal Codes window disappears, and the WordPerfect window returns to its familiar state.

7 **Close the Toy Letter.wpd (or Toy Letter2.101.wpd) document by choosing File➪Close from the menu bar.**

You haven't made any changes, so you don't need to save it.

WordPerfect's most popular codes

The Reveal Codes window lets you see how WordPerfect formats your document. So far, you've seen some basic codes. Table 10-1 shows some of the codes that you're most likely to run across in your documents and that you'll be working with in the rest of this unit.

Table 10-1	Codes You See Frequently
Code	**Meaning**
HRt	Hard return (you create it when you press Enter)
SRt	Soft Return (WordPerfect creates it automagically when text goes past the end of a line)
Tab	Various different types of tab stops exist, as you see in Unit 11
Font	Specifies font (typeface) in use for text after the code
Font Size	Specifies the size of the letters
Lft Margin	Defines white space on the left of the paper
Rgt Margin	Defines white space on the right of the paper
HPg	Hard page break (you create it when you press Ctrl+Enter to start a new page)
SPg	Soft page break (WordPerfect creates it when you type past the end of a page)

(continued)

Notes:

Notes:

Table 10-1	(continued)
Code	**Meaning**
Just	Specifies whether text is flush left, centered, flush right, or justified
Bold	Makes text bold
Und	Makes text underlined
Italc	Makes text italicized

on the test

Many codes are either *hard* or *soft*. This distinction is as follows:

- *Hard* codes are those that you type. WordPerfect never deletes these codes until you specifically tell it to. For example, pressing Enter creates a HRt (Hard Return) code, and pressing Ctrl+Enter creates a HPg (Hard Page) code.

- *Soft* codes are usually created by WordPerfect to make the text flow properly. For example, WordPerfect's word wrap feature inserts Soft Return codes (SRt) when you type past the end of a line and Soft Page codes (SPg) when you type past the bottom of a page. WordPerfect may put them in and take them out at will. As you edit a paragraph, for example, WordPerfect inserts and deletes Soft Return codes so that your lines are all about the same length.

Looking at formatting codes

Most documents have more codes than the Toy Letter.wpd letter because they contain more formatting (and you thought that Toy Letter had plenty!). Take a look at another document: Proposal.101.wpd (or Proposal4.101.wpd, if you didn't do Unit 9).

on the CD

1 **Open Proposal.101.wpd, which you see in Figure 10-2.**

Looks nice, doesn't it? This document uses lots of fancy fonts, using methods you learned in Unit 9.

2 **Display the Reveal Codes window by pressing Alt+F3 or choosing View⇨Reveal Codes from the menu bar.**

3 **Now take a deep breath and look at the codes in this document.**

Move the cursor around to see more. (Remember, familiarity breeds contempt, which is probably better than what you're feeling right now!) You may immediately notice codes you haven't seen before. Among them are Font (which tells WordPerfect which font to use), Font Size, and Bold.

4 **Move your cursor around the document. Notice that some codes have blunt points rather than being simple rectangles; these are paired codes.**

The blunt points indicate beginnings (when the point faces right) and ends (when the point faces left) of formatting.

codes with blunt points are paired

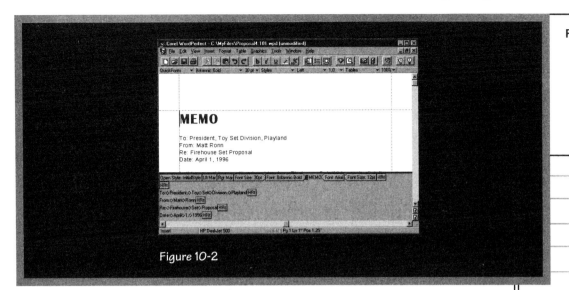

Figure 10-2

Figure 10-2: Here is Proposal.101.wpd, with the character formatting codes that you added in the last unit revealed in the Reveal Codes window.

5 Make the Reveal Codes window bigger by clicking and dragging the top border of the Reveal Codes window up.

Move your pointer around near the border between the Typing area and the Reveal Codes window until the pointer turns into a double-ended arrow. Then click the mouse button and hold it down. You can now move the border up or down, making the Reveal Codes window larger or smaller. Release the mouse button to leave the window border where it is.

Intuitively, if you move the border all the way to the bottom of the Typing area, the Reveal Codes window disappears. Counter-intuitively, if you move the border all the way to the top of the Typing area, the Reveal Codes window still disappears, instead of taking up the whole window.

6 Move your cursor back to the beginning of the document by pressing Ctrl+Home.

Notice that you don't get to the beginning of the codes; you just get to the beginning of the text.

7 Now move your cursor to the right one step at a time.

Things get very interesting: As you move the cursor with the Reveal Codes window open, the cursor moves one step at a time through the *codes*. If you look in the Typing area, you may have to press the right-arrow key several times before the cursor moves to the next letter.

Using the arrow keys is the best way to move through the Reveal Codes window (you can also use PgUp and PgDn). You can use the mouse to position your cursor in the Reveal Codes window, but often, positioning the cursor in the regular window and then using the arrow keys is easier.

8 Move the cursor to the beginning of the word Memo. **Move the cursor to the left, one character at a time, and notice that some codes, when they're to the right of the cursor, expand to show you more detail.**

For example, when the cursor is to the left of the Margin code, the code expands to tell you exactly what the margin setting is. You can't actually move the cursor to the left of the initial style code, but the code does expand when you press the left arrow to move the cursor there — in fact, the cursor is still to the right of the code.

☑ Progress Check

If you can do the following, you've mastered this lesson:

❑ Reveal codes.

❑ Recognize a code from regular text in the Reveal Codes window.

❑ Learn more about a code by positioning the red block cursor to the left of it.

❑ Change the size of the Reveal Codes window.

9 **After you've seen enough, get rid of the Reveal Codes window by choosing <u>V</u>iew⇨Reveal <u>C</u>odes from the menu bar or pressing Alt+F3.**

The Reveal Codes window disappears, leaving you with simple, comforting text.

10 **Close the document by choosing <u>F</u>ile⇨<u>C</u>lose from the menu bar.**

You've looked at advanced formatting codes using the Reveal Codes window, moved your cursor in the Reveal Codes window, learned how to see more detail about a code, and expanded the Reveal Codes window.

Lesson 10-2   Deleting Codes

Understanding codes is important because they can really make a mess of your document. If they're in the wrong places, codes can create formatting havoc. Looking at them can help you figure out what happened.

Something to be aware of is that WordPerfect usually inserts the code where your cursor is when you give a formatting command. Codes are inserted at the cursor when you give commands for margin changes, font changes, changes in tab settings, and other formatting commands. Entering codes throughout the document can be useful, but sometimes the result is not what you expect. If you enter a code in the wrong place, looking at codes helps you figure out what's up with your document. Better still, it may enable you to impress your colleagues by figuring out how to fix *their* documents.

If you find during the course of typing and editing your documents that something is formatted wrong or acts peculiar, you need to look at the codes in your document. Maybe your tabs aren't acting like they used to, or suddenly you notice your left margin shifted a smidgen in the middle of your document. To fix the formatting in your document, you need to either delete a code or alter it. This lesson describes how to delete codes, and the next lesson describes how to alter them.

heads up

Saving your document before you do too much with codes is a good idea — messing things up is easy. Save the document by pressing Ctrl+S. If you mess things up, close your document without saving and open the document again. You get the version that you saved before you started playing with codes.

Lesson 9-2 describes how to change fonts in the middle of your document. When you use the Font and Font Size buttons (or the Font dialog box), WordPerfect creates codes named *Font* and *Font Size*. If a Font or Font Size code creeps into the middle of your document, it can make things look strange. And figuring out what's wrong can be hard!

Often, what you need to do is delete a misplaced code. WordPerfect has at least three ways to do that when you have the Reveal Codes window open and you've found the code that you want to delete:

◆ Move the cursor immediately before the code and press Delete.

◆ Move the cursor immediately after the code and press Backspace.

Delete and Backspace delete codes

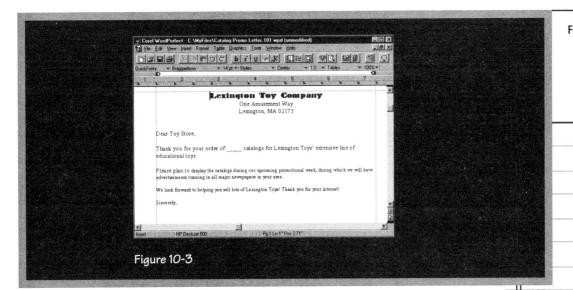

Figure 10-3

Figure 10-3: A bogus Font Size code has crept into the Catalog Promo Letter.101.wpd document!

♦ Click on the code and drag it to somewhere outside the Reveal Codes window (codes die from lack of oxygen when they leave the Reveal Codes window).

Now take a look at a document with an error in it — it's the Case of the Misplaced Code.

on the CD

1 **Open Catalog Promo Letter.101.wpd, which you see in Figure 10-3.**

2 **Notice that halfway through the second paragraph, the type size suddenly changes.**

The second paragraph in the body of the letter switches from 12- to 10-point type, right after the words *Please plan to*, and it looks terrible. Someone must have clicked the Font Size button by accident.

3 **Reveal codes by pressing Alt+F3 or choosing View⇨Reveal Codes or using your favorite method.**

4 **Move your cursor to the place where the font size changes.**

The easiest way to find where the size changes is to move the cursor while watching the Font Size button.

Look for the Font Size code where the type gets smaller, right after the words *Please plan to* in the second paragraph.

You know that you're looking for a font size code because you can see that the problem is differing font size. Some codes (those that control the way an entire paragraph looks) are always at the beginning of a paragraph, making them a little easier to find. Character formatting codes can appear anywhere in a paragraph, so they can be tricky to find.

The author of this letter may have wanted to change the font size for the whole letter but forgot to move the cursor to the beginning of the letter. You can fix the problem with a stroke of a key.

5 **Delete the Font Size code by looking in the Reveal Codes window and moving the red block cursor immediately before it. Then press Delete to delete the code.**

The font size in the second part of the letter changes to match the font in the first part of the document.

or drag code outside window to delete

Alternatively, you can also move the cursor to the position immediately after the code and press Backspace. And perhaps the funnest way to delete a code is to click on it and drag it out of the Reveal Codes window.

6 Close the document by choosing File⇨Close from the menu bar. Go ahead and save the changes to the document — you improved it significantly.

Congratulations! You found a problem, looked for the code that caused it, and deleted the code.

Following are a few other notes about deleting codes:

heads up

▸ When you're in the Reveal Codes window, you can easily delete a code. When the Reveal Codes window isn't visible, WordPerfect usually doesn't let you delete codes: it just skips over them and deletes the next visible character.

▸ When you delete a paired code, you only have to delete one. The other disappears, too — it dies of grief, we suppose. For example, if you delete the Bold code at the beginning of a section of bold text, the Bold code at the end disappears, too.

extra credit

Searching for codes

You may find that looking for codes using your eyes and the Reveal Codes window is just too frustrating. WordPerfect offers another way. You can use Edit⇨Find and Replace to find a code, or to find it and replace it with a different code or with nothing.

After you see the Find and Replace Text dialog box, WordPerfect has two ways to look for codes: using the Type⇨Specific Codes command and using the Match⇨Codes command, both chosen from the menu bar at the top of the Find and Replace Text dialog box.

If you want to look for a code that contains specific settings, use the Type⇨Specific Codes command. For example, you can search for Font Size codes that set the size to exactly 12-point and replace them all with Font Size codes that set the size to 14-point. If you want to look for a code regardless of its specific settings, use the Match⇨Codes command. For example, you can search for all Font Size codes.

Both commands display additional dialog boxes where you can specify the code that you're looking for and its settings.

delete one paired code and both disappear

☑ Progress Check

If you can do the following, you've mastered this lesson:

❑ Find a problematic code in the Reveal Codes window.

❑ Delete a code.

Lesson 10-3

Altering Codes

To create many codes, you give a command that displays a dialog box. You choose settings in that dialog box and click on OK — voilà! A code! For example, you can create Font and Font Size codes using the Font dialog box.

What if you want to change the information in the code? For example, if you create a Margin code that changes the margins to 1 inch on each side and you want to change them to 1.5 inches later, how do you edit the code?

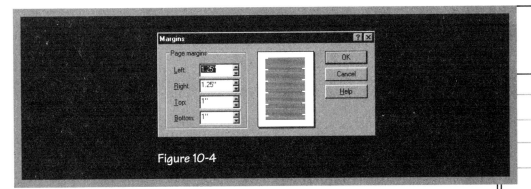

Figure 10-4

Figure 10-4: The Margins dialog box lets you set all the margins.

Notes:

By double-clicking on most codes, you can display the same dialog box you use to create the code in the first place (or the dialog box you bypassed by using a Toolbar or Power Bar button). By changing the settings in the dialog box, you change the code. This procedure is better than creating a new code with different settings because you don't end up with extra formatting codes lying around in your document.

heads up

Don't try changing paired codes (for example, a line or two that has a different font) by using the double-clicking method — WordPerfect just doesn't act the way you'd expect. Instead, select the text and apply the new formatting to it.

Changing a Margin code

Try changing a Margin code setting by double-clicking on the code. Follow these steps to make the margins in the Proposal document a little smaller.

on the CD

1 **Open Proposal.101.wpd or Proposal4.101.wpd again.**

You see it in Figure 10-2.

2 **Reveal your codes by choosing View⇨Reveal Codes or by pressing Alt+F3.**

3 **Find the Rgt Mar (Right Margin) code.**

It's very near the beginning of the document. In fact, it's a few codes to the left of the red box that represents your cursor in the Reveal Codes window.

4 **Double-click on the Rgt Mar code.**

WordPerfect displays the Margin dialog box (Figure 10-4).

5 **Change the left and right margins to 1.05".**

Select the current value and type the new margin sizes or use the arrows to select smaller values.

If you change the margins to be the same as the default value (1"), the margin codes will disappear completely — they're not needed anymore.

6 **Click on OK or press Enter to close the Margin dialog box.**

The dialog box closes and the code changes.

7 **Close and save the document.**

☑ Progress Check

If you can do the following, you're ready to move on to the next lesson:

❑ Double-click on a code in the Reveal Codes window.

❑ Alter a Margin code using the Margins dialog box.

If you double-click on a code in the Reveal Codes window by mistake and you see an unexpected dialog box appear on your screen, you can always press Escape to make it go away.

In this lesson, you learned how to change a code (and therefore the formatting of the document) by double-clicking to display the dialog box and changing values in the dialog box.

Recess

Congratulations! You are now a member of the Mystical WordPerfect Codes Cabal. The secrets of the codes are known only to an initiated few — use them wisely. In fact, you might want to quit WordPerfect and take a walk to let your head clear. Choose File➪Exit to leave the WordPerfect Codes Zone.

Unit 10 Quiz

For each of the following questions, circle the letter of the correct answer or answers. Remember, we may include more than one right answer for each question!

1. **WordPerfect codes are . . .**

   A. Confusing — you need a secret decoder ring to decipher them.

   B. Visible in the Reveal Codes window.

   C. Formatting commands stored in your document.

   D. Useful in figuring out snafued documents.

   E. Better than sex.

2. **To display the Reveal Codes window . . .**

   A. Light a candle, dim the lights, and intone a special incantation.

   B. Press Alt+F3.

   C. Choose View➪Reveal Codes.

   D. Click the right mouse button and choose Reveal Codes from the QuickMenu that appears.

   E. Click and drag the black bar at the top or bottom of the scroll bar.

3. **To delete a code . . .**

   A. Press Delete anytime you think you're near one.

   B. Click and drag it out of the Reveal Codes window.

   C. With the Reveal Codes window open, press Delete or Backspace when the red cursor is immediately before or after the code.

   D. Delete its partner.

   E. Yell that you would like it to leave . . . please.

4. **Matt's Firehouse Set features. . .**

    A. A full-size operative ladder truck.

    B. Captain Kate.

    C. Firefighters rescuing a cat from a tree.

    D. Chief Matt.

    E. No fair testing on content.

5. **You can tell which codes are paired, because . . .**

    A. The codes gaze longingly at each other.

    B. Both codes have the same name (for example, both say *Bold*).

    C. The codes aren't rectangular in the Reveal Codes window: Instead, they have pointed ends that point toward each other.

    D. The codes are right next to each other.

    E. The first code appears where formatting starts, and the second code appears where it ends.

Unit 10 Exercise

1. Open the document Flyer.101.wpd. It's a flyer about a toy show, suitable for posting on bulletin boards (see the following figure).

2. Delete most of the Font and Font Size codes from the document. (The funnest way is to drag each code out of the Reveal Codes window, making the code vanish.)

3. Using the Font and Font Size commands that you learned in Unit 9, format the flyer with the fonts and sizes of your choice. Remember, it's about a toy show, so go wild (but not *too* wild — using more than two or three fonts makes documents look amateurish).

    (**Hint:** If you want to center a line, put your cursor at the beginning of the line and press Shift+F7. You learn this officially in Unit 11, but we thought we'd sneak it in here.)

4. Save the flyer.

5. (Optional) Print the newly formatted flyer.

Formatting Lines and Paragraphs

Objectives for This Unit

- ✓ Setting spacing between lines and paragraphs
- ✓ Setting margins
- ✓ Indenting paragraphs
- ✓ Left-, right-, and center-justifying text
- ✓ Setting tab stops

Prerequisites
- ▶ Opening documents (Lesson 2-2)
- ▶ Selecting text (Lesson 5-1)
- ▶ Using WordPerfect codes (Unit 10)

- ▶ Policy.101.wpd
- ▶ Policy2.101.wpd
- ▶ Policy3.101.wpd
- ▶ Proposal.101.wpd
- ▶ Proposal4.101.wpd
- ▶ Tour Group.101.wpd
- ▶ History of Circuses2.101.wpd

on the CD

This unit covers how to format your lines and paragraphs, how to make tables using tabs, and how to change the position of text on the page. Many of these features are useful when your term paper has to be a certain length and your favorite TV show is on in 20 minutes.

For most of the topics in this unit, it's useful to see the ruler bar, which you see in Figure 11-1. The ruler bar sits below the Power Bar (which is below the Toolbar, which is below the menu bar). WordPerfect may not display it — you might have to ask for it by choosing View⇨Toolbars/Ruler, clicking on Ruler Bar, and clicking on OK or by pressing Alt+Shift+F3. The ruler bar shows you the tabs and margins that are in effect in your document where the cursor is (and because you haven't learned how to change tabs and margins yet, they should be the settings throughout the document). If you get tired of having the ruler bar fill valuable typing space, make it go away by using the same command that displayed it.

The ruler bar shows you tabs and margins. Using your mouse and the ruler bar, you can change tab and margin settings. But as with everything else in WordPerfect, you have more than one way to do these things — you can change tabs and margin settings by using commands and dialog boxes, too.

Alt+Shift+F3 to show ruler bar or make it disappear

Figure 11-1: The ruler bar rules the world of tabs and margins.

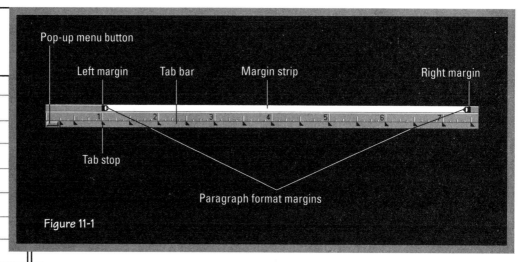

Figure 11-1: The ruler bar rules the world of tabs and margins.

Pop-up menu button

Left margin   Tab bar   Margin strip   Right margin

Tab stop

Paragraph format margins

Figure 11-1

The ruler bar has three parts:

on the test

▶ **The margin strip:** The white strip that sits above the ruler. The dark, outside markers show you the *left and right margins* (look at them before you load a document — they're probably set at 1 inch and 7.5 inches). The tiny black triangles just inside the margin markers on the margin strip show the *paragraph format margins*.

▶ **The ruler:** Marks off the page in eighths of an inch.

▶ **The tab bar:** Shows *tab stops* with differently shaped triangles. A tab stop is where the cursor goes when you press the Tab key — tabs allow you to align text vertically on the page. The triangles that appear on the ruler bar in Figure 11-1 show the positions of normal tab stops — every half inch. Other types of triangles show where right tabs, decimal tabs, and other types of tab stops appear. Don't worry — you find out about them in this unit.

Now that you are familiar with the ruler bar, let's fool around with formatting lines and paragraphs, starting with setting the vertical spacing.

ruler bar shows margins and tab stops

Lesson 11-1

Setting Spacing between Lines and Paragraphs

If you write for a teacher or an editor, you probably have to double-space your text to leave space for extra comments and corrections. (Not that you ever make a mistake!) As always, WordPerfect offers more than one way to change the line spacing in your document. The easiest way — the Line Spacing button on the Power Bar — takes care of the most frequently used options (single, double, and somewhere in between), and the Line Spacing dialog box can do all that and much, much more.

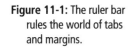

Line Spacing button on Power Bar

Alternatively, you may want to set spacing between your paragraphs. Many people like to leave one blank line between paragraphs. Rather than press Enter an extra time when you end a paragraph, you can tell WordPerfect to leave an extra line between paragraphs. You tell WordPerfect how you want to space paragraphs by using the Paragraph Format dialog box.

heads up

Pay attention to where your cursor is when you change the spacing in a document — WordPerfect inserts a Spacing code at the cursor, and that affects the text that comes after it. If you want to change the line spacing for a section of text rather than the whole document, you can select text before changing the spacing: WordPerfect inserts Spacing codes before and after the selected text.

on the test

Here's the best way to set spacing: Put a Spacing code at the beginning of the document that applies to most of the text in the document. For paragraphs that need different spacing, select them and change their spacing. In fact, this works for nearly any kind of formatting, not just line spacing.

Changing line spacing with the Power Bar

In this exercise, you change the spacing in a policy statement to double spacing, using the Policy.101.wpd document.

on the CD

1 **Load Policy.101.wpd, which you see in Figure 11-2.**

2 **With the cursor at the tippy-top (use Ctrl+Home to get there if you need to), click on the Line Spacing button on the Power Bar.**

The Line Spacing button is the one with a number on it, usually 1.0 (for single spacing). When you click on it, a menu drops down with four choices: 1.0, 1.5, 2.0, and Other.

3 **Click on 2.0 to double-space the text after the cursor.**

2.0 means double-spacing — one blank line is left between every line of text. Your text should now need twice as much paper to print.

4 **Delete the extra lines between paragraphs.**

The lines between paragraphs have been doubled, too, and have left too large a space between paragraphs.

The Line Spacing button on the Power Bar is the easiest way to change the spacing of your text. When you use double spacing, you can't move your cursor to the blank lines between the lines of the text: they're off limits.

heads up

Note that if you create extra blank lines between your paragraphs, WordPerfect double-spaces them, too, so that you have huge gaps. To avoid these gaps, don't press Enter twice at the end of a paragraph. If you want additional space between paragraphs, see the section "Setting the format for your paragraphs" later in this lesson.

Using the Line Spacing dialog box

The Line Spacing button on the Power Bar is the easiest way to change spacing if you want single, double, or one-and-a-half line spacing. But if you want to specify a different value for line spacing — say, 1.7, because that's what your weird company requires — you can (fortunately for your job security). But the line spacing button isn't going to do the job — you need the Line Spacing dialog box, which appears in Figure 11-3.

Notes:

click on Line Spacing button to change spacing

Figure 11-2: The Policy.101.wpd document.

Figure 11-3: The Line Spacing dialog box.

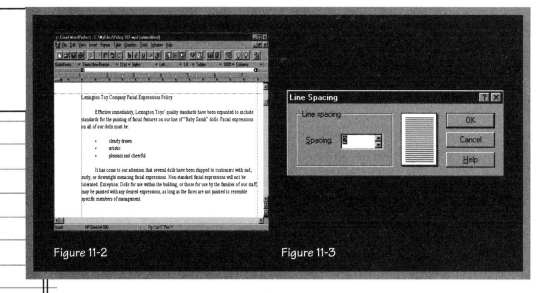

Figure 11-2   Figure 11-3

Display the Line Spacing dialog box by

- ◗ Double-clicking on the Line Spacing button
- ◗ Clicking on the Line Spacing button and choosing Other
- ◗ Choosing Format⇨Line⇨Spacing from the menu

Now change the spacing of the bullet points in Policy.101.wpd:

1 Select all the lines that start with a bullet.

These are short, one-line paragraphs in the middle of the document.

2 Display the Line Spacing dialog box by double-clicking on the Line Spacing button.

Or click on the Line Spacing button and choose Other, or choose Format⇨Line⇨Spacing from the menu. Whichever method you use, WordPerfect displays the Line Spacing dialog box in Figure 11-3.

3 Change the value in the Spacing box to 1.2.

Use the arrows or just type the new value.

4 Click on OK.

The dialog box goes away, and the line spacing of the selected text changes. You may want to add an extra carriage return after the bullet points.

5 Close the Policy.101.wpd document, saving your changes.

When you need to change the line spacing to something other than single, double, and one-and-a-half line spacing, use the Line Spacing dialog box.

Setting the format for your paragraphs

If you always indent the beginning of each paragraph and put an extra line between paragraphs, WordPerfect can do this work for you. Rather than press Tab at the beginning of each paragraph and Enter an extra time at the end of each paragraph, you can tell WordPerfect how you like your paragraphs formatted — all you have to do is press Enter once at the end of each para-

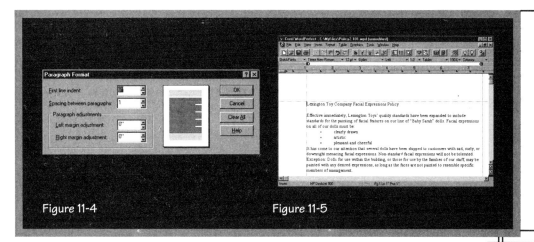

Figure 11-4: The Paragraph Format dialog box lets you tell WordPerfect how you want each paragraph to look.

Figure 11-5: Policy2.101.wpd has no blank lines between paragraphs. You can tell WordPerfect to leave space between paragraphs automagically.

graph. The most important advantage to this automation is that if you change your mind, say, about indenting the beginning of each paragraph, you only have to change one WordPerfect setting instead of going through your document deleting the tab at the beginning of each paragraph. Another advantage is that it saves you keystrokes: when you press Enter, indicating to WordPerfect that you've ended a paragraph, WordPerfect automagically puts in an extra line and indents the next paragraph!

Take a look at the Paragraph Format dialog box, where you tell WordPerfect how you want paragraphs to look. Display the Paragraph Format dialog box by choosing Format⇨Paragraph⇨Format from the menu bar (sounds redundant to us). Figure 11-4 shows the Paragraph Format dialog box.

on the CD

You can format the paragraphs in Policy2.101.wpd to be indented and have one line between paragraphs. It's the same as Policy.101.wpd without extra blank lines between the paragraphs.

1 **Open Policy2.101.wpd and make sure that your cursor is at the top of the document.**

The document appears in Figure 11-5.

If you make changes in the Paragraph Format dialog box settings with the cursor halfway through the document, you affect only the paragraph that the cursor is in and the ones after it. So get that cursor up to the top!

2 **Display the Paragraph Format dialog box by choosing Format⇨Paragraph⇨Format from the menu bar.**

The Paragraph Format dialog box, which you can see in Figure 11-4, has four options. It usually makes the most sense to use the first two, First line indent and Spacing between paragraphs, to format all the paragraphs in a document. (Do so by displaying and changing the settings on this dialog box when the cursor is at the top of the document.) The two Paragraph adjustments settings are more often used for indenting one or more paragraphs somewhere in the middle of a document — for example, for a quote.

3 **Change the First line indent setting to 0.500".**

That is, tell WordPerfect to indent the first line of each paragraph by half an inch. This indent is the equivalent of putting a tab at the beginning of each paragraph.

You can do so by selecting the current setting and typing **.5**, or by clicking on the up arrow button next to the setting until it reads .500". Don't press Enter after you're finished, though, because the dialog box will disappear — instead, press Tab to move to the next setting on the dialog box.

[handwritten margin notes:]
use Paragraph Format dialog box to set paragraph spacing and indent

display Paragraph Format dialog box by choosing Format→Paragraph→Format from the menu bar

Notes:

4 Change the Spacing between paragraphs setting to 2.

You're telling WordPerfect to double-space your paragraphs (not the lines within paragraphs). This value leaves a whole blank line between paragraphs (a value of 1.5 would leave half a blank line between paragraphs).

5 Click on OK.

The dialog box goes away, and the paragraphs in the document are instantly indented and more widely spaced. For most of the document, the indentation looks great, but the title is indented, too, and it looks downright strange.

6 Select the title of the document, which shouldn't be indented.

As with most formatting, you can change the format of the whole document by giving the formatting command when the cursor is at the beginning of the document (which puts in a single code), and then correct selected parts of the document by selecting those parts, giving the formatting command again and correcting the settings (which puts in paired codes).

7 Display the Paragraph Format dialog box again by choosing Format⇨Paragraph⇨Format from the menu bar.

The dialog box appears with the settings that you just entered because these are the settings that are in effect for the paragraphs you selected.

8 Change the First line indent setting back to 0, and the Spacing between paragraphs to 1.

This changes the settings to what you want to use for the selected text.

9 Click on OK.

Now the title is no longer indented and double spaced.

10 Press Ctrl+S to save your improvements to the Policy2.101.wpd document.

The Paragraph Format dialog box allows you to tell WordPerfect how you want paragraphs to look. If you prefer to indent your paragraphs manually, make sure that you use the Tab key to do so, and not spaces. Using spaces marks you as a word-processing tyro, and besides, like using the Paragraph Format dialog box, using tabs gives you the advantage of being able to make a change just once to affect the indentation of every paragraph. If you change the location of the tab stop, all the text that has a tab in it moves to the new tab stop. (Lesson 11-4 covers setting tab stops.)

☑ Progress Check

If you can do the following, you've mastered this lesson:

❑ Change the line spacing of your whole document.

❑ Change the spacing of a few paragraphs.

❑ Change the spacing between paragraphs.

❑ Automatically indent the first line of each paragraph.

extra credit

Making a fancy first letter

A great way to jazz up the first paragraph of a document, or of each section of a document, is to make the first letter bigger. You have a *drop cap* when the first letter of a paragraph is at least twice as big as the rest of the letters in the paragraph and takes up two or more lines.

WordPerfect makes this fancy effect really easy: Move your cursor to the beginning of the paragraph and choose Format⇨Drop Cap from the menu bar or press Ctrl+Shift+C. WordPerfect inserts a Dropcap Definition code and displays the Drop Cap feature bar, with buttons that let you control the size, font, and position of the large first letter. Click on the Close button on the feature bar after you're finished.

Setting Margins

The left and right margin settings tell WordPerfect how much white space to leave along the sides of the paper. If you're artistic, you probably think that margins nicely frame your erudite text. Another good reason to use margins is that most printers can never manage to print close to the edge of the paper. But in actuality, we have no idea why margins are the norm. WordPerfect is usually set to leave an inch on each side of the page unless you tell it otherwise.

The ruler bar tells you where your left and right margins are at the cursor position in the document. You can also use the ruler bar to change left and right margins.

WordPerfect has three ways to change the left and right margins:

- ◆ Click and drag the margin guidelines (the blue dotted lines in the typing area).
- ◆ Move (click and drag) the margin marker on the margin strip.
- ◆ Use the Margins dialog box.

Changing margins by using guidelines

In general, when you change the margins in a document, WordPerfect cares where your cursor is. If it's at the top of the document, margins will be changed for the whole document, but if you use one of the three methods to change the margins when the cursor is somewhere in the middle of the document, you change the margins from that point on. You can also select text before you change margins to change them for just the selected text. When you change margins, WordPerfect inserts a Margin code.

on the CD

Go ahead and change the margins for Policy2.101.wpd. Open the document if it's not already open. (If you didn't follow the steps in Lesson 11-1, open Policy3.101.wpd to see a version of the document with tasteful paragraph spacing.)

If you're a mouse aficionado or if you're trying to fit a precise amount of text on a line, you may prefer to change left and right margins by using the dotted blue guidelines. Using guidelines is the exception to the rule that the code is inserted where the cursor is — when you click and drag guidelines, the margins change from where you changed the guidelines.

Following is how to change the margins by using the mouse and the guidelines (sounds kind of like the Prince and the Pauper):

1 **Move your mouse to the guideline for the left margin even with the first line of the document. Watch for the pointer to turn into a double-headed arrow with a vertical bar through the center.**

This transformation is how the mouse indicates that it's ready to click and drag the guidelines to change the margins.

2 Click and hold down the mouse button, move the margin — indicated by the number in the yellow box that pops up — to 1.25 inches.

3 Release the mouse button when the margin position is correct.

WordPerfect moves the text around to fit within the new margins.

4 Repeat Steps 2–4 for the right margin.

Perhaps the easiest way to change margins is to use guidelines. This method is useful when you're eyeballing the margins but not so convenient when you know to the tenth of an inch how wide the margins should be.

to change margins, click and drag the dotted blue guidelines

Using the Margins dialog box

Another way to change margins is to use the Margins dialog box.

1 Move your cursor to the top of the document.

The quickest way is to press Ctrl+Home.

2 Choose Format➪Margins from the menu bar.

The Margins dialog box in Figure 11-6 is displayed. You can also display the Margins dialog box by

 ▶ Pressing Ctrl+F8

 ▶ Double-clicking on the margin strip of the ruler bar

 ▶ Clicking the right mouse button when the mouse pointer is on the ruler bar or in the left margin and choosing Margins from the QuickMenu that appears

3 Change the values in the Left and Right boxes to 1.50" (that is, an inch and a half).

When the number in a box is highlighted, you can type a new value. Press Tab to move to the next margin setting (at which point the setting in the box will change to display hundredths of an inch, that is, 1.50"). You can also change the margin settings by clicking on the up and down triangles — each click changes the margin setting by a tenth of an inch.

As you change the margins, the diagram on the right of the dialog box changes to reflect the new margins so that you can see the effect of your changes.

Format→Margins to set all margins

4 Change the top margin to 1.20".

The top and bottom margins don't have to be the same. In fact, the left and right margins don't have to be the same, either! An inch all around is a good place to start from when you're not sure what margins to use.

5 Click on OK.

The margin changes take effect, and WordPerfect repaginates the document if necessary — that is, it moves line breaks and page breaks around as necessary to make the text fit.

on the test

If you're changing all four margins, an easy way is to do it in one step and use the Margins dialog box.

Another way to change left and right margins is to use the margin strip on the ruler bar: Click on the black blob at the far left of the margin strip or the gray area to its left, and drag the margin to its new position (try not to click on the little triangles on the margin strip — the paragraph format margins).

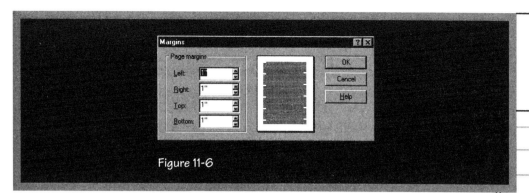

Figure 11-6

Figure 11-6: The Margins dialog box lets you set all four margins and shows you a cute picture of your page.

extra credit

Perfect fit

If making a document a particular size is your problem, WordPerfect has the feature for you. the WordPerfect Make It Fit feature shrinks or expands margins, font size, and line spacing so that a document fits on the number of pages that you specify. To use it, choose Format⇨Make It Fit, or click on the Make It Fit button on the Toolbar. Use the dialog box to tell WordPerfect how many filled pages you want and what settings it can change to get the document to that size, choosing any or all of the following: margins, line spacing, and font size. Click on OK, and WordPerfect goes to work. Technically, you can use this feature to expand your two-page essay into the ten pages required by old Professor Curmudgeon, but if you ask us, we think he'll probably notice that each page has only one sentence. If you change your mind, choose Edit⇨Undo to get back your old settings.

Indenting paragraphs

The easiest way to indent a paragraph is to use the Indent key — the F7 function key. You can also use the Paragraph dialog box, which appears when you click on the box (called a *QuickSpot*) in the left margin next to the paragraph.

You can also indent selected paragraphs by changing the left and right margins for the paragraphs. Select the paragraphs and then change the margins, using either the guidelines, the Margins dialog box or the paragraph format margins on the margin strip (the triangles) on the ruler bar. WordPerfect puts a Margin code at the beginning of the selected text to change the margins and at the end of the selected text to change them back again. You could also use the Paragraph Format dialog box (Format⇨Paragraph⇨Format) to adjust the left and right margins.

on the CD

To change the margins of the last paragraph in Policy2.101.wpd:

1 Put your cursor at the very beginning of the paragraph that you want to indent.

For example, move to the beginning of the last paragraph.

2 Press F7.

Alternatively, you can choose Format⇨Paragraph⇨Indent from the menu bar, but pressing F7 is so much easier.

WordPerfect indents the paragraph one tab stop. This format looks great for quotations and other material that needs to be set off from the rest of the text.

Another way to indent a paragraph is to click on the Edit Paragraph QuickSpot and change the Indent setting on the Paragraph dialog box. (See Figure 11-7.)

Notes:

Make It Fit button.

F7 indents paragraph

Figure 11-7: Click on an
Edit Paragraph
QuickSpot to see the
Paragraph dialog box.
The settings apply to
one paragraph only.

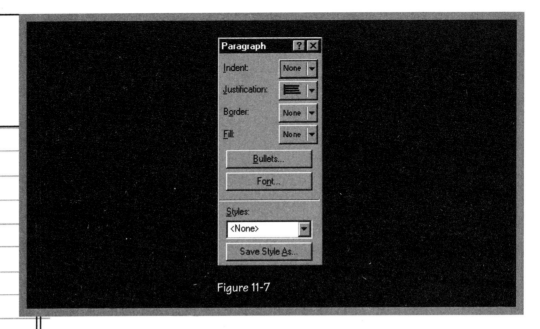

Figure 11-7

3 **Close and save the Policy2.101 document.**

To indent a paragraph, just move the cursor to the beginning of the paragraph
and press F7. WordPerfect inserts a Hd Left Ind (*hard left indent*) code where
the cursor is.

If you want to indent the paragraph from both the left and right margins (the
traditional way of indenting a quotation), press Ctrl+Shift+F7. For a hanging
indent, in which the first line of the paragraph is *not* indented but the rest of
the paragraph is, press Ctrl+F7.

extra credit

QuickSpots

QuickSpots are a new feature in WordPerfect 7 — they give you easy access to formatting
commands. The QuickSpot you will see most often is the Edit Paragraph QuickSpot — it
appears in the left margin next to the paragraph the mouse pointer is pointing to. When
the mouse pointer passes over a QuickSpot, a label pops up to tell you what kind of
QuickSpot it is (for example, Edit Paragraph). Tables and boxes also have QuickSpots.

To use a QuickSpot, simply click on it and make changes to the settings. When you click on
an Edit Paragraph QuickSpot, the changes in the settings will apply only to that paragraph.
When you're done with any of the QuickSpot dialog boxes, click on the close button in the
upper-right corner.

Clicking on the Edit Paragraph QuickSpot displays the Paragraph dialog box, which is a
good way to indent a paragraph, add bullets, or change paragraph justification. If you like
QuickSpots, go ahead and use them — if you don't, there's always another way to change
the settings.

☑ **Progress Check**

If you can do the following,
you've mastered this lesson:

❏ Change the margins of the
whole document.

❏ Change the margins for
part of a document.

❏ Indent a paragraph.

Recess

If you're ready to try that new Anadama bread recipe, exit WordPerfect.

If you have time for another lesson while it's rising, open WordPerfect and
continue with the next lesson.

Making bullets

WordPerfect has two ways (at least) to make paragraphs that begin with bullets: the manual way and the automatic way. To use the manual way, format the paragraph with a hanging indent by moving the cursor to the beginning of the paragraph and pressing Ctrl+F7. Then type an asterisk and press Tab so that the asterisk is at the left margin and the rest of the paragraph is indented. WordPerfect automatically changes your asterisk into a bullet.

If you don't like the bullet that WordPerfect uses, you can choose your own from lots of cool characters by pressing Ctrl+W. This key combination displays the WordPerfect Characters dialog box. You can see different sets of characters by changing the Character Set setting near the top of the dialog box. Insert a character in your document by clicking on it and then clicking on the Insert and Close button.

The automatic way to put a bullet in front of a paragraph or a number of selected paragraphs is to click on the Insert Bullet button on the Toolbar. WordPerfect inserts a bullet character and indents the rest of the paragraph in a wink.

The Paragraph dialog box (the one that appears when you click on the QuickSpot next to a paragraph) also allows you to put a bullet in front of a paragraph — and it gives you choices about how your bullet should look.

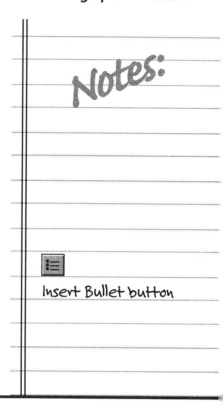

Notes:

Insert Bullet button

Centering and Right-Aligning Text

Lesson 11-3

So far, everything you've typed has been *left justified*. Justification has nothing to do with how well you make your argument — it has to do with how each line in a paragraph lies between the margins. Left justification means that the beginning of each line of text starts at the left margin so that the right side of the text has an uneven edge (unless you have the necessary poetic talent combined with technical understanding of proportionally spaced fonts to make every line the same length). This method of formatting is also called *ragged right*.

on the test

WordPerfect gives you five ways to place each paragraph on the page between the margins: left justified, right justified, centered, full justified, and all justified:

- *Left justified* is the most common way to align text. It means that the left side of the text lines up against the left margin, and the right side is ragged (uneven).

- *Right justified* means that the right side of the text lines up against the right margin. The left edge of the text is uneven.

- *Centered* text is centered between the left and right margins.

- *Full justified* text has extra spaces inserted so that each line starts at the left margin and continues all the way over to the right margin (except the last line of the paragraph, which is only justified on the left side). The extra spaces are tiny, and WordPerfect sticks them in evenly across the line, so you don't (usually) notice that they're there.

- *All justified* text is the same as full-justified, but the last line is justified, too. (See the extra credit sidebar in this lesson.)

Most people use left justified most of the time, with the occasional centered heading. Others prefer the neatness of full justification. All justification is generally only used to get a heading to fill the line — it looks weird for normal paragraphs.

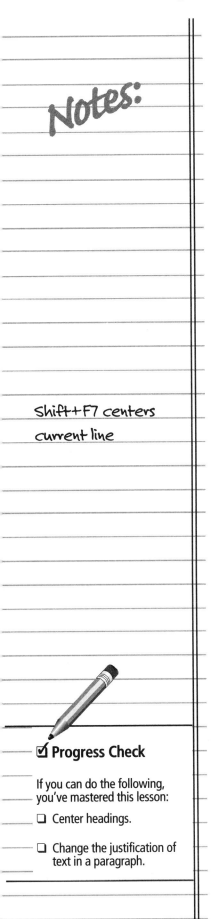

Shift+F7 centers
current line

Progress Check

If you can do the following,
you've mastered this lesson:

❑ Center headings.

❑ Change the justification of
text in a paragraph.

heads up

WordPerfect has two different ways to set text between the margins, and the difference is somewhat confusing. The two different methods put in different codes, which help you know that they're really different. One way, which works on one line at a time (so it's good for headings), is to use the Format⇨Line commands. The other way, which is better for whole paragraphs, is most easily accessed by the Justification button on the Power Bar. In this lesson, you see how to use both of them, as well as finding out when you might need one or the other.

Centering a heading

on the CD

The easiest way to center a heading is to use the Format⇨Line⇨Center command (which you can also do by pressing Shift+F7), which sticks a Hd Center on Marg code into the heading. Go through these steps, using the letter Proposal.101.wpd, the proposal that you formatted in Unit 9:

1 Open Proposal.101.wpd.

If you didn't follow the lessons in Unit 9, open Proposal4.101.wpd.

2 Put the cursor at the very beginning of the line that you want to center — in this case, the first line of the document.

The one that says MEMO.

3 Press Shift+F7 or choose Format⇨Line⇨Center.

The text jumps to the middle of the page.

Shift+F7 is the easiest way to center headings. Just make sure that the cursor is at the beginning of the line that you want to center or that you have selected the line or lines to center.

Changing the justification of paragraphs

As with most formatting commands in WordPerfect, WordPerfect cares where your cursor is when you change the justification. If no text is selected, WordPerfect inserts a Just code where your cursor is, and the code affects the text that comes after it. If you select text, WordPerfect inserts Just codes at the beginning and the end of the text so that the justification affects only the selected text. One caveat: Justification works only paragraph by paragraph, so if you select one sentence in a paragraph and center it, WordPerfect centers the whole paragraph.

To justify text, use the Justification button on the Power Bar or the Format⇨Justification command. The Justification button is in the middle of the Power Bar and usually displays the word *Left* to show that your text is left justified. You can also change the justification of a paragraph by using the Paragraph dialog box — click on the QuickSpot next to the paragraph and change the justification setting.

To try out justification, make all the paragraphs full justified. Feel free to try out all the other kinds of justification, too.

on the CD

1 In Proposal.101.wpd (or Proposal4.101.wpd), put your cursor at the beginning of the body of the memo.

Since the only place full justification makes a difference is in the body of the letter (because that's the only place with full lines of text), you can have your cursor anywhere from the "To" line to somewhere in the body of the first paragraph, and you get exactly the same effect.

2 **After your cursor is in place, click on the Justification button on the Power Bar (it's in the middle) and select Full from the drop-down menu.**

WordPerfect adds lots of tiny spaces to the text of your letter so that all the lines are the same length. Pretty clever, huh?

3 **Save and close the Proposal.101.wpd document.**

The easiest way to change the justification of a paragraph is to use the Justification button on the Power Bar while your cursor is in the paragraph that you want to justify. If you select a paragraph first, WordPerfect turns the new justification on at the beginning of the paragraph and returns to the original justification for the next paragraphs.

Of course, WordPerfect has other ways to put in the full justification code: You can choose Format⇨Justification⇨Full from the Menu or press Ctrl+J (Ctrl+L left justifies, Ctrl+R right justifies, and Ctrl+E centers a paragraph).

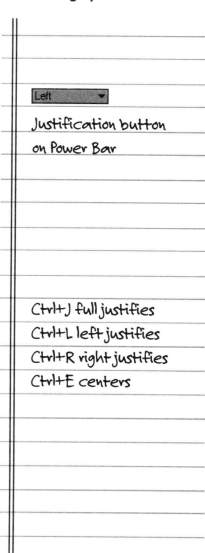

Justification button on Power Bar

Ctrl+J full justifies
Ctrl+L left justifies
Ctrl+R right justifies
Ctrl+E centers

extra credit

Using all justification

In Proposal.101.wpd, (or Proposal4.101.wpd), the *MEMO* line is good for trying all justification. Edit it to the long version of the word, *Memorandum,* (capitalized or not — it's up to you) and delete the centering code. Now select the line and choose All from the Justification button on the Power Bar. The word now fills the top of the page, from margin to margin — looks pretty cool here, although you can see how it would look pretty strange most of the time.

Setting Tab Stops

So what is a *tab stop,* anyway, and how does it differ from, say, a bus stop? Well, as long as you brought it up, we can tell you that they do have similarities — a bus stop is a place where a bus stops when you stand there, and a tab stop is a place where your cursor stops when you press the Tab key. You can put as many tab stops along the route as you want. Tab stops are a matter of convenience, but they're also the best way to line up text vertically (unless you use a table, which is usually even better and is described in an extra credit sidebar in this unit). Using spaces to put text in the same position on different lines just won't cut it — it marks you as an amateur, and besides, lining your columns up when you're using proportionally spaced fonts (where each letter takes up a different amount of space) is almost impossible.

WordPerfect usually starts with a tab stop every half inch. How can you tell? Because that's what those little triangles on the ruler bar are. To be more precise, those little triangles are *left tab stops,* just one of the many varieties of tab stops that WordPerfect has to offer. See Table 11-1 to learn about different kinds of tab stops.

Notes:

Table 11-1		Types of Tab Stops
Type	**What It Looks Like**	**What It Does**
Left	◣	Text starts after the tab stop (this one works the way tab stops on a typewriter do).
Right	◢	Text is right-aligned with the tab stop, so when you tab to a right tab stop and start typing, the text moves backward across the page, and the last letter you type is flush right against the position of the tab stop.
Center	▲	What you type is centered on the tab stop.
Decimal	▲	Useful for a column of numbers; decimal points are aligned with the tab stop.

All the types of tab stops described in Table 11-1 are also available with *dot leaders,* meaning that a line of dots leads up to the tabbed text. Dotted tabs appear on the ruler bar with dots under them.

The ruler bar shows the tabs that apply at the point in the document where your cursor is. Different parts of a document can have different tab stops, especially if you use tabs to make tables. When you change even just one tab stop, WordPerfect puts a Tab Set code into your document that contains the position of all the tab stops that are defined at that point. Always position your cursor or select text before setting tabs.

on the test

put cursor before text that tab stops will apply to, or select text

If you want to change tabs for the whole document, put the cursor at the top of the document and change the tabs. WordPerfect inserts a Tab Set code that affects all the text after the code. If you're changing tabs for only a portion of the document and you'll want your old tab stops back afterward, select that portion of the document and change the tab stops. WordPerfect inserts two Tab Set codes — one at the beginning of the selected text to change tab stops and one at the end to change them back.

As usual, WordPerfect gives you more than one way to change tab settings: you can use the Tab Set dialog box or the *tab bar* on the ruler bar. The Tab Set dialog box method might scare you off, so stick with the ruler bar method, which is easy.

If your document has tab stops (and it will unless you delete them all), you can use tabs in your text. If you press the Tab key, WordPerfect puts a Tab code in your text, and the next text you type appears at the next tab stop across the line. If you change the positions of the tab stops after you've typed something, the text moves to match.

To learn how to use tab stops, you clear the tab stops in a document and then put in your own.

Clearing tabs

Setting and moving tabs consists of playing with the triangles on the *tab bar,* the bottom part of the ruler bar. You can click and drag the triangles along the tab bar to move the tab stops, click and drag them off the tab bar to delete them, or simply click on the tab bar to create them.

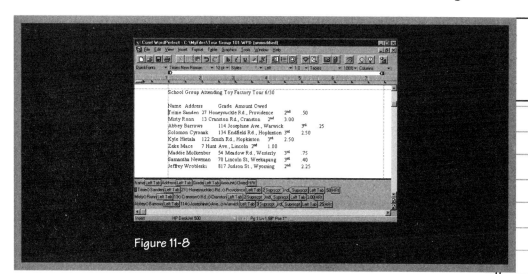

Figure 11-8

on the CD

In this exercise, you start playing with tab stops by deleting all the existing tab stops so that you can put in your own. You use the Tour Group.101.wpd document, which contains information in a columnar table that uses lots of tabs.

1 Open Tour Group.101.wpd.

Figure 11-8 shows the document. It looks lousy, because the tab stops aren't defined correctly to make nice, neat columns. In the Reveal Codes window at the bottom of the figure, you can see that Tab codes (Left Tab codes, to be precise) appear between the columns of the table.

Between each entry in the second, third, and fourth columns is exactly *one* tab — no spaces, and no bunches of tabs. That is, the typist pressed the Tab key only once between each entry, exactly as it should have been done. The table looks lousy because the columns don't line up — you can fix that problem by moving the tab stops.

2 If the ruler bar isn't on-screen, choose View⇨Toobars/Ruler from the menu bar, click on ruler bar and then click on OK, or press Alt+Shift+F3.

You may not normally like to have the ruler bar displayed, but for setting tabs, it's a necessity.

3 Put your cursor where you want to clear the tab stops. In Tour Group.101.wpd, move to the beginning of the document.

After you create the Tab Set code that clears the tab stops (a tab set code with no tabs defined), it will appear where the cursor is now.

If the document isn't empty, remember that the tab stops will be deleted from where your cursor is now until the next Tab Set code is encountered (none are there yet, but you'll soon learn how to put them in).

4 Click on the button at the far left of the tab bar part of the ruler bar (the part with the little triangles along it). A QuickMenu appears (see Figure 11-9).

Alternatively, you can choose Format⇨Line⇨Tab Set to display the daunting Tab Set dialog box. If you do, skip Step 5 and just click on the Clear All button and then click on OK to close the dialog box.

heads up

Note: The ruler part of the ruler bar has its own QuickMenu that contains a Tab Set command. That's not the QuickMenu that you want now, because it has no command for clearing tab stops. Instead, put the pointer on the little

Figure 11-9: The Tab QuickMenu appears when you click on the pop-up menu button on the left of the tab bar or right-click anywhere on the tab bar.

Figure 11-10: With no tab stops, the tabs disappear, and WordPerfect sticks in temporary line breaks instead.

Notes:

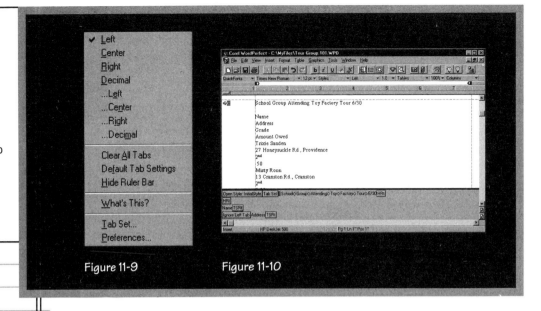

Figure 11-9   Figure 11-10

box at the far left of the tab strip and click on the right mouse button, or right-click on the tab strip.

5 **Choose Clear All Tabs.**

Blammo — no more tab stops. In fact, each item appears on a separate line — the table looks just terrible (see Figure 11-10). But don't panic: you'll put in some new tab stops in a minute. The Tab codes are still there in your document, just waiting for tab stops where they can stop!

Notice that WordPerfect puts a symbol in the margin, called a tab icon — this is to tell you that you did something with tabs at this point in the document. These markers make backing up in your document to find where you messed up your tabs much easier. And if you click on a tab icon, it displays a tab strip across the document, showing the location of the tabs set at this point.

You can clear all the tab stops by right-clicking on the tab bar of the ruler bar and choosing Clear All Tabs from the QuickMenu that appears.

Setting tabs

Now you set a few tabs so that the text looks a little neater.

1 **Make sure that your cursor is at the beginning of the document.**

WordPerfect creates a Tab Set code wherever your cursor is when you create the tab stop. To format the text into columns with tab stops, your cursor must be before the beginning of the text to be formatted.

2 **Click on the button at the left of the tab bar to display the Tab QuickMenu (refer to Figure 11-9). Make sure that Left has a check next to it.**

The QuickMenu indicates the kind of tab that you'll create. Left is usually the default, so you probably won't have to change anything. The . . . Left setting creates a left tab with a dot leader, which is not what you want right now.

3 **Put a left tab stop at 2.5 inches by clicking on the tab bar at that measurement.**

That is, click on the gray-tab-bar part of the ruler bar, just below the 2.5 inch tick on the ruler. The left margin of this document is at 1 inch, so a tab stop at 2.5 inches produces a column one-and-a-half inches wide.

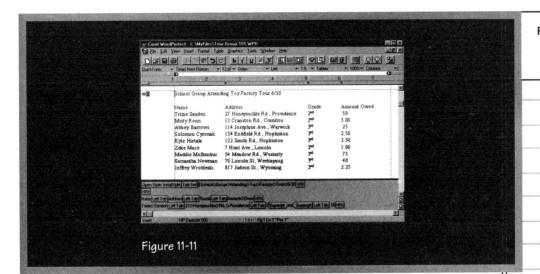

Figure 11-11: You've set tab stops so that the columns look good.

Figure 11-11

A triangle appears on the tab bar, indicating that you've created a tab stop. The first column, *Name*, is now an inch and a half wide, and the second column has moved over to the next tab stop, which starts at 2.5 inches on the ruler.

4 Make two more tab stops at 5 and 6 inches by clicking on the tab bar.

Make sure that your cursor is still at the beginning of the document before you click! Two more triangles appear, indicating left tab stops. The text looks pretty good now — something like Figure 11-11.

on the test

Setting tab stops is easy — just click on the tab bar part of the ruler bar. The hard part is remembering to put your cursor *before* the text you want to format before setting your tab stops. If you want to have the same tab stops for your whole document, move your cursor to the top of the document whenever you work with tab stops.

Moving and deleting tab stops

Moving or deleting tab stops is easy — just drag them around on the tab bar. To delete a tab stop, drag it off the tab bar and it vanishes into the mist. Continue playing with the same document you've been using (Tour Group.101.wpd).

1 With your cursor at the beginning of the document, make another tab stop at 4 inches by clicking on the tab bar.

Ooh, looks bad. Now the second column, *Address*, isn't wide enough to fit all the addresses.

2 Move the tab stop over to 4.75 inches by clicking on the 4-inch tab stop and dragging it to the right along the tab bar.

It looks a little better, but you really don't need that tab stop at all.

3 Delete the 4.75-inch tab stop by dragging it off the tab bar.

Drag its little triangle down into the typing area, where it disappears after you let go of the mouse button.

The easiest way to move or delete tab stops is by dragging the tab stop triangles around on the tab bar.

click on tab bar to create tab stop

drag tab stops left or right on tab bar to change

drag tab stops off tab bar to delete

Notes:

click on a tab stop to change its type (left, right, center, and so on)

Changing how tab stops work

WordPerfect has four types of tab stops, as you see in Table 11-1: left, right, center, and decimal. You can also tell WordPerfect to create *dot leaders* for a tab stop — that is, a row of dots leading up to the text at that tab stop. So far you've just made boring left tab stops. Now you can gussy them up a bit.

1 As usual, make sure that your cursor is at the top of the document.

Before changing your tab stops, make sure that your cursor is upstream of (before) the part of the document that needs different tab stops.

2 To change the tab stop at 6 inches to a decimal tab stop, first choose decimal tab from the tab QuickMenu.

The easiest way to see the Tab QuickMenu is to click on the small button on the far left of the tab strip, and choose Decimal from the choices.

3 Now click the tab stop at 6 inches, to turn it into a decimal.

Your document should now look like Figure 11-12. Pretty goofy, huh? The Amount Owed column head is now right justified to the tab (because that's how decimal tabs work with text). You'll fix it in a minute.

To change the type of a tab stop, change the type of tab you're creating by changing the setting on the tab QuickMenu. Then click on its triangle on the tab bar to change the type of tab that it is.

You can also change the settings of a tab stop by double-clicking on it — the Tab Set dialog box appears (see Figure 11-13). It shows all the settings for the tab stop that you double-clicked, and you can change the tab by changing settings on the Tab Set dialog box and clicking on OK.

heads up

If your tabs aren't working like you think they should (for instance, decimals aren't lining up at the decimal tab), reveal codes and see if WordPerfect has replaced tab codes with indent codes. This is occasionally a useful feature, and occasionally an annoyance. To fix this problem, delete the indent code and press Tab again.

Fixing column titles

One column heading looks a little odd (take a look at Figure 11-12). The Amount Owed column is decimal aligned, but the column heading doesn't have a decimal point in it, so WordPerfect right-aligns it. It looks lousy that way. Fix it by making the tab stop a center tab stop just for the line that contains the column headings.

To set the tabs for part of a document, select the part and then set the tabs. WordPerfect inserts Tab Set codes at the beginning and end of the selected part of the document, setting the tabs for only that part.

1 Select the line that contains the column headings for the table.

Carefully select only the line that you want to change the tab stops for — the data part of the table looks fine, so you don't want to change the tab stops there.

2 Change the tab type to center on the tab QuickMenu.

Click on the tab strip button to see the tab QuickMenu.

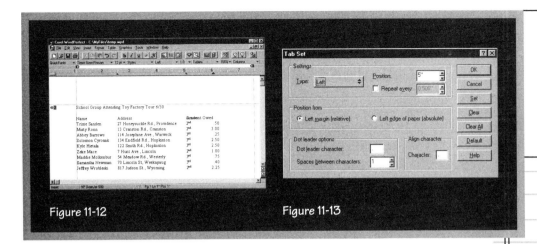

Figure 11-12   Figure 11-13

3 Click on the last tab stop to change it to a center tab stop for the selected text.

Voilá! The title moves, and the data stays put. The Amount Owed heading is now centered over the column. If you want to, you could make all the column titles centered over their columns.

4 Choose View⇨Reveal Codes to see where WordPerfect inserted Tab Set codes into the document.

Remember, move your cursor just to the left of a code to see the details about it. When your cursor is just to the left of a Tab Set code, you see the positions of the tab stops that the code defines. At the beginning of the document is a Tab Set code that says

```
Tab Set: (Rel)+1.5"L, +4"L, +5"D
```

This mysterious gobbledygook says that it's a Tab Set code, that tab stops are measured relative to the left margin, and that the tab stops are at 1.5 inches (a left tab stop), 4 inches (a left tab stop), and 5 inches (a decimal tab stop).

You also see a pair of Tab Set codes at the beginning and the end of the column headings line, changing the Amount Owed tab stop to a center tab stop, just for that line.

You also have two tab set symbols in the margin, indicating that there are tab settings in two lines of the document. In fact, there are three tab set codes, but two of them are on one line — one to set the initial tabs, one to set the tabs for the column titles, and one to change them back to the initial values again.

5 Close and save the Tour Group.101.wpd document.

If the line of columns headings is still selected, WordPerfect asks if you want to save just the selected text, or the whole document. If it asks this question, choose Entire file to save the whole document.

You may need to set column heading tab stops that are different from the tab stops for the columns themselves. If so, select the column headings and then change the tab stops.

to set tab stops for part of a document, select that part beforehand

Notes:

use formatting
commands to
format text in
table cells

select parts of a
table by clicking
when the pointer
turns into a big arrow

☑ **Progress Check**

If you can do the following,
you've mastered this lesson:

❏ Clear all the tab stops.

❏ Set tab stops.

❏ Move tab stops.

❏ Delete individual tab
   stops.

❏ Set tab stops for selected
   text, like column
   headings.

extra credit

Using the splendiferous table feature

In WordPerfect, you can easily use the Table feature to make a great-looking table that you can easily adjust later to make presentable. Adding or deleting rows or columns is a piece of cake, as is adjusting column widths.

Here's a little terminology: A table is made up of *cells,* much like a spreadsheet. A cell is like a tiny document — it will hold as much as you put in it, and you are by no means limited to one line of text (or numbers, or whatever you're putting in your table).

You can easily make a table — the Power Bar has a key named Tables that gives you a grid so that you can tell WordPerfect how big to make your table. If you prefer, you can choose Table ⇨ Create from the menu bar or press F12. You can even turn tabbed text into a table by selecting the text and pressing F12.

After you have a table, you can begin to type in it. Move your cursor to the next cell by pressing the Tab key. Your cursor moves rightward to the next cell unless it's in the last column, in which case it moves to the first cell on the next line. If no next line exists, WordPerfect creates one. Alternatively, you can always use your mouse to position the cursor.

Format the contents of a table cell in the same way that you format regular text — you can make it centered or right justified, change the font, or make it bold or italic or underlined.

You can format text by selecting just the text or by selecting the cell or cells where it is. Selecting entire rows and columns to format can be tricky. Move the pointer around the table until it turns into a big arrow and then

▶ Click once when the pointer points left or up to select a cell

▶ Double-click when the pointer points up to select a column

▶ Double-click when the pointer points left to select a row

▶ Triple-click when the pointer points left or up to select the whole table

▶ Click and drag to select a number of contiguous cells

Tip: WordPerfect has a whole menu of commands about tables — just choose Table from the menu bar. If you need to do something that we don't cover here, have a look at those menu choices and see if they don't let you do exactly what you need. The table QuickMenu has the same choices on it — display it by clicking the right mouse button when the cursor is in a table. Tables also have QuickSpots that display the Tools dialog box — it may give you the settings you're looking for.

Here's how to make a brand new table:

1. **Put your cursor where you want the table to appear.**

2. **Create a table by clicking on the Table button on the Power Bar and holding the mouse button down.**

   A grid appears, with a label at the top. The label initially says No Table. The grid is a clever way to let you tell WordPerfect how big a table you want.

3. **Point to the cell in the tiny grid that indicates the lower-right corner of the table that you want and let go of the mouse button.**

   For example, if you want a table that is four columns wide and three rows long, point your mouse to the cell in the fourth column of the third row. As you move the mouse pointer around the grid, the label tells you the dimensions of the table that you're about to create.

   A table appears in the typing area, with the number of rows and columns you indicated.

(continued)

Tip: If you find that creating a table with the itsy-bitsy grid requires more motor control than you have, choose Table➪Create from the menu bar (or press F12) to display the Create Table dialog box.

Now you're ready to type text in the cells of the table. Click your mouse pointer in the cell and type! Press Tab to move to the next cell.

Adjust the column widths by moving the mouse pointer slowly near the vertical divider (if cells are selected, you'll change only the column width for the selected cells). After it turns into a vertical line with two horizontal arrows, click the mouse button, hold it down, and drag the column divider where you want it.

Inserting and deleting rows and columns is easy: To delete a row or column, select it, press delete, and use the dialog box to tell WordPerfect exactly what you want to delete. To insert a row or column, choose Table➪Insert from the menu. You can even do easy and wonderful formatting by using the Table Speed Format (Table➪SpeedFormat).

Unit 11 Quiz

For each of the following questions, circle the letter of the correct answer or answers. Remember, there may be more than one right answer for each question!

1. **The margin strip of the ruler bar is . . .**

   A. The white part of the ruler bar.

   B. The upper-third of the ruler bar.

   C. The part of the ruler bar that shows you where your left and right margins are set.

   D. The part of the ruler bar that you can use to change your left and right margins.

   E. The sleazy, marginal part of town where the strip joints are.

2. **Before you change margins, tabs, or spacing in your document . . .**

   A. Give a small prayer to the deity of your choice (and save the document because deities help those who help themselves).

   B. Put your cursor at the very end of the document so that if you make a mistake, it won't mess up anything.

   C. Put the cursor just before the part of the document that you want to format.

   D. Select the part of the document that you want to format.

   E. Ah, to heck with it — no one will ever read it anyway.

Notes:

3. **Which button is this?**

    A. Three Sideways Exclamation Points.

    B. Slice and Dice Text.

    C. Insert Bullet.

    D. Intercom.

    E. Decimal Align.

4. **Right justification means . . .**

    A. Proving that you're right.

    B. Being a good conservative orator.

    C. Spacing words across the line the right way.

    D. Moving lines of text to the right so that they all end at the right margin.

    E. The same thing as *ragged left*.

5. **To make a tab stop . . .**

    A. Type code=tab stop.

    B. Click on the tab bar part of the ruler bar.

    C. Choose Format⇨Line⇨Tab Set from the menu bar, enter the position and type of the tab stop, click on the Set button, and click on OK.

    D. Right-click on the tab bar and choose Tab Set from the QuickMenu that appears.

    E. Yell, "Stop, tab!"

6. **In *Peter Pan*, the three children who travel to Neverland are named . . .**

    A. Wendy, John, and Michael.

    B. Huey, Dewey, and Louie.

    C. Winken, Blinken, and Nod.

    D. Aladdin, Belle, and Ariel.

    E. Larry, Moe, and Curly.

Unit 11 Exercise

For inclusion with Lexington Toys' Old-Time Circus Set, you need to format a history of circuses. Use the same file you spellchecked in Unit 7.

1. Open the document History of Circuses2.101.wpd, which appears in the following figure. (The text is the same as History of Circuses.101.wpd, but the paragraph formatting is different, and the document

Lexington Toy Company
Old-Time Circus

Join with us now as we journey back to the days of yesteryear, when the circus was an exotic and magical place. The history of the circus is long and proud. Circuses began in the days of the Romans, when Roman emperors sought to placate angry mobs by providing scintillating entertainment.

The circus was re-introduced to Europe and England by one Philip Astley in 1768. His traveling circus toured Europe and amazed crowds with acrobatics and equestrian acts. Thus was the modern circus reborn!

The circus reached its epitome under the direction of the great P.T. Barnum, noted Unitarian, Connecticut state representative, and circus entertainer extraordinaire. He billed his circus as "The Greatest Show on Earth," in part because it was so large that it had acts performed simultaneously in three separate rings under one huge tent. In the words of B.B. "Chip" Elliot, Barnum's nephew,

"P.T. Barnum was a giant in the area of organization, marketing, and shear hucksterism. Not only could he have sold refrigerators to the Inuit, they would have enjoyed them."

has been checked for spelling, grammatical errors, purity, and wholesomeness.)

2. Set the left and right margins 1.5 inches in from the edges of the paper.

3. Change the paragraph formatting to leave an extra line between paragraphs and to indent each paragraph half an inch.

4. Center the title.

5. Set the justification for the rest of the document to full justification.

6. Format the quotation (the fifth paragraph) so that it is indented an additional half-inch from both margins.

7. Save the document.

Notes:

Formatting Pages

Objectives for This Unit

✓ Centering text on a page

✓ Numbering pages

✓ Adding headers and footers to your documents

✓ Controlling where page breaks occur

Prerequisites

▶ Using WordPerfect commands (Lesson 2-2)

▶ Using dialog boxes (Lesson 2-3)

▶ Starting a new page (Lesson 3-1)

▶ Understanding WordPerfect codes (Lesson 10-1)

▶ Changing margins (Lesson 11-2)

on the CD

▶ Fire Set Proposal.101.wpd

▶ Fire Set Proposal2.101.wpd

▶ Fire Set Proposal3.101.wpd

The other units in Part III deal with character, line, and paragraph formatting. This unit steps back to look at the larger picture — how WordPerfect formats entire pages and documents. When a document gets longer than one page, you'll want to tell WordPerfect to leave nice-looking margins at the tops and bottoms of pages, number your pages, or even put titles, dates, or other information at the top and bottom of each page. All of this is called *page formatting*.

on the test

To format pages, you use these commands:

▶ Format⇨Page to tell WordPerfect what size paper you're using, center text vertically on the page, and prevent WordPerfect from splitting text onto two pages, among other tasks

▶ Format⇨Margins to set the top and bottom margins for each page (or any of the other methods you used in the last unit)

▶ Format⇨Page Numbering to number your pages

▶ Format⇨Header/Footer to tell WordPerfect to include text at the top and bottom of each page

In this unit, you'll review how to set top and bottom margins as well as learn how to center text on a page, which you may want to do with a title page or a table. You'll also learn how to number your pages and add headers and footers to your document. In the last lesson, you'll learn how to tell WordPerfect not to put page breaks where they'll be awkward — otherwise known as *bad breaks*.

heads up

Most of the commands described in this unit affect the entire document — for example, you usually want the same top and bottom margins for each page of a document. Like other WordPerfect formatting commands, these commands insert invisible WordPerfect codes into your document where your cursor is located. To ensure that the formatting codes affect the entire document, be sure to move your cursor to the top of the document before you use each command or be conscious of putting the cursor before the part of the text that you want to format.

Lesson 12-1

Controlling Your Top and Bottom Margins

Notes:

Format→Margins or Ctrl+F8 to set top and bottom margins

If you think that you might already know how to set top and bottom margins, you're probably right. You learned how to set margins in Lesson 11-2, when you set the left and right margins for your document. But for the sake of completeness (after all, this is the unit on formatting pages), we'll quickly go over setting margins here, as well as telling you how to center text vertically on a page.

You can change the margins in lots of ways. Pick your favorite:

 ▶ Choose Format⇨Margins from the menu bar.

 ▶ Press Ctrl+F8.

 ▶ Double-click on the margins strip of the ruler bar (see Lesson 11-2).

 ▶ Click and drag the dotted blue guidelines.

Centering text vertically on the page

on the CD

In this unit, you'll edit the Fire Set Proposal.101.wpd document, a proposal to be presented to the Lexington Toys board for consideration. The document consists of the introductory pages of a long proposal (we've omitted much of the body of the proposal, for the sake of brevity). The document needs lots of formatting. The beginning of Fire Set Proposal.101.wpd is shown in Figure 12-1.

What if you want to create a title page with its information centered vertically on the paper? Or you're writing a report in which Table 3 occupies a page by itself — it might look better with equal amounts of white space above and below it.

You could press Enter at the top of the page to insert a bunch of carriage returns and center the text by eye, but WordPerfect can center text vertically on a page for you. Using WordPerfect's command to center text on a page is a better idea than using carriage returns because the WordPerfect center page command carefully leaves the same amount of space above and below the text on the page and keeps it that way even if you change the size of the font or some other type of formatting.

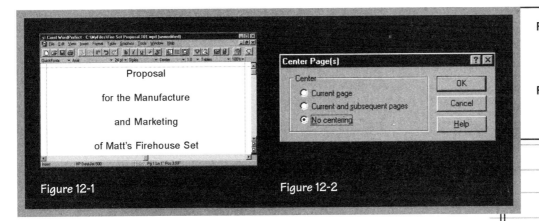

Figure 12-1

Figure 12-2

Figure 12-1: The Fire Set
Proposal.101.wpd
document may look a
little familiar.

Figure 12-2: Would you like
your page centered
vertically?

on the CD

The first page of the Fire Set Proposal.101.wpd document is a title page that
may look better if the information is centered vertically on the page. Follow
these steps:

1 Move your cursor to the top of the page to be centered.

Otherwise, you'll end up centering the wrong page! When you give the
command to center a page, WordPerfect inserts a code at the top of the
current page (the one the cursor is on).

2 Choose Format⇨Page⇨Center from the menu bar.

The Center Page(s) dialog box appears, as shown in Figure 12-2.

**3 If not already selected, click on Current page to center the current
page vertically.**

on the test

If you later decide that you don't want the page centered, display the Center
Page(s) dialog box again and change the choice to No centering. You can also
use reveal codes to delete the code, or you can double-click on the code to go
to the Center Page(s) dialog box and then choose No centering.

4 Click on OK.

WordPerfect inserts the centering code, and the text on the page moves down
to the center. If you're in Page View, the text may have seemed to disappear (it
depends how big your WordPerfect window is) — it didn't; it just moved
further down the page. You may want to use Two Page view or zoom to Full
Page to see the formatting better (use the View menu or the Page/Zoom Full
button on the Toolbar).

**5 Press Ctrl+S or click on the Save icon on the Toolbar to save the
Fire Set Proposal.101.wpd document.**

The best way to center text on a page vertically is to use the Center Page(s)
dialog box by choosing Format⇨Page⇨Center from the menu.

*Format→Page→Center
to center text
vertically on page*

*remember:
double-click on a
code to edit its
settings*

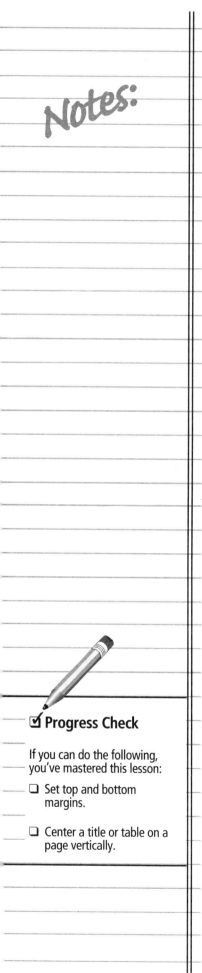

extra credit

Telling WordPerfect how big your paper is

If you switch to a different size of paper, you must tell WordPerfect so that it can format your pages to fit the paper. Even if you want to use your normal paper, you can tell WordPerfect that you'd like to print sideways on the page. WordPerfect (and computers in general) use these two terms to describe which way the text runs on the paper:

▶ **Portrait:** The usual orientation, in which the shorter sides of the paper are at the top and the bottom (like you have with a *portrait* of a person)

▶ **Landscape:** Sideways, in which the longer sides of the paper are at the top and the bottom (like you have with a wide view of a *landscape*)

If you always print on 8 ½-x-11-inch paper in portrait orientation, you never need to set the page size, because that's the kind of paper that WordPerfect is set up to deal with. But if you want to print in landscape mode or on a different size of paper, you need to use the Format⇨Page⇨Page Size command to tell WordPerfect about it.

Follow these steps to tell WordPerfect about the paper that you plan to print your document on:

1. **Press Ctrl+Home to move your cursor to the beginning of the document.**

   You'll be inserting a WordPerfect formatting code that should go at the beginning of the document, so move your cursor there before giving the command.

2. **Choose Format⇨Page⇨Page Size from the menu bar.**

   WordPerfect displays the Paper Size dialog box, which includes a list of Page definitions. This list differs depending on what sizes of paper your printer can cope with.

3. **Move the highlight to the Page definitions entry that describes the paper that you want to use.**

   When you choose a Page definition, the Orientation box shows a diagram of how the document will appear on the page.

4. **Click on the OK button.**

WordPerfect inserts a Paper Sz/Typ code that specifies the paper size and orientation (see Unit 10 for information about codes).

☑ Progress Check

If you can do the following, you've mastered this lesson:

❑ Set top and bottom margins.

❑ Center a title or table on a page vertically.

Recess

Ready to stop so soon? You've already learned some good stuff — controlling the white space at the top and bottom of the page can make your documents look more professional. If you do need to stop, close WordPerfect by choosing File⇨Exit from the menu bar (or use another method, if you prefer). Remember to exit the program and Windows if you want to turn the computer off! And come back soon for the next lesson.

Numbering Pages

Whenever you write something that's more than a couple of pages long, numbering the pages is a good idea. Don't you hate it when someone gives you a long report to read with no page numbers, and you drop the pages on the floor? Without page numbers, getting your pages back in order is a real chore.

heads up

Some word-processing tyros get the urge to type a number at the bottom of each page. Don't do it! This is a mistake that will cause you grief if you add a sentence to the first page of your document and cause the page number at the bottom of page 1 to slide to the top of page 2 and so forth for the rest of the document. Don't even try to figure out what your document will look like if you decide to change your font.

Instead, ask WordPerfect to put the page numbers on for you. Believe us, automated page numbering is much less complicated than spending your life moving page numbers around!

WordPerfect has — you'll never believe this — two different ways to number pages. The first way is to use the Format⇨Page Numbering command, which is perfect when all you care about is getting numbers on the page. The alternative is the Format⇨Header/Footer command, which allows you to add page numbers to headers and footers. The Header/Footer command is ideal when you want not only page numbers but a title, the date, or other information at the top or bottom of each page.

This lesson describes how to create just plain page numbers using the Format⇨Page Numbering⇨Select command. You'll find out how to make fancier headers and footers that may or may not include page numbers by using the Header/Footer command in Lesson 12-3.

> Format→Page
> Numbering→Select
> to number pages

By the way, it doesn't matter *where* on the page your cursor is when you give a page numbering command. WordPerfect is clever enough to put the page numbering code at the top of the current page.

We'll guide you through putting page numbers in the Fire Set Proposal.101.wpd document — you'll start by putting ordinary page numbers on every page. But after you're finished, the introduction will be numbered separately from the body of the proposal, the numbering style will be different in each part (introduction and body), the numbering will start over for the body of the proposal, and the cover page won't have a page number on it. Ready to start with the simple stuff?

Putting numbers on your pages

When all you want is page numbers, this is the way to do it:

on the CD

1 **If you don't have Fire Set Proposal.101.wpd open, open it now.**

Refer to Figure 12-1 for a picture of the document.

2 **Put your cursor anywhere on the second page.**

The title page doesn't need a page number.

Figure 12-3: When all you want is just plain page numbers, use the Select Page Numbering Format dialog box.

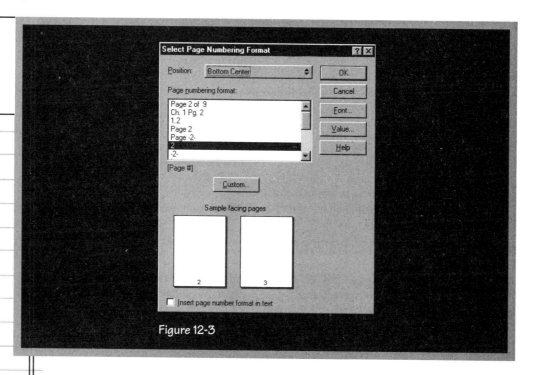

Figure 12-3

3 **Choose Format➪Page Numbering➪Select from the menu bar.**

WordPerfect displays the Select Page Numbering Format dialog box, shown in Figure 12-3.

4 **Change the Position setting to tell WordPerfect where to print the page numbers. Set it to Bottom Center (it might already be set to Bottom Center, in which case you can leave it alone).**

Our favorite setting is Bottom Center or Bottom Right, but you may certainly choose something else (far be it from us to squelch your creativity).

5 **Check the Page numbering format. The selected format should look like plain 2.**

You have lots of choices here, but keeping things simple is often a good idea. You may want to scroll through the options, though, just to see what's there.

6 **Click on OK to exit the Select Page Numbering Format dialog box.**

Now page numbers appear at the bottom of each page. (The numbers don't appear in Draft view — switch to Page view or Two Page view to see them. The easiest way to see page numbers if you're in Draft view is to use the Page/Zoom Full button.)

heads up

Page numbers start on the page where the page numbering code is, but the number printed on that page is the actual page number. So if you insert a page numbering code on the second page of the document, the page number that appears on that page is 2. You'll learn how to change the number WordPerfect starts on in a later exercise.

After you tell WordPerfect in the Select Page Numbering Format dialog box that you want a position for page numbers, WordPerfect enters a Pg Num Pos code into your document. That code tells WordPerfect that you want numbers on the page that the code is on and all the pages after that — even ones you haven't written yet.

Tip: If you set the <u>P</u>osition setting in the Select Page Numbering Format dialog box to one of the Alternating settings (Top <u>O</u>utside Alternating, Top <u>I</u>nside Alternating, Bottom O<u>u</u>tside Alternating, or Bottom In<u>s</u>ide Alternating), WordPerfect puts the page numbers on a different side for odd- and even-numbered pages. When you print the documents on two sides of the paper, the page numbers are in the outside or inside corners of the pages — very professional! (Whether or not the text lives up to the format is up to you.)

extra credit

Changing the font of page numbers

You can change the font used for the page numbers, make its bigger or smaller, or bold, or italic. Click on the <u>F</u>ont button in the Select Page Numbering Format dialog box. If you don't change the font, WordPerfect uses the document initial font (see Lesson 9-2), which usually looks just fine.

Using Roman page numbers

Introductory material is often numbered with small Roman numerals. Here's how to do it for the Fire Set Proposal document.

1 **Move your cursor to the beginning of page 2 (that's where you put the page numbering code).**

2 **Reveal codes by pressing Alt+F3.**

3 **Find the Pg Num Pos code.**

This is the code that you put into the document when you used the Select Page Numbering Format dialog box in the lesson on putting numbers on your pages.

If you have trouble finding the Pg Num Pos code, you can try using the Find and Replace Text dialog box to look for it. Press F2, choose <u>M</u>atch⇨C<u>o</u>des from the dialog box menu, find the Pg Num Pos code in the list of codes, <u>I</u>nsert it into the <u>F</u>ind box, and click on <u>F</u>ind Next. You'll still need to have the Reveal Codes window open — this isn't a way to avoid having to look at codes!

4 **Double-click on the Pg Num Pos code.**

The Select Page Numbering Format dialog box appears.

5 **Scroll down the Page <u>n</u>umbering format setting to find the plain old, small Roman numeral — it looks like ii.**

For the beginning pages of a long document, lowercase Roman numerals are traditional, so that's what we recommend choosing.

6 **Click on OK to leave the Select Page Numbering Format dialog box with a sigh of relief.**

Now WordPerfect puts lowercase Roman numerals at the bottom of the pages.

The Page <u>n</u>umbering format setting on the Select Page Numbering Format dialog box allows you to change your page numbers to Roman numerals or to letters.

Notes:

Figure 12-4: The Values
dialog box — for page
numbers, not the other
kind.

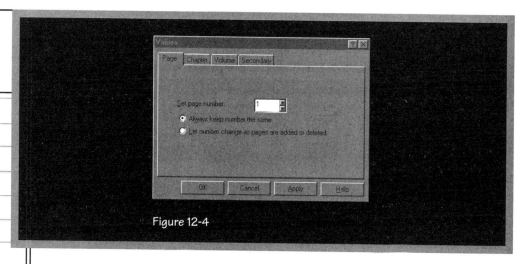

Figure 12-4

Fixing page numbers — number and format

heads up

Look at the page numbers of the document. The whole document has small Roman numerals for page numbers — not surprising, because that's what you ordered, but it's not exactly what you want, either. Page 7 starts the body of the proposal, and ideally the number on that page should be 1. Fortunately, fixing the page number isn't hard — you'll insert another page numbering code that tells WordPerfect to start numbering in regular Arabic numbers on this page starting with the number 1.

1 **Move your cursor to the top of Page 7.**

This is the first page of the body of the proposal. You can get to page 7 by using Go To — double-click on the last part of the status bar or press Ctrl+G — then type 7 and press enter. Voilà! Page 7.

2 **Display the Select Page Numbering Format dialog box.**

Same old, same old. Choose Format➪Page Numbering➪Select from the menu.

3 **Now change the Page numbering format to regular old Arabic numbers — choose** 7.

That selection changes the way the number looks (Arabic instead of Roman numerals), but you still want to change the value of the number on this page.

4 **Click on the Value button on the Select Page Numbering Format dialog box.**

This displays the Values dialog box (and don't we often wish that our friends and family had one of these so that we could set *their* values!), also available for your viewing pleasure in Figure 12-4. Fortunately, you don't need to worry about the tabs at the top of the dialog box — the settings you need are already displayed (on the Page tab).The other tabs are for very long documents, and you get to ignore them completely.

5 **Change the Set page number setting to 1 and check that the radio buttons are set to Always keep number the same.**

Because you are on the first page of the body of the document, you want the page numbers to start at 1 on this page, even if more pages are added to the "front matter" (as they say in the publishing biz) — that is, the table of contents, list of figures, and summary of the proposal. The other setting, Let number change as pages are added or deleted, lets you skip a page number so that you can add material that you may not be able to put in a WordPerfect document, such as a table or figure (although these days, you can put just about anything in a WordPerfect document).

6 **Click on OK in the Values dialog box and OK in the Select Page Numbering Format dialog box.**

You're back to your document. Have a look at the page numbers and see if they look like they should.

7 **Save your Fire Set Proposal document by pressing Ctrl+S. (By now, you should be in the habit of pressing Ctrl+S every few minutes, just in case of disaster.)**

If your page numbers aren't behaving like you want them to, give the Format⇨Page Numbering⇨Select command again on the page where the numbering should be different, and change the settings to insert a new code.

extra credit

A picture is worth a thousand words

You can add pictures to your document by creating a graphics box. You need to have a picture to add, of course, in the form of a graphics file. WordPerfect comes with a bunch of sample pictures, and you can buy graphics files, too, or find them on the Internet.

Here's how to display a picture in your document:

1. **Move your cursor where you want the picture to appear.**

2. **Create an image box by choosing Graphics⇨Image from the menu bar or by clicking on the Image button on the Toolbar.**

   The Insert Image dialog box appears. It looks very similar to the Open dialog box because it lets you select a file that contains the image. The Insert Image dialog box shows the files in the directory where Corel Office 7 graphics are stored — probably c:\MyFiles\Graphics. (If you didn't install them, check the Corel WordPerfect Suite 7 CD-ROM or diskettes).

3. **Scroll down the list and select a file or change to the folder that has the file you want.**

4. **Insert the file by double-clicking on it or selecting the one you want and clicking on the Insert button.**

   WordPerfect loads the graphics file into the image box that you've created. Your document now contains an image box with a picture. WordPerfect also adjusts the size and shape of the box to fit the picture.

You can edit a box in one of the following ways: Right-click on the graphics box to display the QuickMenu and then use the menu options to make your edits, or click on the Edit Box QuickSpot to display the Edit Box dialog box. Use either of these methods to add a caption, border, or other fancy stuff. To move a graphics box, select it (so that little boxes appear around its edges) and drag it where you want it.

Lesson 12-3   Adding Headers and Footers

Notes:

Once you get the knack of this word-processing thing, you may want to try all sorts of things that you never did with your typewriter. Headers and footers are a convenient way to put important (or boring) information on every page — a header goes at the top and a footer at the bottom (only yoga aficionados who spend a lot of time standing on their heads find this confusing).

For example, you may want your name or initials to appear on every page because you're afraid that your boss or coworker may try to steal your work and present it as his or her own. You may want to loudly proclaim that a document is only a draft, thus shielding yourself from criticism ("Well, you knew I was still working on it; it said 'Draft' on every page!"). Headers and footers can contain not only text but also the time, date, page number (yes, this is the other way to number pages), and even graphics.

on the test

Tip: Being in Page view when you're working with headers and footers helps — you can't see them in Draft view except when you're creating or editing them. As you may recall, Page view (which is probably what you're in anyway) displays what will be printed, including a header at the top of each page and a footer at the bottom. If you prefer Draft view (as we often do), stick with that and remember that headers and footers don't appear.

WordPerfect lets you have up to two different headers and footers at a time in a document. For example, you can have different headers (Header A and Header B) and footers (Footer A and Footer B) for even- and odd-numbered pages. If you work with long documents, you may have a header (or footer) for the first part of the document and a different one later on. WordPerfect lets you set up different headers and footers for different parts of a document — just move your cursor to the page where you want the header or footer to start and then give the command to create the header or footer. If the new header replaces the old, use the same letter (for example, Header A) that you used for the old header. If the new header is in addition to the old, use the other header. You're limited to two headers and two footers at a time (one for even pages, another for odd, if you like to do it that way). You can replace the contents of a header or footer at any time with new text, or discontinue it.

> *headers and footers can contain text, page numbers, current date, lines, and graphics*

Mostly we have just one header or footer at a time (forget the odd and even thing), so you can stick with using Header A and Footer A and reusing them when you want a different header for a different set of pages. You can also have both headers and/or footers on the same page — but they appear in the same space at the top of the page, so you need to be careful that the text of one doesn't overlap the text of the other.

Creating a header or footer

on the CD

It's time to add headers to the Fire Set Proposal.101.wpd document. The headers include the title of the document and the date. You don't need to include a page number in your headers, because you already defined page numbers for the document in Lesson 12-2. (If you didn't define page numbers, open Fire Set Proposal2.101.wpd, which has them defined.)

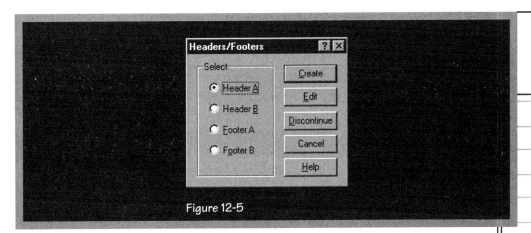

Figure 12-5

Figure 12-5: WordPerfect lets you create two different headers and two different footers.

To put a header or footer in your document, follow these steps:

1 **Move your cursor to the top of the first page on which you want the header or footer to appear. For the proposal that you're editing, move to page 2.**

That is, the real page 2 — the second page of the document. The real page 2 says "Presented to Lexington Toys Board of Directors."

2 **Choose Format➪Header/Footer from the menu bar.**

The Headers/Footers dialog box (see Figure 12-5) appears.

3 **Choose the header or footer that you'll create — in this case, Header A.**

If you want something to appear at the top of the page, choose Header A or Header B, and if you want something at the bottom, choose Footer A or Footer B. If you plan to use only one header or footer at a time for the document, stick with Header A or Footer A.

4 **Click on the Create button in the Headers/Footers dialog box.**

WordPerfect displays a new bar with buttons on it at the top of the typing area and stands prepared to receive the text of your header or footer. Figure 12-6 shows the WordPerfect window with the Headers/Footers feature bar. Your cursor appears where the header will appear on the page (if you're in page view) — the header area is outlined with a tasteful pink dotted line.

5 **Type the text of your header or footer:** Fire Set Proposal.

You can control how your text looks in all the usual ways — changing font size, text style, and so on. If you want more than one line in the header or footer, feel free to use the Enter key to start a new line.

6 **Press Alt+F7 to get ready to type some text to appear at the right margin.**

It's the old flush-right command (alternatively, you can choose Format➪Line➪Flush Right from the menu bar).

Format→Header/Footer to create or edit header or footer

Figure 12-6: WordPerfect gives you a row of buttons — the Header/Footer feature bar — that you can use when creating headers and footers.

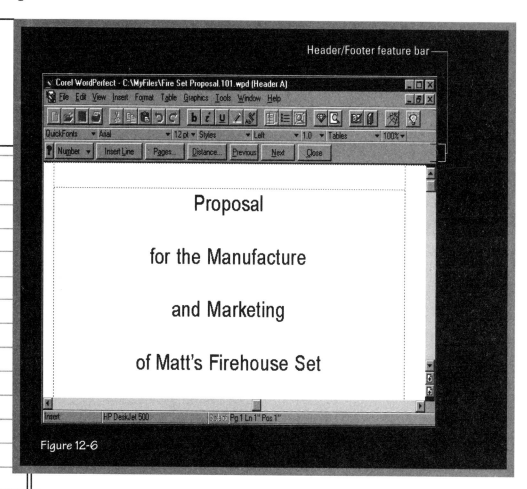

Figure 12-6

Ctrl+Shift+D inserts code for current date (changes every day)

Ctrl+D inserts today's date (doesn't change)

7 **To insert the date, choose Insert⇨Date⇨Date Code from the menu bar. (Or press Ctrl+Shift+D).**

WordPerfect inserts a code (a Date code, to be precise) that always shows the current date. If you open this document tomorrow, WordPerfect updates the code to show tomorrow's date.

If you want to insert today's date as text so that the date is *not* automatically updated, choose the command Insert⇨Date⇨Date Text instead (or Ctrl+D).

8 **Click on the Close button on the Headers/Footers feature bar after you're done editing your header or footer.**

WordPerfect inserts a Header A (or Header B or Footer A or Footer B) code where the cursor is. Move forward in the document — you see the same header on every page starting with page 2.

extra credit

Dressing up your headers and footers

You can use all of WordPerfect's formatting commands to format the text of your headers and footers. Here are some formatting tips:

- To make a three-part header or footer with some text left-justified, some centered, and some right-justified, type the first part of the header, use Shift+F7 to center the next part, press Alt+F7, and type the right-justified part.

- If you want a line in your header (perhaps to separate the text of the header from the text in the document), click on the Insert Line button. This gives you a basic single horizontal line. If you're interested in getting fancier, check out the options by choosing Graphics⇨Edit Line to display the Edit Graphics Line dialog box.

- If you want the header or footer to appear on only odd or even pages, use the Pages button on the Header/Footer feature bar to specify Odd Pages, Even Pages, or Every Page. When you click on the Pages button, a dialog box appears giving you those three options. If you print a header on even pages, you'll probably want to define another header to print on just odd pages.

Here are some other things you might want to do with a header or footer:

- To edit a header or footer, double-click on the code or click in the header or footer wherever it appears; the changes you make in one will be reflected on all the pages that the header or footer appears. You can also display the Headers/Footers dialog box, choose the header or footer to edit, and click on the Edit button.

- If you change your mind about a header or a footer, delete the code that defines it.

- To discontinue a header or footer (so that it doesn't appear past a certain page), go to the first page that the header or footer should not appear on, display the Headers/Footers dialog box, choose the header or footer you want to discontinue, and click on the Discontinue button.

- To create a header or footer to replace one used on earlier pages, go to the first page that the new header or footer will appear on, display the Headers/Footers dialog box, select the same header or footer that you created for prior pages, and use Create to create a new one.

- To redisplay the feature bar, choose Format⇨Headers/Footers and click on the Edit button on the Headers/Footers dialog box.

To put a header or footer in your document, choose the Format⇨Headers/Footers command, format the header, and click on the Close button on the Header/Footer feature bar. The header or footer appears on every page of the document, starting with the page on which you defined it.

on the test

Remember that we told you that you can use headers and footers to number pages? To put a page number in your header or footer, click on the Number button on the Header/Footer feature bar and choose Page Number.

Figure 12-7: This dialog box lets you suppress what you've gone to great pains to create.

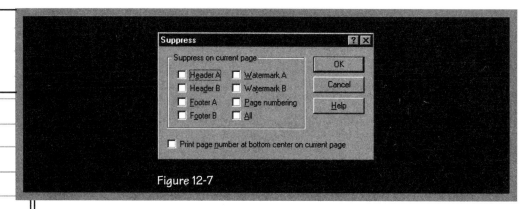

Figure 12-7

Suppressing headers and footers on the first page

on the test

Suppressing headers and footers on the first page of a document is standard. Suppressing them means that they don't appear, and this is often done because the first page of a document already has all the information that is in the header or footer — headers and footers just clutter up the initial presentation of a document.

on the CD

In the Fire Set Proposal.101.wpd document that you've been slaving over for the last few lessons, you created a header starting on page 2. Now you decide to suppress the header on the page that begins the actual proposal. This is the first page of the actual proposal, and it already has a title, so it doesn't really need a header.

1 Move your cursor to the page on which you don't want the header or footer to appear. In this case, it's the page after page 6, the page with the centered title "Matt's Firehouse Set."

heads up

You can suppress headers and footers on any page — just move your cursor to the page. Be aware, though, that the Suppress code that you're about to insert may end up on a different page if you insert or delete text, so it's a good idea to put the code near the text that will always be on the page that shouldn't have headers and footers — that's usually the title.

2 Choose Format⇨Page⇨Suppress from the Menu.

The Suppress dialog box appears (shown in Figure 12-7), with suppression options (something that some governments seem to have easy access to).

3 Choose what to suppress by clicking on it to put a check mark in the box. The header that you created is Header A, so click on Header A.

If you want no headers or footers and you've embedded the page number in one or the other, but would still like a page number, notice that you can choose that option at the bottom of the dialog box.

4 Click on OK to close the dialog box.

The header you created disappears from this page, but still appears on other pages.

Format→Page→
Suppress to skip
printing header or
footer on current
page

5 **Save Fire Set Proposal.101.wpd by pressing Ctrl+S.**

If your dog kicks your computer's plug out of the wall right now, you'll lose all the work that you've done on this document. Why risk it, even if you don't have a dog? Save early and often!

The Format⇨Page⇨Suppress command allows you to skip printing headers and footers on specific pages.

extra credit

Creating footnotes and endnotes

Use footnotes or endnotes when you reference other people's work in your text. Footnotes and endnotes are mostly used by scholarly types (or people who aren't but somehow ended up in school writing papers anyway). A footnote or endnote is a number in the text and a reference or annotation that the number refers to. The only difference between a footnote and an endnote is that footnotes appear at the bottom of the page that contains the reference, and endnotes appear at the end of a document.

WordPerfect makes footnotes and endnotes easy to use — it numbers them for you automatically so that when you add a note to the text, WordPerfect juggles the numbers to make them appear in order with the correct reference. For footnotes, it also figures out how much space is needed at the bottom of each page for the footnotes on that page.

Not everyone needs to use footnotes or endnotes — if you need to use them, you know it, so here's how to do it:

1. **Put your cursor where the footnote or endnote number should appear.**

   Usually, you should place the cursor after the period ending the sentence that contains the reference.

2. **Choose Insert⇨Footnote (or Endnote)⇨Create.**

   WordPerfect displays a footnote or endnote typing area, with a new row of buttons. The cursor appears after the footnote or endnote number.

3. **Type the reference or annotation.**

   Don't change the reference number, because keeping footnotes in the correct order is one of the things that WordPerfect does best.

4. **Choose Close from the Footnote or Endnote button bar.**

   WordPerfect returns you to your regular text. If you're in Page view, footnotes appear at the bottom of the page and move to a new page if the footnote number moves (because of added text, say). If you move the block of text with the reference number in it, WordPerfect changes the number, if needed, and keeps the references in the right order.

To edit a footnote or endnote, choose Insert⇨Footnote (or Endnote)⇨Edit from the menu (if you're in Page view, you can simply click on the note to edit it). WordPerfect asks you which number you want to edit (it doesn't matter too much, because once you're in the footnote or endnote area, you can navigate to find the note that you're looking for). Click on OK to display and edit the note. Click on Next or Previous to go to the next or previous note. If you accidentally delete a note, use the Note Number button to restore it. Click on Close after you're finished.

To delete a footnote or endnote, delete the reference number in the text.

Notes:

☑ Progress Check

If you can do the following, you've mastered this lesson:

❑ Put headers and footers in your document.

❑ Include today's date in a header or footer.

❑ Omit the header or footer for a certain page.

Lesson 12-4	Avoiding Bad (Page) Breaks

When you want to end one page and start another, insert a hard page break code by pressing Ctrl+Enter. In general, though, you should let WordPerfect choose where to put page breaks.

But what about when WordPerfect inserts a page break in a place that looks just terrible, like between a heading and the first paragraph of the section that follows the heading? Or in the middle of a table? When WordPerfect (or any word processor) inserts a page break in a silly-looking place, it's a *bad break*. This lesson is about avoiding bad breaks.

on the test

Luckily, you can avoid bad breaks in your documents by telling WordPerfect about sections of your document that should not be broken into separate pages. WordPerfect has an unusually appropriate name for the dialog box that allows you to tell WordPerfect where *not* to put page breaks — it's called the Keep Text Together dialog box.

heads up

You'll learn to avoid two kinds of bad breaks:

- A page break that occurs after the first line of a paragraph (the lone line is called an *orphan*) or before the last line (the lone line is called a *widow*) — leaving one line of a paragraph all by itself at the top or bottom of a page is bad form

- A page break that occurs right after a heading so that the heading is sitting by itself at the bottom of the page while the text that goes with it appears on the next page

You can avoid both of these problems by using the Keep Text Together dialog box, which you display by choosing Format⇨Page⇨Keep Text Together from the menu bar.

heads up

Try not to enter a hard page break (Ctrl+Enter) to avoid a bad break. Hard page breaks can cause trouble later if you're still editing your document and the position of the page break changes. Use the Keep Text Together dialog box instead.

Preventing widows and orphans

on the test

Widows and *orphans* are single lines that get separated from the rest of the paragraph that they belong to (think of each paragraph as a family). Keep families together in the following way:

on the CD

1 **If it's not already open, open the Fire Set Proposal.101.wpd document, which you'll edit during this lesson.**

As you recall, the document is the beginning of a proposal for reinstating Matt's Firehouse Set. (If you haven't done the exercises in this unit, open Fire Set Proposal3.101 instead — it includes page numbers and a header — the work you skipped.)

2 **Move the cursor to the beginning of the document by pressing Ctrl+Home.**

As always, WordPerfect inserts a code that affects only the text after it. Insert the code at the tippy-top of the document so that widows and orphans are prevented throughout the document.

(margin notes)

bad break = page break in lousy-looking place

F<u>o</u>rmat→<u>P</u>age→<u>K</u>eep Text Together to control bad breaks

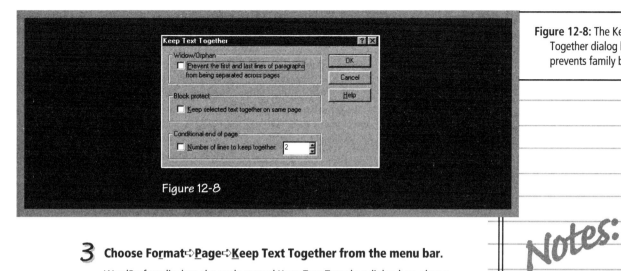

Figure 12-8

Figure 12-8: The Keep Text
Together dialog box
prevents family breakups.

Notes:

3 **Choose Format⇨Page⇨Keep Text Together from the menu bar.**

WordPerfect displays the aptly named Keep Text Together dialog box, shown
in Figure 12-8.

4 **Click on the box next to Prevent the first and last lines of paragraphs from being separated across pages.**

A check mark now appears in the box.

5 **Click on OK to leave the dialog box.**

WordPerfect inserts a Wid/Orph:On code where your cursor was when you
started this command. (Aren't you glad you don't have to remember the codes?)

Use the Keep Text Together dialog box to prevent the first and last lines of
paragraphs from being separated across pages — otherwise known as
preventing widows and orphans.

Keeping text together

You may want to keep blocks of text together. For example, tables look
terrible with a page break in the middle. WordPerfect has just the thing for
these occasions: it's called Block Protect. When you have a chunk of text that
you want to keep on one page, you can select the text and tell WordPerfect to
protect the block — that is, avoid inserting a page break within the block.

on the CD

In Fire Set Proposal.101.wpd, Table 1 starts at the bottom of page 8 (which
has the number 2) and ends at the top of the last page. That is, the table spans
pages 2 and 3. The table looks lousy that way — the last part of the table is
difficult to read when the column headings appear on the previous page. It's
time to fix this bad break:

1 **Select the text that should appear together on the page — that is, all of Table 1, including its heading.**

Start selecting text with *Table 1: Components and Approximate Height* and
keep selecting down through the whole table. (The table starts at the bottom
of the second-to-last-page of the document, which is numbered page 2.)

2 **Display the Keep Text Together dialog box by choosing Format⇨Page⇨Keep Text Together from the menu bar.**

The dialog box is shown back in Figure 12-8. The middle section of the dialog
box is called Block protect and allows you to tell WordPerfect to keep selected
text all on the same page (it protects the selected block of text).

3 Click on the box next to **Keep selected text together on same page** so that a check mark appears in the box.

4 Click on OK to leave the **Keep Text Together** dialog box.

Word Perfect inserts Block Pro codes at the beginning and the end of the selected text and moves the table down to the top of the last page of the document.

WordPerfect's Block Protect feature allows you to tell WordPerfect to keep the selected text all on one page.

Keeping heads with bodies

You've learned how to keep families together; read on to find out how to keep sections from getting decapitated. Specifically, you'll learn how to keep a heading with at least some of the text that follows. To perform this feat, you insert a Condl EOP (*Conditional End of Page*) code in your document, which says to WordPerfect, "If this line falls within *x* lines of the end of the page, take the whole kit and caboodle and put it on the next page." You get to determine how many lines *x* is.

on the CD

Unlike preventing widows and orphans, which can be done once for the whole document, WordPerfect has to be told each time that a heading needs to be kept with some of the next paragraph. With Fire Set Proposal.101.wpd open, follow these steps to tell WordPerfect not to separate a heading from the paragraph that follows:

1 Move your cursor to the beginning of a heading that has less than two lines of the next paragraph with it on the same page.

The Buildings heading at the bottom of the page numbered 1 is probably hanging out all by its lonesome. (If you can't find one, create it by adding some random carriage returns — just for this exercise, though. We may not have made this exercise work for everyone, because you all have different setups and different printers.)

2 Choose Format⇨Page⇨Keep Text Together from the menu.

WordPerfect displays the Keep Text Together dialog box, a familiar sight by now. (Take a look at Figure 12-8 if it's not.)

3 In the **Conditional End of Page** section of the dialog box, click on the little box to the left of the label **Number of lines to keep together.**

A check mark appears in the box to tell WordPerfect that you're interested in inserting a Condl EOP code.

4 Enter 4 in the box to the right of the **Number of lines to keep together** label.

This tells WordPerfect how many lines to keep together — if you have a heading with a blank line after it, enter **4** in the box to keep the heading, the blank line, and two lines of the following paragraph on the same page.

select text, then select Keep selected text together on same page in Keep Text Together dialog box

heading should always have 2+ lines of text after it on same page

5 **Choose OK to leave the dialog box.**

WordPerfect enters the Condl EOP code in your document. The heading that was by itself at the bottom of the page jumps to the top of the next page, where it can hang out with the text it refers to.

6 **Save the Fire Set Proposal.101.wpd document by pressing Ctrl+S.**

A conditional end of page code is the best way to keep a heading with the text that follows.

heads up

Have some consideration for WordPerfect when you use the Keep Text Together features — WordPerfect has to put page breaks somewhere! If you insert too many Condl EOP codes, especially ones in which you type a large number for the number of lines to keep together, WordPerfect may have trouble figuring out where it *can* insert a page break! You may end up with large white spaces at the bottoms of pages.

Tip: Inserting a code at the beginning of every heading just to avoid a bad page break is annoying. Isn't there a better way? Yes — use a very useful feature called *styles*. Styles let you tell WordPerfect to protect all the headings in your whole document with just one command. The time-saving way to keep headings with text is to finish your document and then start at the beginning, go through the document to find where WordPerfect has left a heading hanging lonely at the end of a page, and insert a Condl EOP code. Check out *WordPerfect 7 For Dummies* by Margaret Levine Young and David C. Kay (published by IDG Books Worldwide) for more information on styles.

Well done! You've learned how to spiff up your documents in a bunch of new ways, including setting top and bottom margins, numbering pages, creating headers and footers, and avoiding bad page breaks.

Recess

Speaking of breaks . . . you're ready for the quiz! But take a break to clear your brain before you do so. You've gotten to the end of this book, and you are now an official Seasoned WordPefect Pro! You've done great work and learned a lot that will make your documents look professional.

☑ **Progress Check**

If you can do the following, you've mastered this lesson:

❑ Prevent widows and orphans (and achieve other worthy social goals).

❑ Keep a block of text together on a page.

❑ Keep a heading with some of the text that follows.

Unit 12 Quiz

For each of the following questions, circle the letter of the correct answer or answers. Remember, there may be more than one right answer for each question!

1. **To display the Margins dialog box, you can . . .**

   A. Choose Format⇨Margins from the menu bar.

   B. Press the Margins key on the keyboard (if you can find it).

   C. Press Ctrl+F8.

   D. Hold down the Ctrl, Alt, and Shift keys while typing the word *margin*.

Notes:

    E. Double-click on the margins strip of the ruler bar.

2. A header is . . .

    A. A soccer play.

    B. A yoga posture.

    C. Something that appears at the top of every page of a document.

    D. A section title.

    E. Something that appears at the bottom of odd pages of a document.

3. The four major types of foods are . . .

    A. Meat and fish, grains, vegetables and fruit, and dairy products.

    B. Light-colored foods (like potatoes and pasta), dark-colored foods (like tomatoes and grapes), stuff to drink, and snacks.

    C. Sugar, salt, chocolate, and caffeine (but what about grease?).

    D. With fries, without fries, salad dressing on the side, and over easy.

    E. Pepperoni, onions, mushrooms, and anchovies.

4. Block protect . . .

    A. Is something that your neighborhood watch does.

    B. Is frequently seen in nursery schools and play groups.

    C. Keeps a block of text together on a page.

    D. Is what to use when you don't want a page break in the middle of a table.

    E. Is performed using the Format⇨Page⇨Keep Text Together command.

5. In this unit you learned . . .

    A. How to use letters instead of page numbers.

    B. How to put page numbers on only odd-numbered pages.

    C. How to suppress page numbers on a particular page.

    D. How to change the value of the printed page number.

    E. How to change the font the page number is printed in.

6. Which of the following are not positions in which WordPerfect can place page numbers?

    A. Bottom Center

    B. Alternating Top

    C. No Page Numbering

    D. Third Base

    E. Shortstop

Unit 12 Exercise

1. Type a title page for your next novel, the one about how a secret agent single-handedly averts World War III. Include the title of the novel, the name of the author (you), and the name of the publisher.

2. Insert a page break after the title page.

3. On page 2, type the copyright information. Indicate that this is the sixth printing of your book because the first five printings sold out. Thank your mother, father, and cat for helping you write the book. Also thank the authors of *Dummies 101: WordPerfect 7 For Windows 95* for helping you learn to use WordPerfect.

4. Center the title page vertically.

5. Start numbering the pages on page 2.

6. Save the document as Novel.wpd.

7. (Optional) Insert a page break after page 2 and write an entire novel (or make it a short story, if you're a little short on time). Make sure that page numbers appear on each page.

8. (Optional) Save and print the novel, hire a literary agent, and submit the novel to a publisher.

Part III Review

Unit 9 Summary

- **Formatting characters:** To make characters bold, italic, or underlined, select the text to be formatted and click on the Bold, Italic, or Underline button on the Toolbar. Alternatively, use the keystrokes Ctrl+B, Ctrl+I, or Ctrl+U.

- **Formatting text:** To format text that is about to be written, click on the appropriate button or press the corresponding keys — then as you type, the text will be formatted.

- **Changing fonts:** Change the font of selected text by selecting the text, clicking on the Font button on the Toolbar, and choosing a new font. Change the font for the rest of the document by using the same steps with no text selected.

- **Using QuickFonts:** Use the QuickFonts button to change the font of selected text to a recently used font.

- **Changing type size:** Change the type size by clicking on the Font Size button on the Power Bar and choosing a new font size. When text is selected, the size of the selected text changes; when no text is selected, the size of the type changes for the rest of the document.

- **Identifying font and font size:** The Font and Font Size buttons show the name and size of text where the cursor is.

- **Changing the initial font:** Change the initial font of a document by choosing Format⇨Document⇨Initial Font and changing the font in the Document Initial Font dialog box.

- **Changing capitalization:** Change the capitalization of text that you've already typed by selecting the text and choosing Edit⇨Convert Case from the Menu.

- **Copying character formatting:** Copy character formatting by selecting some formatted text, clicking on the QuickFormat button on the Toolbar, choosing Characters or Headings, and selecting the text that you want to format in the same way.

Unit 10 Summary

- **Revealing codes:** Reveal codes by pressing Alt+F3 or choosing View⇨Reveal Codes from the menu bar. Make the Reveal Codes window go away by using the same technique.

- **Deleting a code:** Delete a code by putting the cursor (the red block in the Reveal Codes window) next to the code and pressing Delete or Backspace. Alternatively, click on the code and drag it out of the Reveal Codes window. When the Reveal Codes window isn't visible, you can't delete codes.

- **Expanding a code:** Expand a code to see more details about it by putting the cursor immediately to its left.

- **Changing code settings:** Change the settings in a code by double-clicking on it to display the appropriate dialog box. Change the settings in the dialog box and the code changes also.

Part III Review

Unit 11 Summary

▶ **Changing line spacing:** Double-space (or otherwise change the spacing between lines) by clicking on the Line Spacing button on the Power Bar.

▶ **Displaying the Ruler Bar:** Display the ruler bar by pressing Alt+Shift+F3, or by choosing View⇨Toolbars/Ruler from the menu bar and clicking on the ruler bar in the dialog box to put a check mark next to it.

▶ **Formatting paragraphs:** Use the Paragraph Format dialog box to set paragraph formatting for the whole document. Display the dialog box by choosing Format⇨Paragraph⇨Format from the menu bar.

▶ **Setting margins:** Set margins in the Margins dialog box — display it by choosing Format⇨Margins, or by pressing Ctrl+F8, or by clicking and dragging the dotted blue guidelines — but make sure that the cursor is where the new margins should begin!

▶ **Indenting paragraphs:** Indent paragraphs by putting the cursor at the beginning of the paragraph to be indented and pressing F7 (indent), Ctrl+F7 (hanging indent), or Ctrl+Shift+F7 (double indent).

▶ **Justifying text:** Justify text in the paragraph the cursor is in (or selected paragraphs) by clicking on the Justification button on the Power Bar.

▶ **Setting tab stops:** Set tab stops by clicking on the tab strip of the ruler bar. Delete a tab stop by dragging the tab off the tab strip.

▶ **Centering headings:** Center headings by pressing Shift+F7 at the beginning of the heading.

Unit 12 Summary

▶ **Centering text:** Center text on a page by choosing Format⇨Page⇨Center from the menu bar.

▶ **Numbering pages:** Number pages by choosing the Format⇨Page Numbering⇨Select command from the menu bar or by putting a page number in a header or footer by using the Number button on the Header/Footer feature bar.

▶ **Adding headers and footers:** Add headers and footers by choosing the Format⇨Header/Footer command.

▶ **Controlling page breaks:** Control page breaks by making use of the Keep Text Together dialog box — display it by choosing Format⇨Page⇨Keep Text Together from the menu.

Part III Test

The questions on this test cover all of the material presented in Parts I, II, and III, Units 1-12.

True False

T F 1. There are at least three different ways to make text bold, italic, or underlined.

T F 2. If text is bold, it's impossible to make it underlined, too.

T F 3. The word *it's* is spelled wrong in this sentence: "WordPerfect is great but it's manual is not so hot."

T F 4. If you press the Caps Lock key by mistake, the only way to fix the text you wrote is to retype it correctly.

T F 5. Fonts only come in one size.

T F 6. Double-clicking on a code is a really cool way to change the settings.

T F 7. The best line in *Star Wars* is when Han Solo tells Princess Leia that he loves her and she says, "I know."

T F 8. Codes always look the same, no matter where the cursor is.

T F 9. The best way to double-space a document is to type it and then go back and press Enter twice at the end of every line.

T F 10. The best way to add page numbers is to type each page number at the bottom of each page.

Multiple Choice

For each of the following questions, circle the correct answer or answers. Remember, there may be more than one right answer for each question!

11. **Add page numbers to a document by:**

    A. Adding them to a header or footer.

    B. Typing them at the bottom of each page.

    C. Printing the document and then hand writing the correct number on each page.

    D. Choosing Format⇨Page Numbering⇨Select from the menu bar.

    E. Inserting a Pg Num Pos code at the point in the document where the page numbers should begin.

12. **Which of the following movies was Susan Sarandon not in?**

    A. *Little Women*

    B. *Witches of Eastwick*

    C. *The Big Easy*

    D. *The Client*

    E. *The Rocky Horror Picture Show*

13. **Which of the following can't you do with the Keep Text Together dialog box?**

    A. Prevent widows and orphans.

    B. Keep selected text on the same page.

    C. Keep a heading with at least some of the section that follows it.

    D. Insert a page break after the title page.

    E. Keep a designated number of lines together on the same page.

14. **Which of the following colors do not appear in the Reveal Codes window?**

    A. Black

    B. Yellow

    C. White

    D. Gray

    E. Red

Part III Test

15. Which of the following makes your document seem shorter?

A. A larger font

B. Smaller margins

C. Changing line spacing to 2.2

D. Smaller paper

E. A bigger, longer title

16. Which of the following are enemies of the Federation?

A. The Borg

B. The Klingons

C. The Romulans

D. The Bajorans

E. The Vulcans

17. WordPerfect does not use a code to

A. Change margins.

B. Change font size.

C. Center text on a page vertically.

D. Center text on a page horizontally.

E. Save a document.

18. Which of the following cannot be done using a choice from the Format menu?

A. Change the font of selected text.

B. Add a header or footer.

C. Change margins.

D. Indent a paragraph.

E. Copy selected text.

Matching

19. Match up the following buttons with the corresponding tasks:

A. Arial ▼

B. 1.0 ▼

C. Left ▼

D. 50

E. ☰

1. Add bullets at the beginning of each paragraph.

2. Change font.

3. Check spelling.

4. Change line spacing.

5. Change the justification of the text.

20. Match up the features with the part of the screen they appear on.

A. Tab stops.

B. Codes.

C. Bold button.

D. Font button.

E. Printer you're using.

1. Power bar.

2. Toolbar.

3. Status bar.

4. Reveal Codes window.

5. Ruler bar.

21. Match up the following keyboard shortcuts with the corresponding tasks.

A. Alt+F3.

B. F3.

C. Ctrl+Z.

D. F7.

E. Ctrl+X.

1. Save As.

2. Undo.

3. Reveal Codes.

4. Cut.

5. Indent.

22. Match the following authors with their books:

A. J.R.R. Tolkien.

B. Madeline L'Engle.

C. David Brin.

D. Ursula LeGuin.

E. Anne McCaffrey.

1. *The Ship Who Sang.*

2. *Earth.*

3. *The Dispossessed.*

4. *A Wrinkle in Time.*

5. *The Two Towers.*

Part III Lab Assignment

Create an invitation to a party welcoming the members of the press to a party announcing the new line of Houdini Magic Toys (or some other kind of event, if you like).

Step 1: Create the text

Use our example as a model, or create your own text.

Step 2: Edit and format

Center the text vertically on the page.

Center the lines on the page, as you think appropriate. Make at least one line all justified, so that it spreads from margin to margin.

Change font and font size and character formatting to make the most important text stick out and to make the flyer eye catching.

Step 3: Save the document

Save the document with the name Invite.wpd.

Answers

Part I Test Answers

Question	Answer	If You Missed It, Try This
1.	False	Review Lesson 1-4.
2.	True	Review Lesson 1-2.
3.	False	Just try it.
4.	True	Review Lesson 2-1.
5.	False — unless your printer can print on post-cards or unless you cut the paper into postcard size pieces after you've printed on it.	Review Lesson 4-2.
6.	We don't know, we're not writing comic strips.	
7.	True	Review Lesson 3-4.
8.	False — you wish.	Review Lesson 4-1.
9.	False	Review Lesson 2-3.
10.	True	Review Lesson 3-1.
11.	A, C	Review Lesson 1-5.
12.	A, B, C, E	Review Lesson 2-1.
13.	B	Take time out to read *Peanuts*.
14.	A, B, C	Review Lesson 1-4.
15.	C	Review Lesson 1-2.
16.	B, C, D	Review Lesson 1-1.
17.	E	Review Lesson 2-3.
18.	D	Watch more game shows (just kidding).
19.	A, 3	Review Unit 1 and the beginning of Unit 2.
	B, 5	
	C, 2	
	D, 1	
	E, 4	

Question	Answer	If You Missed It, Try This
20.	A, 5	Review Lesson 1-2, Lesson 2-3, and Lesson 3-2.
	B, 3	
	C, 1	
	D, 2	
	E, 4	

Part II Test Answers

Question	Answer	If You Missed It, Try This
1.	False	Review the beginning of Unit 8.
2.	False — in WordPerfect, there are always at least three ways to do anything!	Review Lesson 5-1.
3.	False — it helps with serious errors, but doesn't change your style.	Review Lesson 7-4.
4.	True	Review Lesson 6-3.
5.	True	But he also hosts a kids' TV show, *Mister Rogers' Neighborhood.*
6.	Nah (just kidding) — True	Review Lesson 7-1.
7.	True	Review Lesson 5-3.
8.	False	Review the beginning of Unit 5.
9.	False	Review Lesson 6-1.
10.	True	Review Lesson 7-1.
11.	A, B, D	Review the beginning of Unit 8.
12.	A, B, D	Review Lesson 5-2.
13.	B	Trust us on this one.
14.	A, B	Review Lesson 5-3.
15.	B, C	Review Lesson 8-5.
16.	A, B, C, D	Review Lesson 7-1.
17.	B, D, E	Review Lesson 6-3.
18.	A, B, C, D, E	It always pays to be open-minded!
19.	A, 2	Review Lesson 5-2, Lesson 5-3, Lesson 7-1, and Lesson 7-4.
	B, 5	
	C, 4	
	D, 1	
	E, 3	

Question	Answer	If You Missed It, Try This
20.	A, 3	Review Lesson 1-4, Lesson 2-1, and Lesson 5-2.
	B, 5	
	C, 1	
	D, 4	
	E, 2	
21.	A, 2	Review Lesson 1-3, Lesson 3-3 Lesson 5-2, and Lesson 5-3.
	B, 1	
	C, 4	
	D, 5	
	E, 3	
22.	A, 2	Get out there and watch some television!
	B, 5	
	C, 4	
	D, 1	
	E, 3	

Part III Test Answers

Question	Answer	If You Missed It, Try This
1.	True	Review Lesson 9-1.
2.	False	Review Lesson 9-1.
3.	True, it is spelled wrong.	Check your handy copy of *Strunk and White*.
4.	False	Review Lesson 9-3.
5.	False	Review Lesson 9-2.
6.	True	Review Lesson 10-3.
7.	True	Watch the movie.
8.	False	Review Lesson 10-1.
9.	False	Review Lesson 11-1.
10.	False	Review Lesson 12-2 and 12-3.
11.	A, D, E	Review Lesson 12-2 and 12-3.
12.	C	Rent them and watch the credits (although the movies are all pretty good).
13.	D	Well, you could, but there are far easier ways to do it (Lesson 12-4).
14.	B — but it's still pretty drab.	Press Alt+F3 and have a look.
15.	B, or just use Perfect Fit.	Review Lessons 9-2, 11-1, and 11-2.
16.	A, C	*Star Trek: The Next Generation* reruns are on at least once a day in most viewing areas. They make a good break from taking silly tests.

Question	Answer	If You Missed It, Try This
17.	E	Review Lesson 10-1.
18.	E	Get out and see some *good* movies.
19.	A, 2	Review Lessons 7-1, 9-2, 9-3, 11-1, and the extra credit sidebar "Making Bullets" in Unit 11.
	B, 4	
	C, 5	
	D, 3	
	E, 1	
20.	A, 5	
	B, 4	
	C, 2	
	D, 1	
	E, 3	
21.	A, 3	
	B, 1	
	C, 2	
	D, 5	
	E, 4	
22.	A, 5	Visit the Fantasy/Science Fiction section of your local library.
	B, 4	
	C, 2	
	D, 3	
	E, 1	

Index

◗ Symbols ◗

◗ A ◗

◗ B ◗

◗ C ◗

D U M M I E S   P R E S S™

IDG BOOKS WORLDWIDE

10/31/95

The Fun & Easy Way™ to learn about computers and more!

Windows® 3.11 For Dummies® 3rd Edition
by Andy Rathbone

ISBN: 1-56884-370-4
$16.95 USA/
$22.95 Canada

SUPER STAR

Mutual Funds For Dummies™
by Eric Tyson

ISBN: 1-56884-226-0
$16.99 USA/
$22.99 Canada

SUPER STAR

DOS For Dummies® 2nd Edition
by Dan Gookin

ISBN: 1-878058-75-4
$16.95 USA/
$22.95 Canada

SUPER STAR

The Internet For Dummies® 2nd Edition
by John Levine & Carol Baroudi

ISBN: 1-56884-222-8
$19.99 USA/
$26.99 Canada

VIII FINALIST

Personal Finance For Dummies™
by Eric Tyson

ISBN: 1-56884-150-7
$16.95 USA/
$22.95 Canada

SUPER STAR

PCs For Dummies® 3rd Edition
by Dan Gookin & Andy Rathbone

ISBN: 1-56884-904-4
$16.99 USA/
$22.99 Canada

VIII FINALIST

Macs® For Dummies® 3rd Edition
by David Pogue

ISBN: 1-56884-239-2
$19.99 USA/
$26.99 Canada

SUPER STAR

The SAT® I For Dummies™
by Suzee Vlk

ISBN: 1-56884-213-9
$14.99 USA/
$20.99 Canada

SUPER STAR

Here's a complete listing of IDG Books' ...For Dummies® titles

Title	Author	ISBN	Price
DATABASE			
Access 2 For Dummies®	by Scott Palmer	ISBN: 1-56884-090-X	$19.95 USA/$26.95 Canada
Access Programming For Dummies®	by Rob Krumm	ISBN: 1-56884-091-8	$19.95 USA/$26.95 Canada
Approach 3 For Windows® For Dummies®	by Doug Lowe	ISBN: 1-56884-233-3	$19.99 USA/$26.99 Canada
dBASE For DOS For Dummies®	by Scott Palmer & Michael Stabler	ISBN: 1-56884-188-4	$19.95 USA/$26.95 Canada
dBASE For Windows® For Dummies®	by Scott Palmer	ISBN: 1-56884-179-5	$19.95 USA/$26.95 Canada
dBASE 5 For Windows® Programming For Dummies®	by Ted Coombs & Jason Coombs	ISBN: 1-56884-215-5	$19.99 USA/$26.99 Canada
FoxPro 2.6 For Windows® For Dummies®	by John Kaufeld	ISBN: 1-56884-187-6	$19.95 USA/$26.95 Canada
Paradox 5 For Windows® For Dummies®	by John Kaufeld	ISBN: 1-56884-185-X	$19.95 USA/$26.95 Canada
DESKTOP PUBLISHING/ILLUSTRATION/GRAPHICS			
CorelDRAW! 5 For Dummies®	by Deke McClelland	ISBN: 1-56884-157-4	$19.95 USA/$26.95 Canada
CorelDRAW! For Dummies®	by Deke McClelland	ISBN: 1-56884-042-X	$19.95 USA/$26.95 Canada
Desktop Publishing & Design For Dummies®	by Roger C. Parker	ISBN: 1-56884-234-1	$19.99 USA/$26.99 Canada
Harvard Graphics 2 For Windows® For Dummies®	by Roger C. Parker	ISBN: 1-56884-092-6	$19.95 USA/$26.95 Canada
PageMaker 5 For Macs® For Dummies®	by Galen Gruman & Deke McClelland	ISBN: 1-56884-178-7	$19.95 USA/$26.95 Canada
PageMaker 5 For Windows® For Dummies®	by Deke McClelland & Galen Gruman	ISBN: 1-56884-160-4	$19.95 USA/$26.95 Canada
Photoshop 3 For Macs® For Dummies®	by Deke McClelland	ISBN: 1-56884-208-2	$19.99 USA/$26.99 Canada
QuarkXPress 3.3 For Dummies®	by Galen Gruman & Barbara Assadi	ISBN: 1-56884-217-1	$19.99 USA/$26.99 Canada
FINANCE/PERSONAL FINANCE/TEST TAKING REFERENCE			
Everyday Math For Dummies™	by Charles Seiter	ISBN: 1-56884-248-1	$14.99 USA/$22.99 Canada
Personal Finance For Dummies™ For Canadians	by Eric Tyson & Tony Martin	ISBN: 1-56884-378-X	$18.99 USA/$24.99 Canada
QuickBooks 3 For Dummies®	by Stephen L. Nelson	ISBN: 1-56884-227-9	$19.99 USA/$26.99 Canada
Quicken 8 For DOS For Dummies® 2nd Edition	by Stephen L. Nelson	ISBN: 1-56884-210-4	$19.95 USA/$26.95 Canada
Quicken 5 For Macs® For Dummies®	by Stephen L. Nelson	ISBN: 1-56884-211-2	$19.95 USA/$26.95 Canada
Quicken 4 For Windows® For Dummies® 2nd Edition	by Stephen L. Nelson	ISBN: 1-56884-209-0	$19.95 USA/$26.95 Canada
Taxes For Dummies™ 1995 Edition	by Eric Tyson & David J. Silverman	ISBN: 1-56884-220-1	$14.99 USA/$20.99 Canada
The GMAT® For Dummies™	by Suzee Vlk, Series Editor	ISBN: 1-56884-376-3	$14.99 USA/$20.99 Canada
The GRE® For Dummies™	by Suzee Vlk, Series Editor	ISBN: 1-56884-375-5	$14.99 USA/$20.99 Canada
Time Management For Dummies™	by Jeffrey J. Mayer	ISBN: 1-56884-360-7	$16.99 USA/$22.99 Canada
TurboTax For Windows® For Dummies®	by Gail A. Helsel, CPA	ISBN: 1-56884-228-7	$19.99 USA/$26.99 Canada
GROUPWARE/INTEGRATED			
ClarisWorks For Macs® For Dummies®	by Frank Higgins	ISBN: 1-56884-363-1	$19.99 USA/$26.99 Canada
Lotus Notes For Dummies®	by Pat Freeland & Stephen Londergan	ISBN: 1-56884-212-0	$19.95 USA/$26.95 Canada
Microsoft® Office 4 For Windows® For Dummies®	by Roger C. Parker	ISBN: 1-56884-183-3	$19.95 USA/$26.95 Canada
Microsoft® Works 3 For Windows® For Dummies®	by David C. Kay	ISBN: 1-56884-214-7	$19.99 USA/$26.99 Canada
SmartSuite 3 For Dummies®	by Jan Weingarten & John Weingarten	ISBN: 1-56884-367-4	$19.99 USA/$26.99 Canada
INTERNET/COMMUNICATIONS/NETWORKING			
America Online® For Dummies® 2nd Edition	by John Kaufeld	ISBN: 1-56884-933-8	$19.99 USA/$26.99 Canada
CompuServe For Dummies® 2nd Edition	by Wallace Wang	ISBN: 1-56884-937-0	$19.99 USA/$26.99 Canada
Modems For Dummies® 2nd Edition	by Tina Rathbone	ISBN: 1-56884-223-6	$19.99 USA/$26.99 Canada
MORE Internet For Dummies®	by John R. Levine & Margaret Levine Young	ISBN: 1-56884-164-7	$19.95 USA/$26.95 Canada
MORE Modems & On-line Services For Dummies®	by Tina Rathbone	ISBN: 1-56884-365-8	$19.99 USA/$26.99 Canada
Mosaic For Dummies® Windows Edition	by David Angell & Brent Heslop	ISBN: 1-56884-242-2	$19.99 USA/$26.99 Canada
NetWare For Dummies® 2nd Edition	by Ed Tittel, Deni Connor & Earl Follis	ISBN: 1-56884-369-0	$19.99 USA/$26.99 Canada
Networking For Dummies®	by Doug Lowe	ISBN: 1-56884-079-9	$19.95 USA/$26.95 Canada
PROCOMM PLUS 2 For Windows® For Dummies®	by Wallace Wang	ISBN: 1-56884-219-8	$19.99 USA/$26.99 Canada
TCP/IP For Dummies®	by Marshall Wilensky & Candace Leiden	ISBN: 1-56884-241-4	$19.99 USA/$26.99 Canada

For scholastic requests & educational orders please call Educational Sales at 1. 800. 434. 2086

FOR MORE INFO OR TO ORDER, PLEASE CALL ▶ 800. 762. 2974

For volume discounts & special orders please call Tony Real, Special Sales, at 415. 655. 3048

The Internet For Macs® For Dummies,® 2nd Edition	by Charles Seiter	ISBN: 1-56884-371-2	$19.99 USA/$26.99 Canada
The Internet For Macs® For Dummies® Starter Kit	by Charles Seiter	ISBN: 1-56884-244-9	$29.99 USA/$39.99 Canada
The Internet For Macs® For Dummies® Starter Kit Bestseller Edition	by Charles Seiter	ISBN: 1-56884-245-7	$39.99 USA/$54.99 Canada
The Internet For Windows® For Dummies® Starter Kit	by John R. Levine & Margaret Levine Young	ISBN: 1-56884-237-6	$34.99 USA/$44.99 Canada
The Internet For Windows® For Dummies® Starter Kit, Bestseller Edition	by John R. Levine & Margaret Levine Young	ISBN: 1-56884-246-5	$39.99 USA/$54.99 Canada

MACINTOSH

Mac® Programming For Dummies®	by Dan Parks Sydow	ISBN: 1-56884-173-6	$19.95 USA/$26.95 Canada
Macintosh® System 7.5 For Dummies®	by Bob LeVitus	ISBN: 1-56884-197-3	$19.95 USA/$26.95 Canada
MORE Macs® For Dummies®	by David Pogue	ISBN: 1-56884-087-X	$19.95 USA/$26.95 Canada
PageMaker 5 For Macs® For Dummies®	by Galen Gruman & Deke McClelland	ISBN: 1-56884-178-7	$19.95 USA/$26.95 Canada
QuarkXPress 3.3 For Dummies®	by Galen Gruman & Barbara Assadi	ISBN: 1-56884-217-1	$19.95 USA/$26.99 Canada
Upgrading and Fixing Macs® For Dummies®	by Kearney Rietmann & Frank Higgins	ISBN: 1-56884-189-2	$19.95 USA/$26.95 Canada

MULTIMEDIA

Multimedia & CD-ROMs For Dummies,® 2nd Edition	by Andy Rathbone	ISBN: 1-56884-907-9	$19.99 USA/$26.99 Canada
Multimedia & CD-ROMs For Dummies,® Interactive Multimedia Value Pack, 2nd Edition	by Andy Rathbone	ISBN: 1-56884-909-5	$29.99 USA/$39.99 Canada

OPERATING SYSTEMS:

DOS

MORE DOS For Dummies®	by Dan Gookin	ISBN: 1-56884-046-2	$19.95 USA/$26.95 Canada
OS/2® Warp For Dummies,® 2nd Edition	by Andy Rathbone	ISBN: 1-56884-205-8	$19.99 USA/$26.99 Canada

UNIX

MORE UNIX® For Dummies®	by John R. Levine & Margaret Levine Young	ISBN: 1-56884-361-5	$19.99 USA/$26.99 Canada
UNIX® For Dummies®	by John R. Levine & Margaret Levine Young	ISBN: 1-878058-58-4	$19.95 USA/$26.95 Canada

WINDOWS

MORE Windows® For Dummies,® 2nd Edition	by Andy Rathbone	ISBN: 1-56884-048-9	$19.95 USA/$26.95 Canada
Windows® 95 For Dummies®	by Andy Rathbone	ISBN: 1-56884-240-6	$19.99 USA/$26.99 Canada

PCS/HARDWARE

Illustrated Computer Dictionary For Dummies,® 2nd Edition	by Dan Gookin & Wallace Wang	ISBN: 1-56884-218-X	$12.95 USA/$16.95 Canada
Upgrading and Fixing PCs For Dummies,® 2nd Edition	by Andy Rathbone	ISBN: 1-56884-903-6	$19.99 USA/$26.99 Canada

PRESENTATION/AUTOCAD

AutoCAD For Dummies®	by Bud Smith	ISBN: 1-56884-191-4	$19.95 USA/$26.95 Canada
PowerPoint 4 For Windows® For Dummies®	by Doug Lowe	ISBN: 1-56884-161-2	$16.99 USA/$22.99 Canada

PROGRAMMING

Borland C++ For Dummies®	by Michael Hyman	ISBN: 1-56884-162-0	$19.95 USA/$26.95 Canada
C For Dummies,® Volume 1	by Dan Gookin	ISBN: 1-878058-78-9	$19.95 USA/$26.95 Canada
C++ For Dummies®	by Stephen R. Davis	ISBN: 1-56884-163-9	$19.95 USA/$26.95 Canada
Delphi Programming For Dummies®	by Neil Rubenking	ISBN: 1-56884-200-7	$19.99 USA/$26.99 Canada
Mac® Programming For Dummies®	by Dan Parks Sydow	ISBN: 1-56884-173-6	$19.95 USA/$26.95 Canada
PowerBuilder 4 Programming For Dummies®	by Ted Coombs & Jason Coombs	ISBN: 1-56884-325-9	$19.99 USA/$26.99 Canada
QBasic Programming For Dummies®	by Douglas Hergert	ISBN: 1-56884-093-4	$19.95 USA/$26.95 Canada
Visual Basic 3 For Dummies®	by Wallace Wang	ISBN: 1-56884-076-4	$19.95 USA/$26.95 Canada
Visual Basic "X" For Dummies®	by Wallace Wang	ISBN: 1-56884-230-9	$19.99 USA/$26.99 Canada
Visual C++ 2 For Dummies®	by Michael Hyman & Bob Arnson	ISBN: 1-56884-328-3	$19.99 USA/$26.99 Canada
Windows® 95 Programming For Dummies®	by S. Randy Davis	ISBN: 1-56884-327-5	$19.99 USA/$26.99 Canada

SPREADSHEET

1-2-3 For Dummies®	by Greg Harvey	ISBN: 1-878058-60-6	$16.95 USA/$22.95 Canada
1-2-3 For Windows® 5 For Dummies,® 2nd Edition	by John Walkenbach	ISBN: 1-56884-216-3	$16.95 USA/$22.95 Canada
Excel 5 For Macs® For Dummies®	by Greg Harvey	ISBN: 1-56884-186-8	$19.95 USA/$26.95 Canada
Excel For Dummies,® 2nd Edition	by Greg Harvey	ISBN: 1-56884-050-0	$16.95 USA/$22.95 Canada
MORE 1-2-3 For DOS For Dummies®	by John Weingarten	ISBN: 1-56884-224-4	$19.99 USA/$26.99 Canada
MORE Excel 5 For Windows® For Dummies®	by Greg Harvey	ISBN: 1-56884-207-4	$19.95 USA/$26.95 Canada
Quattro Pro 6 For Windows® For Dummies®	by John Walkenbach	ISBN: 1-56884-174-4	$19.95 USA/$26.95 Canada
Quattro Pro For DOS For Dummies®	by John Walkenbach	ISBN: 1-56884-023-3	$16.95 USA/$22.95 Canada

UTILITIES

Norton Utilities 8 For Dummies®	by Beth Slick	ISBN: 1-56884-166-3	$19.95 USA/$26.95 Canada

VCRS/CAMCORDERS

VCRs & Camcorders For Dummies™	by Gordon McComb & Andy Rathbone	ISBN: 1-56884-229-5	$14.99 USA/$20.99 Canada

WORD PROCESSING

Ami Pro For Dummies®	by Jim Meade	ISBN: 1-56884-049-7	$19.95 USA/$26.95 Canada
MORE Word For Windows® 6 For Dummies®	by Doug Lowe	ISBN: 1-56884-165-5	$19.95 USA/$26.95 Canada
MORE WordPerfect® 6 For Windows® For Dummies®	by Margaret Levine Young & David C. Kay	ISBN: 1-56884-206-6	$19.95 USA/$26.95 Canada
MORE WordPerfect® 6 For DOS For Dummies®	by Wallace Wang, edited by Dan Gookin	ISBN: 1-56884-047-0	$19.95 USA/$26.95 Canada
Word 6 For Macs® For Dummies®	by Dan Gookin	ISBN: 1-56884-190-6	$19.95 USA/$26.95 Canada
Word For Windows® 6 For Dummies®	by Dan Gookin	ISBN: 1-56884-075-6	$16.95 USA/$22.95 Canada
Word For Windows® For Dummies®	by Dan Gookin & Ray Werner	ISBN: 1-878058-86-X	$16.95 USA/$22.95 Canada
WordPerfect® 6 For DOS For Dummies®	by Dan Gookin	ISBN: 1-878058-77-0	$16.95 USA/$22.95 Canada
WordPerfect® 6.1 For Windows® For Dummies,® 2nd Edition	by Margaret Levine Young & David Kay	ISBN: 1-56884-243-0	$16.95 USA/$22.95 Canada
WordPerfect® For Dummies®	by Dan Gookin	ISBN: 1-878058-52-5	$16.95 USA/$22.95 Canada

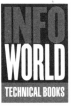

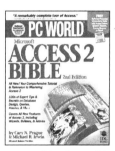

Order Center: **(800) 762-2974** *(8 a.m.–6 p.m., EST, weekdays)*

9/19

Quantity	ISBN	Title	Price	Total

Shipping & Handling Charges

	Description	First book	Each additional book	Total
Domestic	Normal	$4.50	$1.50	$
	Two Day Air	$8.50	$2.50	$
	Overnight	$18.00	$3.00	$
International	Surface	$8.00	$8.00	$
	Airmail	$16.00	$16.00	$
	DHL Air	$17.00	$17.00	$

*For large quantities call for shipping & handling charges.
**Prices are subject to change without notice.

Ship to:

Name _____

Company _____

Address _____

City/State/Zip _____

Daytime Phone _____

Payment: ☐ Check to IDG Books Worldwide (US Funds Only)

☐ VISA   ☐ MasterCard   ☐ American Express

Card # _____ Expires _____

Signature _____

Subtotal _____

CA residents add
applicable sales tax _____

IN, MA, and MD
residents add
5% sales tax _____

IL residents add
6.25% sales tax _____

RI residents add
7% sales tax _____

TX residents add
8.25% sales tax _____

Shipping _____

Total _____

Please send this order form to:
IDG Books Worldwide, Inc.
7260 Shadeland Station, Suite 100
Indianapolis, IN 46256

Allow up to 3 weeks for delivery.
Thank you!

IDG BOOKS WORLDWIDE, INC.
LICENSE AGREEMENT

<u>Read This</u>. You should carefully read these terms and conditions before opening the software packet(s) included with this book ("Book"). This is a license agreement ("Agreement") between you and IDG Books Worldwide, Inc. ("IDGB"). By opening the accompanying software packet(s), you acknowledge that you have read and accept the following terms and conditions. If you do not agree and do not want to be bound by such terms and conditions, promptly return the Book and the unopened software packet(s) to the place you obtained them for a full refund.

1. **License Grant.** IDGB grants to you (either an individual or entity) a nonexclusive license to use one copy of the enclosed software package (collectively, the "Software") solely for your own personal or business purposes on a single computer (whether a standard computer or a workstation component of a multiuser network). The Software is in use on a computer when it is loaded into temporary memory (i.e., RAM) or installed into permanent memory (e.g., hard disk, CD-ROM, or other storage device). IDGB reserves all rights not expressly granted herein.

2. **Ownership.** IDGB is the owner of all right, title, and interest, including copyright, in and to the compilation of the Software recorded on the CD-ROM. Ownership of the Software and all proprietary rights relating thereto remain with IDGB and its licensors.

3. **Restrictions on Use and Transfer.**
   (a) You may only (i) make one copy of the Software for backup or archival purposes, or (ii) transfer the Software to a single hard disk, provided that you keep the original for backup or archival purposes. You may not (i) rent or lease the Software, (ii) copy or reproduce the Software through a LAN or other network system or through any computer subscriber system or bulletin-board system, or (iii) modify, adapt, or create derivative works based on the Software.
   (b) You may not reverse engineer, decompile, or disassemble the Software. You may transfer the Software and user documentation on a permanent basis, provided that the transferee agrees to accept the terms and conditions of this Agreement and you retain no copies. If the Software is an update or has been updated, any transfer must include the most recent update and all prior versions.

4. **Restrictions on Use of Individual Files.** You must follow the instructions — located on the Cheat Sheet at the beginning of this book — to access the files on the CD-ROM. By opening the Software packet(s), you will be agreeing to abide by the licenses and restrictions for use of these files. None of the material on this CD-ROM or listed in this Book may ever be distributed, in original or modified form, for commercial purposes.

5. **Limited Warranty.**
   (a) IDGB warrants that the Software and CD-ROM are free from defects in materials and workmanship under normal use for a period of sixty (60) days from the date of purchase of this Book. If IDGB receives notification within the warranty period of defects in materials or workmanship, IDGB will replace the defective CD-ROM.
   (b) This limited warranty gives you specific legal rights, and you may have other rights which vary from jurisdiction to jurisdiction.

6. **Remedies.**
   (a) IDGB's entire liability and your exclusive remedy for defects in materials and workmanship shall be limited to replacement of the Software, which may be returned to IDGB with a copy of your receipt at the following address: Disk Fulfillment Department, Attn: *Dummies 101: WordPerfect 7 For Windows 95,* IDG Books Worldwide, Inc., 7260 Shadeland Station, Ste. 100, Indianapolis, IN 46256, or call 1-800-762-2974. Please allow 3-4 weeks for delivery. This Limited Warranty is void if failure of the Software has resulted from accident, abuse, or misapplication. Any replacement Software will be warranted for the remainder of the original warranty period or thirty (30) days, whichever is longer.
   (b) In no event shall IDGB or the author be liable for any damages whatsoever (including without limitation damages for loss of business profits, business interruption, loss of business information, or any other pecuniary loss) arising from the use of or inability to use the Book or the Software, even if IDGB has been advised of the possibility of such damages.
   (c) Because some jurisdictions do not allow the exclusion or limitation of liability for consequential or incidental damages, the above limitation or exclusion may not apply to you.

7. **U.S. Government Restricted Rights.** Use, duplication, or disclosure of the Software by the U.S. Government is subject to restrictions stated in paragraph (c) (1) (ii) of the Rights in Technical Data and Computer Software clause of DFARS 252.227-7013, and in subparagraphs (a) through (d) of the Commercial Computer—Restricted Rights clause at FAR 52.227-19, and in similar clauses in the NASA FAR supplement, when applicable.

8. **General.** This Agreement constitutes the entire understanding of the parties and revokes and supersedes all prior agreements, oral or written, between them and may not be modified or amended except in a writing signed by both parties hereto which specifically refers to this Agreement. This Agreement shall take precedence over any other documents that may be in conflict herewith. If any one or more provisions contained in this Agreement are held by any court or tribunal to be invalid, illegal, or otherwise unenforceable, each and every other provision shall remain in full force and effect.

CD-ROM Installation Instructions

The CD-ROM at the back of this book contains the practice files that you'll be using throughout the lessons in this book. It also contains a handy installation program that copies the files to your hard drive in a very simple process.

Note: The CD-ROM does *not* contain Software. You must already have the WordPerfect 7 for Windows program installed on your computer before beginning the lessons in this book.

With Windows 95 running, follow these steps:

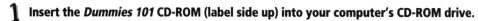

1 **Insert the *Dummies 101* CD-ROM (label side up) into your computer's CD-ROM drive.**

Be careful to handle only the edges of the CD-ROM. The CD-ROM drive is the one that pops out with a circular drawer.

Wait about minute before you do anything else; the installation program should begin automatically if your computer has the AutoPlay feature. If the program does not start after a minute, go to Step 2. If it does, go to Step 5.

 2 **Click on the Start button on the Windows 95 Taskbar (which is usually at the bottom of the screen).**

3 **Click on <u>R</u>un from the menu that appears.**

4 **Type d:\install in the text box of the Run dialog box; then click on the OK button or press Enter.**

Note: If your CD-ROM drive is not your D drive, please substitute the appropriate letter before the colon.

5 **Follow the directions on-screen.**

The installation program guides you through the process, asking some questions along the way. Unless you know what you're doing (and you folks know who you are), go ahead and accept the defaults shown on-screen by clicking on the <u>N</u>ext button when those windows appear. If at any time during the process you need more information, click on the Help button.

If you have problems with the installation process, you can call the IDG Books Worldwide, Inc. Customer Support number: 800-762-2974 (outside the U.S.: 317-596-5261).

After you complete the installation process, all the files you'll need for this book will be ready and waiting for you in the C:\MyFiles folder. You don't have to do anything with the files yet — I'll let you know when you need to open the first file (in Unit 2).

Note: The files are meant to accompany the book's lessons. If you open a file prematurely, you may accidentally make changes to the file, which may prevent you from following along with the steps in the lessons. So please don't try to open or view a file until you've reached the point in the lessons where the book explains how to open the file.

Store the CD-ROM where it will be free from harm so that you can reinstall a file in case the one that's installed on your computer gets messed up.

IDG BOOKS WORLDWIDE REGISTRATION CARD

RETURN THIS REGISTRATION CARD FOR FREE CATALOG

Title of this book: **Dummies 101™: WordPerfect® 7 For Windows® 95**

My overall rating of this book: ❑ Very good [1] ❑ Good [2] ❑ Satisfactory [3] ❑ Fair [4] ❑ Poor [5]

How I first heard about this book:

❑ Found in bookstore; name: [6] _____

❑ Advertisement: [8] _____

❑ Word of mouth; heard about book from friend, co-worker, etc.: [10] _____

❑ Book review: [7] _____

❑ Catalog: [9] _____

❑ Other: [11] _____

What I liked most about this book:

_____
_____
_____

What I would change, add, delete, etc., in future editions of this book:

_____
_____

Other comments:

_____
_____

Number of computer books I purchase in a year: ❑ 1 [12] ❑ 2-5 [13] ❑ 6-10 [14] ❑ More than 10 [15]

I would characterize my computer skills as: ❑ Beginner [16] ❑ Intermediate [17] ❑ Advanced [18] ❑ Professional [19]

I use ❑ DOS [20] ❑ Windows [21] ❑ OS/2 [22] ❑ Unix [23] ❑ Macintosh [24] ❑ Other: [25]_____
(please specify)

I would be interested in new books on the following subjects:
(please check all that apply, and use the spaces provided to identify specific software)

❑ Word processing: [26] _____

❑ Data bases: [28] _____

❑ File Utilities: [30] _____

❑ Networking: [32] _____

❑ Spreadsheets: [27] _____

❑ Desktop publishing: [29] _____

❑ Money management: [31] _____

❑ Programming languages: [33] _____

❑ Other: [34] _____

I use a PC at (please check all that apply): ❑ home [35] ❑ work [36] ❑ school [37] ❑ other: [38] _____

The disks I prefer to use are ❑ 5.25 [39] ❑ 3.5 [40] ❑ other: [41]_____

I have a CD ROM: ❑ yes [42] ❑ no [43]

I plan to buy or upgrade computer hardware this year: ❑ yes [44] ❑ no [45]

I plan to buy or upgrade computer software this year: ❑ yes [46] ❑ no [47]

Name: _____ Business title: [48] _____ Type of Business: [49] _____

Address (❑ home [50] ❑ work [51]/Company name: _____)

Street/Suite# _____

City [52]/State [53]/Zipcode [54]: _____ Country [55] _____

❑ **I liked this book!** You may quote me by name in future IDG Books Worldwide promotional materials.

My daytime phone number is _____

IDG BOOKS

THE WORLD OF COMPUTER KNOWLEDGE

☐ YES!

Please keep me informed about IDG's World of Computer Knowledge.
Send me the latest IDG Books catalog.